International Event-Data Developments: DDIR Phase II

Edited by Richard L. Merritt,
Robert G. Muncaster, and Dina A. Zinnes

Ann Arbor

THE UNIVERSITY OF MICHIGAN PRESS

1996   1995   1994   1993   4   3   2   1

A CIP catalogue record for this book is available from the British Library.

Library of Congress Cataloging-in-Publication Data

International event-data developments : DDIR phase II / edited by
   Richard L. Merritt, Robert G. Muncaster, and Dina A. Zinnes.
         p.   cm.
      Includes bibliographical references and index.
      ISBN 0-472-10427-6 (alk. paper)
         1.   International relations—Research.   I. Merritt, Richard L.
   II. Muncaster, R. G.   III. Zinnes, Dina A.
   JX1291.I468   1993
   327'.072-dc20   93-31232
                                                            CIP

*Dedicated to the memory
of an event-data pioneer:
Edward E. Azar*

Acknowledgments

The entire production of this book, other than copy-editing and printing, was carried out at the Merriam Laboratory for Analytic Political Research, University of Illinois at Urbana-Champaign. Financial support for the work came, in part, from the National Science Foundation through grant NSF SES 90-25130. The project has been, at times, an arduous one, perhaps because we had to "learn as we go" concerning the technology of desktop publishing. It was recently noted that over the course of production of this book one of the authors actually proceeded from president-elect through president to past-president of one of the major scholarly societies.

We owe a special debt of thanks to two people. The first goes to Scot Muncaster for his many hours of work on the graphics that are presented here. The second goes to Lori Lefcourt who has been in sole charge of the production since its inception. Without her organizational skills, technical abilities, and infinite patience, this book would most certainly not have been completed.

Contents

CHAPTER 1

Event Data and DDIR

Richard L. Merritt, Robert G. Muncaster, and Dina A. Zinnes

Abstract

The use of quantitative data for analyzing international political events, while rich in background, did not take off scientifically until the late-1950s with Rummel's DON, McClelland's WEIS, and, somewhat later, Azar's COPDAB. Interest accelerated for about two decades. New research interests, costs in time and money, and sharp criticism from both friendly and hostile analysts led to a hiatus in event-data research during the 1980s. Recent efforts by scientists linked to Data Development for International Research (DDIR) included a sustained effort to rebuild what many view as an important research tool. DDIR Phase I focused on updating, expanding, and developing new national attribute and international conflict data. Meetings held through late summer 1990 led to DDIR Phase II's attention to event data and, by 1991, financial support from the National Science Foundation. Its goals are (1) systematically to enhance and improve currently-existing, high-quality event datasets and (2) to develop computer software that can both facilitate the future generation of such event data and make more datasets more readily accessible to users in the public domain.

The systematic, quantitative study of international and comparative politics has seen dramatic growth in recent years. This explosion in the scientific study of cross-national and international politics has produced an enhanced awareness that datasets are critical for the continuation and further development of these scientific studies. This awareness of the centrality of datasets has been intensified by the developing sophistication of methodology and computer hard- and software which has made such analyses both more feasible and more efficient. The compilation, storage, and retrieval of datasets, however, is costly, and requisite funding has not kept pace with the discipline's increasing needs. This realization led a number of the researchers active in the textual and quantitative study of international and comparative politics to convene a series of meetings in 1983-84 to study the community's data needs. The consensus that emerged from the meetings became the basis for the organization that came to be called Data Development for International Research (DDIR).

The reports and discussions generated by the meetings of 1983-84 led to the development of a coordinated, inter-university proposal to the National Science Foundation. The proposal, submitted in 1985, stressed four data needs: filling in and updating major datasets concerning (1) national attributes and (2) international conflict; and the development of a series of conferences to examine the needs, feasibility, and appropriate strategies for constructing (3) event datasets and (4) datasets for use in the field of international political economy. The proposal was successful and the NSF funding obtained for 1986-89 made it possible to pursue all four objectives.

DDIR Phase I consisted of ten distinct projects at seven universities designed to produce critical datasets for items (1) and (2). At this writing nearly all of these datasets are complete and have been submitted for public distribution to the Inter-University Consortium for Political and Social Research. In addition, DDIR as a scientific institution has taken on more enduring roots. Directed by Richard L. Merritt and Dina A. Zinnes, both at the Merriam Laboratory for Analytic Political Research, University of Illinois at Urbana-Champaign, the organization consists of a 12-person, elected Council which provides professional oversight and programmatic assistance. DDIR has, among other things, published a quarterly newsletter, DDIR-Update, and, through its panels at professional meetings, publications, and recruiting programs, broadened the scope of scientists engaged in quantitative and textual international politics research.

To complete goals (3) and (4), DDIR held several working conferences on event and international political economy data where papers were presented and discussions held to consider how the data needs in these two areas could best be met. The conferences concerning event data led to a second phase in DDIR's research program that sought and obtained NSF support both (1) to enhance systematically currently-existing, high-quality event datasets and (2) to develop computer software to facilitate the future generation of such event data and make such datasets more readily accessible to users in the public domain. The rest of this chapter outlines the overall dimensions of DDIR's second phase, event-data research.

Event Data in Historical Perspective

The concept of an "event" can be seen from several perspectives. At the broadest, most general level, diplomatic historians view the course of international relations as a series of events — démarches, protests, treaties, crises, wars, conferences, and the like. An event in this sense is an occurrence that stands out against the gray background of everyday living. At a more micro level an event is a discrete unit of action, with its own beginning and ending points, delineated by an actor, action, and target. Events seen from the global level are thus nested sequences of yet smaller events at the micro level. The Franco-Prussian war of 1870-71 can be seen in the light of inter alia Bismarck's wars against Denmark and Austria, Ems dispatch, declaration of war, military hostilities, siege of Paris, conclusion of a peace treaty, and such consequences as indemnification, territorial transfer, and formation of the German empire. Each of these in turn can be seen as a congeries of yet smaller events. In the present context an "event" refers to the more micro interpretation.

In the late 19th century, with the flowering of labor unions throughout the industrialized West, government agencies began to gather data on social events. The focus was the strike or lock-out, industrial disputes leading to stoppage of work in some firm or branch of industry. In the United States, the Department of Labor's Bureau of Labor Statistics combed newspapers and other sources to identify work stoppages, sent questionnaires to key participants inquiring about the dimensions of these events, and reported on the number of strikes, workers involved, duration, days idle, and so forth (see U.S. Department of Labor, 1976: 195-202). In the 1930s Harold Lasswell and Dorothy Blumenstock's (1939) study of social unrest and world revolutionary propaganda in Chicago from 1919 to 1934 recorded the number and characteristics of (1) communist-sponsored meetings, demonstrations, parades, and other social gatherings, (2) strikes, (3) group and individual complaints about violations of civil rights, and (4) evictions, foreclosures, and arrests of "radicals."

Two decades later the growing concern with processes of political development and their implication for violence led scholars of international relations to use events to study the correlates of unrest and violence both systematically, that is, across nation-states, and diachronically for a more limited set of countries (Merritt, 1992; but see Mansbach and Vasquez, 1981). The nation-state was the unit of analysis. Researchers tabulated such events occurring within a state's boundaries as demonstrations, coups d'état, and revolutions.

Another area in which event data assumed a central role was in the study of foreign policy decision-making. In the attempt to understand these processes more systematically scientists turned to simulation — putting the foreign policy decision-maker into a "laboratory." These simulations, whether all man, man-computer, or all computer, required event data either to set the stage for the simulation or to test hypotheses in the simulation. As the simulation methodology evolved, the focus shifted from the nation-state as the unit of analysis to interactions between pairs of nation-states and to such ongoing processes as trade, diplomatic exchanges, and the more or less distinct occurrences of threats or militarized interventions.

The History of Event-Dataset Compilation

As the data movement captured the field of international politics, increasing numbers of researchers turned to the compilation of datasets. Evolving research questions, in turn, highlighted the limitations of old datasets and thus led to the creation of new datasets. These datasets can be classified into two types. What might be called the *global* approach to event-data compilation defines the type of event of interest, for example, hostility, specifies coding rules, and, in universal sources such as the *New York Times* or *Facts On File*, codes for the entire international system every single instance meeting the definitional criteria. (Regional studies pursued the same procedures but focused primarily on regional issues and sources.) A very different approach is seen in what can be labeled as the *event-specific* focus. Here, critical events of interest, such as the Suez crisis of 1956, are identified and a wide variety of sources (for example, newspapers, historical treatises) are searched to collect in detail the chronology of events that preceded the key event.

The global vs. event-specific approaches to event data can be seen in the seven major data compilations that have emerged over the years.

Global Event Datasets

Dimensionality of Nations (DON). The earliest event-data project of major proportions began in 1962 at Northwestern University. Rudolph J. Rummel (1964, 1972, 1976) assembled data for 1955-57 on the domestic and foreign conflict behavior of 77 nation-states, originally for use in Harold Guetzkow's Inter-Nation Simulation. The original Dimensionality of Nations or DON project tabulated seven domestic conflict events (e.g., guerrilla wars, number of assassinations), and thirteen foreign conflict variables (e.g., military action, the number of anti-foreign demonstrations, negative sanctions, protests) using five sources: the *New York Times Index*, *New International Yearbook*, *Keesing's Contemporary Archives*, *Facts on File*, and *Britannica Book of the Year*. Rummel's principal concern was with the relationship between *domestic conflict* behavior and *foreign conflict* behavior, and used factor analysis to reduce the multiple indicators to two main variables.

World Event Interaction Survey (WEIS). At roughly the same time Charles A. McClelland initiated at the University of Southern California a comparable but unrelated data enterprise. His World Event Interaction Survey or WEIS (McClelland et al., 1971) focused on the events, or interactions, that took place over time between *pairs* of countries. It used the *New York Times* for a detailed set of 63 mutually exclusive and exhaustive coding categories, designed to capture the type of hostile or cooperative action that one country directs toward another.[1] The extensive historical chronicle of interstate interactions that resulted made it possible to observe patterns in the activities of nation-states and to develop a monitoring system to facilitate the forecasting of future crises.

Conflict and Peace Data Bank (COPDAB). Edward E. Azar's original interest in the recurring Middle Eastern conflicts led him to develop the Conflict and Peace Data Bank or COPDAB (Azar, 1970; Azar and Sloan, 1975). Although it began with a regional focus it was extended to cover global international events. Building on earlier work by Robert C. North, Lincoln E.

Moses, and their collaborators (Moses et al., 1967; Choucri and North, 1975), Azar defined events as occurrences between or within nation-states that were distinct from the constant flow of "transactions" (such as trade or mail flow). Each event record, specifying which public source reported *who* did or said *what* to *whom* and *when*, is classified into one of 15 categories that represent a unidimensional scale from high cooperation through neutral events (category 8) to high hostility.

Comparative Research on the Events of Nations (CREON). Another important event dataset, Comparative Research on the Events of Nations or CREON, developed by Charles F. Hermann and his colleagues (1973) primarily at The Ohio State University, sought to examine the correlates of foreign policy behavior. Focusing on events that characterized different foreign policy positions of states, the coding categories were somewhat different from those developed for WEIS or COPDAB. The central research questions concerned the relationship between attributes of states and types of foreign policies, eliminating the need for costly time-series data.

World Handbook of Political and Social Indicators. In the late 1970s, Charles Lewis Taylor and David A. Jodice's (1983) World Handbook III provided for 136 nation-states in 1948-77 daily event data for *domestic* political events only. The event categories include political unrest (e.g., protests, riots), state coercive behavior (e.g., government sanctions, political executions), and governmental change (e.g., elections, executive transfers). World Handbook III also separately compiles for each nation-state statistical indicators of political, economic, and social change, thus helping to define the broader context within which coded events occur.

Event-Specific Datasets

Behavioral Correlates of War (BCOW). The Behavioral Correlates of War or BCOW dataset, developed by Russell J. Leng as an offshoot of the Correlates of War, focuses on *militarized crises*, a subset of militarized interstate disputes (MIDs) that are more intense in magnitude (Leng and Singer, 1988). A fine-screened description of all events is provided for the time period prior to each militarized crisis. The coding scheme includes the location of each event; duration and variations in intensity of multi-day events; assignment of physical events to one of 103 categories of military, diplomatic, economic, or unofficial behaviors; and detailed analysis of sequential verbal interactions (allowing identification of bargaining strategies). This detailed itemization of "mini-events" makes this data-collection effort labor-intensive, thereby making it possible to code only a sample of 46 militarized crises selected randomly (but stratified according to characteristics of the crisis and participants) from 1816 to 1980.

SHERFACS. The SHERFACS conflict dataset grew out of Haas's (1968) empirical studies of conflict management of 55 interstate disputes referred to the United Nations for management. Nye (1971), Haas, Butterworth, and Nye (1972), Butterworth and Scranton (1976), and later Butterworth (1980) added cases to the dataset so that by 1980 there were 307 cases of managed interstate *conflict* occurring between 1945 and 1979. Farris, Alker, Carley, and Sherman (1980) added to each of these 307 cases three new kinds of information: *conflict phases* (using the CASCON phase structure developed by Bloomfield and Leiss, 1969), information concerning the management agents (e.g., whether or not the agents accepted, ignored, or deferred a referral), and the actions of all parties, both primary and secondary, involved in the conflict (Alker and Sherman, 1982). Sherman (1987a, 1987b) updated FACS to 1984 and added "internationally recognized" *non-state actors*: domestic, or *subnational*, actors (e.g., Maronite Christians) as well as *transnational* actors (e.g., the Arab League), and *non-national* actors (e.g., Pope Paul or IBM). Based on the types of actors involved, Sherman classified conflicts into *international disputes* (parties on both sides of the issue are internationally-recognized actors) and *domestic quarrels*. The resulting dataset consists of 730 international disputes and 980 domestic quarrels.

Shifting Focus on Event-Data Research

These event-data projects saw enormous use by scholars (particularly Azar's COPDAB).[2] But as usage increased, the fundamental idea underlying event datasets came under fire by critics, both friendly and hostile. Their complaints included the uneven reporting in even the best of sources, reliance on single or a limited number of sources, the conceptual problems underlying a unidimensional scale of cooperative and conflictive behavior, inadequate attention to non-state actors (e.g., trade unions, ethnic groups, and religious communities), the global focus of event-data collections, and the untimeliness of the collections (e.g., COPDAB ends in 1979).

Although such questioning contributed to diminished funding and discouraged previous and new event-data researchers from undertaking new collections, it also led researchers to rethink the implicit assumptions in event-data collection and to explore the possibilities of adopting new computer methodologies to expedite and extend the collection process. Thus the stage was set for a new approach to event data.

As the event-data community looked back over its successes and failures, three points were evident. First, as can be seen from the above characterization, significant differences exist among the event datasets, manifested primarily in the distinct coding rules used by each. Yet each major event dataset to emerge has unique, valuable characteristics that have served the research interests of some part of the community. It would be difficult to argue for the superiority of one event-data collection over all others for all research questions. Yet the costliness of event-data collection seemed to imply the impossibility of funding the further development of all collections.

Second, event-data researchers came to realize that there was a certain amount of duplication in the published-report-to-data transformation. This suggested that some of the enterprise's costliness could be eliminated if it were possible to coordinate efforts by developing a general core data record which could then be fed into each of the more specialized coding rules.

The third factor to be considered was the enormous breakthroughs in the field of computing. The technological progress in this area needed to be tapped. These technologies would not only make event-data collection efforts more efficient and reliable, but, through recent developments in the area of artificial intelligence, could provide radically different approaches to event-data collection. The methodologies emerging in the artificial intelligence arena could provide a basis for exceptionally flexible event coding that would lend itself more readily to multiple research questions.

With these considerations in mind the event-data community decided to develop an NSF proposal focused on a mixed strategy: (1) begin generating a rich and general core dataset; (2) improve the capabilities of key, existing, specialized event datasets; (3) enhance software so as to minimize the time and cost of expanding datasets in the future; and (4) explore the possibilities for new styles of event-data research. This became Phase II of DDIR. The projected pieces of DDIR II are described below.

DDIR II: Event-Data Collection Projects

Figure 1.1 presents the various slices of the event-data development pie.[3] DDIR Phase II unifies the specialized datasets by making the *core-data collection*, called the Global Event-Data System (GEDS), the first step in the data generation process for each. The specialized datasets can be thought of as coding templates that are placed over GEDS. Each individual project updates and/or expands a particular dataset by working from the core dataset, GEDS. The remainder of this section describes briefly the thrust of each of these projects.

The Global Event-Data System (GEDS)

John L. Davies, Ted Robert Gurr, and Chad K. McDaniel of the Center for International Development and Conflict Management (CIDCM), University of Maryland, have established a Global Event-Data System (GEDS) for *computer-assisted identification, abstracting, and coding of daily international and domestic events*, as reported primarily in one comprehensive, on-line news source: Reuters Library Report, with other sources to be added as demand and resources permit. GEDS produces a *core event-data stream* from 1979 forward. It includes: (1) the actions vis-à-vis each other of (a) nation-states, (b) major non-state communities, and (c) international organizations; (2) detailed event summaries and coding, including direct quotations and cross-referencing; and

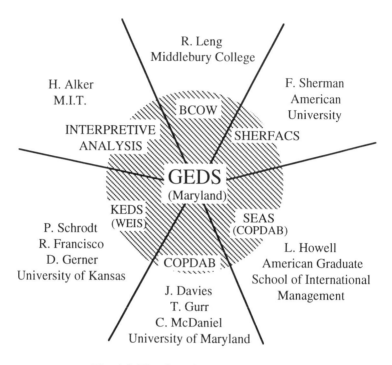

Fig. 1.1 The data development picture

(3) information allowing user access to the full-text source articles where available on-line. The software produced in the GEDS project will permit partially-*automated, continuous updating after 1990* of the core event-data stream. The event-data stream generated by using Maryland's computer-assisted coding procedures on on-line news sources is the basis for each of the specialized projects described below.

Individual Data Projects

Updating and Extending the Conflict and Peace Data Bank (COPDAB), World Event Interaction Survey (WEIS), and Subsequently World Handbook III. The Maryland team, as part of the larger GEDS effort to be carried out at CIDCM, is updating to 1990+ the existing COPDAB dataset, incorporating updated WEIS and World Handbook III (as well as BCOW and SHERFACS) event data as they become available, and adding non-state actors. Given the economies of computerized coding, it is possible to expand from traditional hardcopy (news sources such as the *New York Times* and archives such as *Facts on File*) to the much denser and more even coverage of world events offered by news wire services such as Reuters.

Foreign Policy Behaviors of Southeast Asian States (SEAS). Llewellyn D. Howell at the American Graduate School of International Management will use the GEDS computer-assisted procedures on *regional sources* (e.g., Hong Kong's *Asian Wall Street Journal,* Singapore's *Straits Times,* Malaysia's *New Straits Times, Far Eastern Economic Review,* and *Asiaweek*) to produce a data bank on 10 Southeast Asia states: Malaysia, Singapore, the Philippines, Indonesia, Brunei, Thailand, Vietnam, Cambodia, Laos, and Myanmar (Burma). The event-data stream emerging from this project will be added to the Maryland core event-data stream. This subproject thus enriches the Maryland event-data stream, and provides a basis for comparing for a specific region, Southeast Asia, the coding of global sources vs. regional sources. SEAS uses COPDAB coding rules to focus on interstate behavior and non-state actors.

Kansas Event-Data Sources (KEDS) for Central Europe and the Middle East. At the University of Kansas Philip A. Schrodt, Ronald A. Francisco, and Deborah J. Gerner are experimenting both with fully-automated event coding using machine-readable sources, and with using regional chronologies as an event-data source. The first step is to develop a fully-automated event coding system, KEDS, to use in coding Reuters stories on the Middle East and Central Europe. (This program is described below.) "Human coders" are coding a large set of Reuters stories to permit comparison of human-coded data vs. the machine-coding system. The Kansas team is using the WEIS coding rules. However, it is anticipated that it will eventually be possible for KEDS to work with the GEDS format, thereby permitting WEIS codes to be automatically assigned to GEDS event summaries.

A second step involves the use of inexpensive optical character recognition (OCR) equipment to convert into machine-readable form several regional foreign affairs chronologies. These chronologies will be coded using KEDS and the coverage of these sources compared to that of Reuters. If time and resources permit, the project will also study the coverage of other machine-readable sources such as the *Facts on File* CD-ROM and the forthcoming Foreign Broadcast Information Service (FBIS) CD-ROM.

A third component of the project involves experiments using OCR on microfilmed historical materials. Using the *Times* (London) for the 1936-39 uprising in Palestine, the experiment will determine the extent to which (1) inexpensive OCR equipment can be used with library-grade microfilm and (2) dictionaries developed for coding contemporary materials such as Reuters need modification when dealing with historical materials.

Behavioral Correlates of War (BCOW). Using the core data provided by GEDS for 40 to 55 militarized crises occurring in 1979-90, Russell J. Leng at Middlebury College is applying BCOW data-collection procedures to produce a fine-screened dataset. The BCOW coding rules specify 103 descriptors of each action (such as alert, mobilization, and evacuation) that can take place during a militarized crisis, and code each event-action according to the date of occurrence, actor, target, location, whether the actor was acting unilaterally or together with another state, and "tempo" of the action. The GEDS records will be supplemented by newspaper reports, government publications, historical treatises, and any other source of information concerning the militarized crisis in question.

Non-State Actors in Interstate Conflicts (SHERFACS). Frank L. Sherman at American University is enhancing and updating the SHERFACS dataset: fine-screened accounts of several kinds of episodic conflict situations, both international and domestic with particular emphasis on those conflicts involving collective management (e.g., UN mediation) and non-state actors. SHERFACS will supplement the sources used by GEDS with newspaper reports, government publications, and historical treatises. SHERFACS provides data of a historical, narrative, and quantitative nature with expanded actor-participant identifications which include domestic and non-state political actors as well as nation-states.

Data Development for Interpretive Analysis. Hayward R. Alker, Jr., at the Massachusetts Institute of Technology, is developing methods for the interpretive analysis of detailed event summaries, by adding to the GEDS dataset both narrative depth and varieties of interpretive perspectives for specific conflict episodes. The three data components studied are (1) explicitly coded WEIS/ COPDAB/BCOW/ SHERFACS event data, (2) humanly constructed narrative summaries of each event, and (3) quotations attributed to the principal actors and interactors of the event being described. In addition, original and secondary source stories are being made conveniently accessible for the purposes of detailed textual and interpretive analysis of both quantitative and qualitative, political data.

DDIR II: The Software Component

With major international news sources such as Reuters, Associated Press, and United Press International and local news reports (e.g., as translated by the *FBIS Reports*) either now or soon to be accessible on-line, the retrieval of source stories begs for automation. Moreover, the enormously expanded storage capacity, processing speed, and programming flexibility at the microcomputer level now make it possible to develop an event-coding system which sacrifices neither the comprehensiveness of global coding efforts nor the depth and diversity of coverage of the episodic coding projects. Thus there is an important software component to DDIR. This is described below.

Software for Data Collection

Computer-Assisted and Partially-Automated Coding in GEDS. With a small grant from DDIR I and considerable backing from the University of Maryland, the Maryland team developed and tested a preliminary version of software for computer-assisted entry, coding, and editing of Reuters' on-line source stories to produce GEDS event records (reported in chapter 2 of this volume). Coders enter summary material using data-entry software which prompts, and to some extent verifies the correctness (according to an on-line codebook) of, each step in the coding process. Since the initial summary material that is entered is critical for subsequent work, the Maryland team is developing software for source "pre-reading." It involves machine pre-reading, key-item identification, extraction, and extended code verification procedures. The Maryland team aims to set in place at CIDCM a process for continuously updating GEDS records in the foreseeable future, as well as for back-coding of data from 1979.

Fully-Automated Machine Coding: KEDS. The Kansas team is developing a system that can be used for the fully-automated coding of event data from machine-readable sources such as wire services and CD-ROM. KEDS is a Macintosh program that produces WEIS-coded events directly from Reuters newswire leads downloaded from the NEXIS data service. Unlike partially-automated systems, KEDS codes without any human intervention, though the system can also be used for machine-assisted coding. A fully-automated system's coding is completely consistent and reproducible. Statistical corrections can be applied to aggregated machine-coded data to improve their accuracy in quantitative studies. It also allows an individual researcher to develop a custom event-data coding scheme and code a large amount of existing text.

KEDS utilizes a user-defined dictionary to identify the actors, and then applies simple grammatical rules to determine compound actors, verb phrases, pronouns, and source attribution. The assignment of WEIS codes focuses on the patterns based on the verbs in the sentence. Using coding data from the Middle East, KEDS currently has a dictionary of about 500 actors and 1000 verb patterns. Actor and verb dictionaries are also being developed to code German-language foreign policy chronologies dealing with international politics in Central Europe. While the system was initially developed using Reuters newswire leads as the text source, the input format is very general and most ASCII text files could be formatted to work with KEDS. Future enhancements of KEDS will include the development of coding dictionaries to handle COPDAB codes, front-ends to handle other machine-readable event sources such as *Facts on File* and GEDS, and an MS-DOS version of the program.

Computerized Textual and Interpretive Analysis of Conflict Episodes. Alker's work explores software development for the multi-perspective, interpretive analysis of event histories. This allows subsequent validity- and reliability-oriented comparisons of original sources, GEDS codings, human narrative summaries, speech fragments, and such computational interpretations as are produced. The work builds on publicly available software routines for computational text analysis in the Schank-Abelson tradition. Central to the redefinition of these routines are the development and implementation of an "event-description framework" motivated by Lasswell's work on interactions, and a translation scheme for "filling in" this framework using, in particular, SHERFACS data. The interpretive routines will then operate computationally on this framework to produce event interpretations from a variety of perspectives. At the end of the project an advanced working subset of the proposed interpretive routines, more or less oriented toward SHERFACS's research conceptualizations, will be available to DDIR event-dataset users. A series of papers and appropriate user manuals oriented toward DDIR materials will supplement and illustrate the use of the software.

Extension of Computerized Procedures for the Analysis of BCOW Data. Leng is modifying and enhancing two currently existing software packages developed to analyze BCOW data. Because of the richness of BCOW's coding categories, software is the only efficient way in which to aggregate the data for subsequent analyses. The CRISIS program permits the user to select, count, and scale events along various dimensions. The INFLUENCE program was designed specifically to analyze crisis bargaining. Both programs currently exist only in the environment of a (VAX) mini-computer. The goal of the BCOW subproject of DDIR Phase II is to increase their functionality and availability by converting them to microcomputer environments.

Computerized Preparation of SHERFACS Data for Interpretive Analysis. Sherman is exploring the possibility of fitting the SHERFACS data into the Lasswellian frames which Alker is using for interpretively describing conflict episodes. Computer-assisted or partially-automated coding sequences will transform into the Lasswellian categories the SHERFACS information (and thereby, by extension, the associated event summaries and event categories of GEDS). The software will be compatible with the GEDS data-collection system.

GEDS User Software. The Maryland team is developing GEDS end-user software for browsing, data selection, temporal and spatial aggregation, graphic display, and interfacing with full-text sources and statistical and interpretive software packages.

Reliability Assessments and Validity Analyses

The multiplicity of projects involving different approaches, software, and coding rules suggests the need to compare and integrate the products of the projects. The Illinois team will pursue this. General comparisons across the basic event datasets (COPDAB, WEIS, BCOW, and SHERFACS) will be made to assess the coding schemes' relative validity against the original source texts.[4] Using the Iraqi crisis that became the Persian Gulf war, a Bolshevik and a Liberal ordinary language description of the crisis will be prepared. Each will impose a different interpretation on the ordinary language stream, much like that produced by COPDAB, WEIS, BCOW, or SHERFACS, or perhaps even in the less structured data frames of GEDS. The point is *not* that these datasets are invalid, but rather that they will reflect their coders' perceptions. What is important is that independent analysis take into account the perceptual glasses of coders and coding rules when using the data for their own research. The interpretive differences imposed by the different coding schemes and how they relate to different "meaning interpretations" of the original text are ultimately questions of validity. We shall examine this issue systematically by assessing the BCOW, COPDAB, SHERFACS, WEIS, and GEDS coding schemes against alternate case-study interpretations, as well as Alker's interpretive analyses, of such issues as the Iraqi-Kurdistan crisis.

The Vancouver Conference

Support for DDIR provided in early 1991 by the National Science Foundation[5] enabled the principal investigators to begin working on the various projects described above. The first organizational activity took place at the International Studies Association's 32d Annual Convention, held on 19-23 March 1991 in Vancouver, British Columbia. A pair of panels provided the principal investigators and others a formal opportunity to update and elaborate some of their ideas and ongoing work on event-data collection. This volume contains revised versions of DDIR Phase II papers, most of which were presented at that convention.

The papers address the three principal issues discussed above. Chapters 2-6 constitute state-of-the-art reports on the two main forms of research in the event-data domain: the global and event-specific approaches to data collection. Individual chapters provide event-data researchers with a comprehensive historical background, précis of analyses using such data, and how-to-do-it guides. As a group these papers offer updated information about the varieties of approaches to event-data research. Chapters 7-9 describe new methodologies and conceptualizations.

Global Approach

The volume's first three chapters represent the global approach. Specific contributions by Davies and McDaniel and by Howell and Barnes indicate new work that updates, expands, and improves the quality of Azar's COPDAB data. Tomlinson, besides indicating the roots and scope of new research being carried out in the tradition of McClelland's WEIS, offers a new methodological means to analyze scaled data.

John Davies and Chad McDaniel recount in chapter 2, "The Global Event-Data System," the history of and current issues relating to event-data research as background for developing GEDS event-data records. An illustration (with the original Reuters source article contained in an appendix) focuses on Iraq's announcement in August 1990 of its annexation of Kuwait. The GEDS event records for this example include (a) descriptive event summaries, (b) source coverage, (c) coded actors, including major non-state entities, (d) issues coded by types, (e) a supporting analysis of verbal events, (f) reported casualty data, (g) on-line access to source articles, and (h) coder and editor identification.

In chapter 3, "Event Data for Region-Specific Interactions: A Research Note on Source Coverage," Llewellyn Howell and Gillian Barnes examine preliminary results of GEDS coding of events in Southeast Asia. Their principal concern is with how policy makers and analysts might use data to explore Third World and smaller countries. Focusing on Malaysian foreign policy, they compare GEDS data collection based on five news sources: *New York Times*, the *Times* (London), *Far Eastern Economic Review*, *Straits Times* (Singapore), and Reuters news service. They analyze the frequencies of Malaysian events in a given time period, the balance between cooperative and conflictual events, and the ultimate effects of source choice on analytical outcomes.

Rodney Tomlinson's "Monitoring WEIS Event Data in Three Dimensions" (chapter 4) discusses the use of event scales and exponential smoothing for the coding of WEIS data and the visual analysis of such data with three-dimensional graphics software. This extended review of the development of Charles McClelland's WEIS project through event scales and exponential smoothing methods is important at a time when enterprises such as DDIR are placing greater focus on the science of data collection, and it provides the theoretic underpinnings that went into the development of WEIS scales. Tomlinson's three-dimensional graphical analyses provide a significant new contribution that allows him to draw specific conclusions for three dyads: U.S.-USSR, USSR-Czechoslovakia, and U.S.-United Kingdom. Conventional conflict-cooperation continua are simplistic, he says. An alternative is needed to convey the notion of complex events. Event flows are plotted in *two* dimensions, using vector algebraic composite values of the power and evaluative constructs for each event, and in *three* dimensions, using the actual values of the power and evaluative constructs. The distances between the plots are interpreted in terms of specific states of affairs such as constructive periods and unstable deconstructive periods.

Event-specific Approach

The volume's second section represents the event-specific approach to the analytic study of worldwide events. The chapter by Sherman and Neack reports on the latest stage of earlier research by Ernst Haas, Joseph Nye, Hayward Alker, and Sherman himself. That by Leng explores the current status of the BCOW project, which is an offshoot of Singer's COW.

In chapter 5, "Imagining the Possibilities: The Prospects of Isolating the Genome of International Conflict from the SHERFACS Dataset," Frank Sherman and Laura Neack demonstrate how SHERFACS enables analysts to compare phase *trajectories* or the sequencing of phases of escalation and de-escalation in cases with similar chronological structures. Their goal is to use SHERFACS to examine those factors which distinguish non-hostile from deadly international conflicts since World War II. They conclude that the substantive issues, threats to values, and great power interests are among the more important factors while power equality and ideology are the least important. They also find that the presence of a bipolar rivalry and/or great-power interest in disputes since 1945 has kept international disputes from escalating from "mere" disputes and crises into deadly conflicts.

Russell Leng's chapter 6, "Automated and Machine-Assisted Coding of Event Data: The BCOW Approach," examines the advantages and limitations of automated and machine-assisted coding of event data, using illustrations from the Behavioral Correlates of War (BCOW) project. He focuses on the trade-offs between reliability and validity as the data-generation process becomes increasingly automated, and concludes that, while the gains in reliability and efficiency are dramatic, one needs to be cognizant of the potential losses with respect to validity.

Methodological Advances

The volume's third main thrust, chapters 7-9 as well as the chapters by Davies and McDaniel and Tomlinson, is methodological. In chapter 2 Davies and McDaniel offer a new, semi-automated procedure for coding event data using the COPDAB dataset as a model. The full development of their GEDS procedure will reduce one of the greatest stumbling blocks to event-data research: the cost in time and money required to code data for each new year. Tomlinson's chapter 4 demonstrates three-dimensional graphical methods applied to WEIS data. While both chapters stress the data-collection side of the equation, they also go into its methodological dimensions.

In chapter 7, "Machine Coding of Event Data," Philip Schrodt reports on his efforts to develop automated systems for generating event data. He describes two systems that have been developed to use machine-learning and statistical techniques for natural-language processing, and then outlines testing procedures and results for each. WINR is a statistical-classification scheme that uses a set of pre-coded training cases; it is tested using the text summaries from various WEIS datasets. The Kansas Event-Data System (KEDS) uses procedures for pattern recognition and simple linguistic parsing. English and German dictionaries for use in the parsing routine are currently under development for coding WEIS data. The accuracy of the KEDS system is evaluated using a similar set of WEIS summaries originally coded from the *New York Times*. Finally, Schrodt discusses NEXIS and other machine-readable databases as a source of event data.

Hayward Alker, in chapter 8, "Making Peaceful Sense of the News: Institutionalizing International Conflict-Management Event Reporting Using

Frame-Based Interpretive Routines," explores the development of a news monitoring component of a United Nations oriented conflict warning and analysis system. He considers several frame-based ways of automating interpretive codings of GEDS data records that are relevant to conflict management. These include conflict-characterization frames, conflict-sequence scripts, case-based reasoning about conflict precedents or analogies, and explanation-based learning from new disputes. Of principal concern is the integration of such procedures into SHERFACS coding practices.

The final chapter 9, "Through Rose-Colored Glasses: Computational Interpretations of Events," is Steven Seitz's outline of a strategy — different from semantic parsing (chapter 7) and hermeneutic contextualism (chapter 8) — for the systematic analysis of textual material. His strategy begins with libraries of interpretive frameworks (metaphors and parables) and works backward to the structuring of text streams. Although the volume of textual information is typically large, Seitz shows how a relatively small number of interpretive frameworks can often cover much of the textual material of general interest to political scientists. An interpretive framework that meets the user's goodness-of-fit standards can, in turn, serve as the basis for generating projections that utilize dynamic components of each interpretive framework.

In summary, this volume aims at both reporting the state of the art of event-data research and considering the issues involved in improving the quality of research collections, data-gathering procedures, and analytic methodologies. As the initial product of an active research community, supported under the framework of Data Development for International Research, the chapters presented here clearly represent, we feel, the direction in which research in this domain is heading.

NOTES

This chapter, a revision of DDIR's Phase II proposal submitted in summer 1990 to the National Science Foundation, includes some substantially modified paragraphs drafted by other principal investigators. We are indebted to them for this assistance.

1. WEIS's international event data are publicly available for 1966-77. Some more recent coding is in progress for both international and domestic events; see Tomlinson, chapter 4 in this volume.
2. A survey of dataset usage in 15 major U.S. journals in international and comparative politics in 1974-86 found event datasets third placed (with COPDAB, WEIS, and CREON together citing 61 uses) behind only the Correlates of War (87) and World Handbook (69), with the second volume of World Handbook III including event data (McGowan et al., 1988).
3. Ideally, figure 1.1 should include as a seventh slice an improved version of World Handbook III, which Taylor intends to undertake next year.

4. In standard methodological jargon, "validity" is an assessment of whether one is measuring what one intends to measure. Different coding schemes involve more than different intentions, because the process of structuring information from less structured sources (e.g., a WEIS record vs. a Reuters report) can reasonably be expected incompletely and perhaps inadequately to capture the meaning in the less structured text. We need to examine such issues more systematically as part of the data development research.

5. National Science Foundation Grant NSF SES 90-25130.

REFERENCES

Alker, H. R., Jr. and F. L. Sherman. 1982. "Collective Security-Seeking Practices Since 1945." In *Managing International Crises.* Ed. Frei, D. 113-145. Beverly Hills, CA and London: Sage Publications.

Azar, E. E. 1970. "Analysis of International Events." *Peace Research Reviews* 4, 1: 1-113.

Azar, E. E. and T. J. Sloan. 1975. *Dimensions of Interaction: A Sourcebook for the Study of the Behavior of 31 Nations from 1948 through 1973*, Occasional Paper #8. Pittsburgh, PA: International Studies Association.

Bloomfield, L. P. and A. C. Leiss. 1969. *Controlling Small Wars: A Strategy for the 1970's.* New York: Alfred A. Knopf.

Butterworth, R. L. 1980. *Managing Interstate Conflict, 1945-1979: Data with Synopses*, Final Report, February.

Butterworth, R. L. and M. E. Scranton. 1976. *Managing Interstate Conflict, 1945-1974: Data with Synopses.* Pittsburgh, PA: University of Pittsburgh, University Center for International Studies.

Choucri, N. and R. C. North. 1975. *Nations in Conflict: National Growth and International Violence.* San Francisco, CA: W. H. Freeman.

Farris, L., H. R. Alker, Jr., K. Carley and F. L. Sherman. 1980. "Phase/Actor Disaggregated Butterworth-Scranton Codebook." Cambridge, MA: The Massachusetts Institute of Technology, Center for International Studies. Working paper.

Haas, E. B. 1968. "Collective Security and the Future International System." Monograph No. 1. Monograph Series in World Affairs, Vol. 5, No. 1. Denver, CO: University of Denver.

Haas, E. B., R. L. Butterworth and J. S. Nye. 1972. *Conflict Management by International Organizations.* Morristown, NJ: General Learning Press.

Hermann, C. F., M. A. East, M. G. Hermann, B. G. Salmore and S. A. Salmore. 1973. *CREON: A Foreign Events Data Set*, Sage Professional Papers in International Studies, Vol. 1, Series No. 02-024. Beverly Hills, CA and London: Sage Publications.

Lasswell, H. D. and D. Blumenstock. 1939. *World Revolutionary Propaganda: A Chicago Study.* New York and London: Alfred A. Knopf.

Leng, R. J. and J. David Singer. 1988. "Militarized Interstate Crisis: The BCOW Typology and Its Applications." *International Studies Quarterly* 32, 2 (June): 155-173.

Mansbach, R. W. and J. A. Vasquez. 1981. In Search of Theory: A New Paradigm for Global Politics. New York: Columbia University Press.

McClelland, C. A., R. G. Tomlinson, R. G. Sherwin, G. A. Hill, H. A. Calhoun, P. H. Fenn and J. D. Martin. 1971. "The Management and Analysis of International Event Data: A Computerized System for Monitoring and Projecting Event Flows." Report in support of ARPA/ONR Contract #N00014-67-A-0269-0004 for Short-Term Conflict Prediction. Los Angeles, CA: University of Southern California, School of International Relations. Mimeograph.

McGowan, P., H. Starr, G. Hower, R. L. Merritt and D. A. Zinnes. 1988. "International Data as a National Resource." *International Interactions* 14, 2: 101-113.

Merritt, R. L. 1992. "Measuring Events for International Political Analysis." *International Interactions* 18, 2.

Moses, L. E., R. A. Brody, O. R. Holsti, J. B. Kadane and J. S. Milstein. 1967. "Scaling Data on Inter-Nation Action: A Standard Scale is Developed for Comparing International Conflict in a Variety of Situations." *Science* 156, 3778 (26 May): 1054-1059.

Nye, J. S. 1971. *Peace in Parts: Integration and Conflict in Regional Organization.* Boston, MA: Little, Brown and Company.

Rummel, R. J. 1964. "Dimensions of Conflict Behavior Within and Between Nations." In *General Systems: Yearbook of the Society for General Systems Research.* Ed. von Bertalanffy, L. and A. Rapoport. Vol. 8. 1-50. Ann Arbor, MI: Society for General Systems Research.

___. 1972. *The Dimensions of Nations.* Beverly Hills, CA and London: Sage Publications.

___. 1976. "The Roots of Faith." In *In Search of Global Patterns.* Ed. Rosenau, J. N. 10-30. New York: Free Press.

Sherman, F. L. 1987a. "Four Major Traditions of Historical Events Research: A Brief Comparison." Paper presented at the Second DDIR Event Data Conference. Boston, MA, The Massachusetts Institute of Technology, November 13-15.

___. 1987b. "Partway to Peace: The United Nations and the Road to Nowhere." Ph.D. dissertation. State College, PA: The Pennsylvania State University.

Taylor, C. L. and D. A. Jodice. 1983. *World Handbook of Political and Social Indicators,* 3d ed. New Haven: Yale University Press.

United States Department of Labor. 1976. *BLS Handbook of Methods,* Bulletin No. 1910. Washington, DC: U.S. Department of Labor, Bureau of Labor Statistics.

CHAPTER 2

The Global Event-Data System

John L. Davies and Chad K. McDaniel

Abstract

The Global Event-Data System (GLOBAL or GEDS) is being developed to provide computer-assisted identification, abstracting and coding of daily international and domestic events, as reported primarily in Reuters international newswire service (World Service or Library Report) as well as other sources. GEDS data describe the internal and interactive behavior of all nation-states and the major non-state communities and international organizations, providing both detailed summaries (including direct quotes and cross referencing) and analytical coding for each event. Associated microcomputer software and user manuals will also facilitate user access to the full-text source articles (where available on-line), searching, extraction, manipulation and graphic display of data, as well as interfacing with statistical and interpretive software and related datasets.

GEDS data are being generated initially for the period from 1990, with the aim of establishing a program for continuous near-real-time coding as well as back-coding to 1979. This will provide the basis for a collaborative effort to update and expand earlier, more specialized datasets, including Azar's Conflict and Peace Data Bank (COPDAB), McClelland's World Event Interaction Survey (WEIS), Taylor's World Handbook of Political and Social Indicators (WHPSI), and episodic datasets such as Leng's Behavioral Correlates of War (BCOW) and Sherman's SHERFACS.

At the same time, GEDS is designed to overcome several conceptual and practical limits inherent in older datasets. It provides a significant expansion in density of coverage, and in descriptive and analytical detail as compared to available event-datasets; and partially automated coding of on-line news sources allows improved efficiency and reliability for human coders. Continuous updating of existing datasets from a common data stream thus becomes possible and at the same time qualitative analyses and development and application of new coding schemes are amply supported. Both aspects are critical for meeting the evolving needs of researchers and policy-makers in tracking, analyzing, modelling, or predicting crises and patterns of change in international affairs.

Event-Data Research: Current Status and Issues

There have been many attempts to remedy what Charles Hermann (1982) has called the "intolerable gap" between the concern lavished on explanatory theories of international relations, and the neglect of the need to define and measure with precision the variables to be explained.

Of these, Edward Azar's (1980, 1982) Conflict and Peace Data Bank (COPDAB), Charles McClelland and colleagues' (1971) World Event Interaction Survey (WEIS), and Charles Taylor and David Jodice's (1983) World Handbook of Political and Social Indicators (WHPSI) are the only three comprehensive, global data banks currently (i.e., beyond the mid-1960s) providing access to daily interaction chronologies of international and/or domestic events.

A unique value of these datasets is that they allow tracking, modelling and prediction, based on dynamic statistical analysis, of changes in patterns of international or domestic interaction; and testing of theoretical predictions as to how these changes may be related to other events or variables, on local, regional, or global levels. Thus they continue to be widely used in IR research (see survey by McGowan et al., 1988), despite a substantial and still-growing lag-time between data and current events.

A number of theorists have raised serious questions about the assumptions and strategies underlying the generation of such datasets, and consequent limitations or distortions which may reduce their validity or utility in producing theoretically and practically significant findings (e.g., Alker, 1975; Mansbach and Vasquez, 1981). How these concerns may be addressed through the development of a new and expanded event-data system is discussed in two separate papers (McDaniel and Davies, 1991; Davies and McDaniel, forthcoming). The first paper addresses the more radical, phenomenological critiques which question the possibility that any event data could be constructed that are meaningful outside the interpretive framework of the individual responsible for generating them. The second paper follows from this to describe how the more common and specific criticisms are being addressed through the development of GEDS. The focus of the present paper is more descriptive, reviewing the strategies adopted in the GEDS project in relation to the existing datasets which are to be updated on the basis of the GEDS event summaries.

In the face of such concerns as to the value of event data and related quantitative coding schemes, many researchers have limited themselves either to qualitative, in-depth case-studies focusing on specific countries and periods, or to developing case-oriented data on multiple "historical episodes," which take large-scale events (episodes) such as crises or militarized disputes as the primary units of analysis, rather than small-scale day-to-day interactions (Hermann, 1989).

In order to retain the advantages of detailed tracking and analysis of patterns of change, some of these datasets also incorporate or draw on daily interaction chronologies as a means of describing detailed events within each crisis or dispute — e.g., Leng and Singer's (1988) Behavioral Correlates of War (BCOW), and the FACS/SHERFACS projects (Farris et al., 1980; Alker and Sherman, 1982; Sherman, 1987). However, event patterns that extend beyond each episode are not examined. The COPDAB, WEIS or WHPSI datasets must then be relied on for any analysis of the broader temporal and spatial context within which these episodes arise.

Historically, the limitations on the information processing capacity of any one research group have necessitated a choice between these two strategies: comprehensive, long-term global interaction chronologies with precoded, telegraphic event descriptions; or in-depth descriptive analyses of selected historical episodes which sacrifice comprehensiveness of coverage to avoid some of the difficulties mentioned above.

Hermann (1989) suggests that this has led to the emergence of two distinct research communities with apparently incompatible data requirements. The first group gives priority to the need for comprehensive coverage, and has assumed that differences between the accounts in different sources can be usefully resolved to yield a single brief description and coding of each event; while the second group may seek to avoid any such single characterization, giving priority instead to preserving contextual detail and investigating the diversity of perspectives reflected by different participants or reports. Each approach has been productive, yielding complementary perspectives in the attempt to understand the complex dynamics of international and domestic interactions.

However, recent advances in computer and information technologies have provided a basis for developing a broad consensus on how to meet the needs of both groups through a number of significant upgrades in the event-data generation process. With (1) major international news sources such as Reuters now available on-line, and (2) the enormously expanded storage capacity, processing speed, and programming flexibility now available at the microcomputer level, it has become possible to develop an event coding system which sacrifices neither the comprehensiveness and analytical strengths of global coding efforts, nor the depth, complexity and diversity of coverage of the case-study and episodic coding projects. Moreover, such a unified coding system can be achieved while still reducing the overall cost of data generation, through the development of computer applications which minimize the time needed of human coders, editors and data managers, and through cross-project collaboration to avoid duplication of effort.

The GEDS system is being developed to meet these goals, in collaboration with leading research scholars coordinated through the Data Development for International Research (DDIR) group based at the University of Illinois at Urbana-Champaign. The GEDS project avoids current inefficiencies and duplications of effort by producing a single event-data stream from which COPDAB, WEIS, WHPSI, BCOW, SHERFACS and other/future data coding schemes can be developed, expanded and updated.

Current World Event-Datasets

Of the existing data banks, COPDAB is maintained (along with the GEDS project) at the Center for International Development and Conflict Management (CIDCM) at the University of Maryland, and will be specifically updated as part of this project, with other datasets also being updated through the larger collaborative effort coordinated by DDIR. We thus refer to COPDAB in more detail in reviewing the strengths and weaknesses of these data banks.

COPDAB includes event records of the daily actions of 135 nation-states, both toward one another and within their domestic environments, for the period from 1 January 1948 to 31 December 1978 (some more recent coding has been completed for specific regions). Each event record specifies which public *source* reported *who* did or said *what* to *whom*, and *when;* and in addition to being briefly *summarized* (76 characters total per event), each event is further coded for *issue type* (symbolic, economic, military, etc.) and degree of *cooperation or conflict* involved.

International events are defined by COPDAB as occurrences between nation-states that are distinct enough from the constant flow of "transactions" (e.g., trade, mail flow) to stand out against this background as reportable, or newsworthy (e.g., new trade agreements). Thus, to qualify as an event, an occurrence has to be actually reported in a reputable and available public source (such as a newspaper or chronology). A combination of international sources (e.g., the *New York Times)* and local sources are relied on to maximize coverage and minimize bias in reporting events (Azar, 1975).

Cooperation and conflict are assessed using 15-point International and Domestic Scales, which have been developed and validated in a series of studies (e.g., Azar and Sloan, 1975; Azar and Havener, 1976; Azar and Lerner, 1981). Ordinal scale values are convertible to an interval scale using a weighting system for the degree of cooperation or conflict represented by each scale point (level 8 being neutral). Thus, it is possible to aggregate the data to derive periodic (daily, monthly, yearly, etc.) totals in each of these "dimensions of interaction," yielding time-series data for quantitative analysis of intensity of cooperation or conflict within or between the nations, dyads, or regions of interest. Data can also be selectively analyzed within or across different domains (by issue type as above); and the brief event summaries also are intended to allow for limited qualitative analysis or further coding as desired.

WEIS data, which are publicly available for international events from 1966 to 1977 (with some more recent coding for both international and domestic events in progress), also follows the basic coding scheme of identifying who did or said what to whom and when. Although covering a shorter period than COPDAB (particularly for domestic events), and drawing on only one news source (*New York Times*), WEIS provides two unique codings not provided by COPDAB: events are classified into 63 mutually exclusive and exhaustive categories (e.g., "make substantive agreement" or "non-military demonstration"), capable of being weighted to form scales reflecting a dimension of interest (McClelland et al., 1971); and for the more recent coding of domestic events, subnational actors and targets are identified by role or membership in 57 distinct groupings (VanBeers and Sherwin, 1977).

WHPSI daily event data are available, for domestic political events only, for 136 nation-states for the period 1948 to 1977. Event categories are focused specifically to provide indices of political unrest (e.g., protests, riots), state coercive behavior (e.g., government sanctions, political executions), and governmental change (e.g., elections, executive transfers). Number of deaths from events involving domestic violence are also recorded, and additional codings for event duration, intensity, scale, and impact are included for events from 1968. WHPSI also separately compiles statistical indicators of political, economic, and social change for each state, thus helping to define the broader context within which coded events occur (Taylor and Jodice, 1983).

To date, BCOW provides daily event data only within the boundaries of 40 interstate crises between 1816 and 1980. The GEDS project will facilitate updating from 1980, and also allow an option that some aspects of the BCOW coding scheme could be applied to include all international events rather than only those within selected crises. Unique features of the BCOW coding scheme (beyond the core coding of who does or says what to whom and when) include: location of each event; duration and variations in intensity of multi-day events; assignment of physical events to one of 103 categories of military, diplomatic, economic, or unofficial behaviors; and detailed analysis of sequential verbal interactions (allowing identification of negotiating strategies: Leng and Singer, 1988).

All four of these data banks have been extensively used and cited in published research (McGowan et al., 1988). A cursory review of recent research literature identified more than 70 substantive studies drawing on the COPDAB data alone, and we process new requests for this dataset at CIDCM every month, in spite of the fact that the data are now over ten years behind current events. A primary example is the utilization by the SHERFACS project of COPDAB data for generating phase/actor analyses of international quarrels and disputes (Sherman, 1987).

The extent of this demand reflects the growing number of researchers using event data generally and daily interaction chronologies in particular. Along with this has come the demand for datasets which are sufficiently rich, comprehensive, up to date, and well documented, to overcome current limitations.

While acknowledging the validity of the need for richer data, we also emphasize the value and economy of addressing this need in a manner which supports the updating of existing datasets, thus maintaining and building on time-tested resources of the international research and policy community. Updating existing datasets makes it possible to maintain consistency in analytic strategies, to permit long-run time-series analyses, and thus to facilitate the cumulation of research findings. At the same time, old limitations can be overcome and new research needs met by coordinating and substantially expanding the current coding projects, using more comprehensive sources, and making use of new technologies to develop more efficient, powerful, and reliable real-time coding procedures.

Proposed Improvements on Current Datasets

The following event records illustrate the contrast between the existing COPDAB data and data now being generated through the GEDS coding procedures (see appendix 1 for the Reuters report from which these sample records were coded):

COPDAB:

90080864569094ANNEX3713 FOLLOWING AUG 2 INVASION

The numeric codes give year (90), month (08), day (08), actor (645: Iraq), target (690: Kuwait), news source (94: Reuters), one-word action (annex), issue types (3: military/strategic and 7: political/legal), 15-point international cooperation-conflict scale value (13), and event summary (up to a total record length of 76 characters).

GEDS:

Event Date: 8 Aug 1990

Continuity: Discrete

Summary: #Iraq's ruling Revolution Command Council# ~announced the annexation~ of *Kuwait*, despite the deployment of US combat troops in Saudi Arabia and growing military and economic pressure on Baghdad. In ^Baghdad^, Iraqi leader Saddam Hussein was wildly cheered by the <national assembly> after the announcement. "Thank God we are now one people, one state that will be the paradise of the Arabs," Saddam said. The announcement follows Iraq's Aug 2 invasion of Kuwait, and is said to have been endorsed by the nine-man provisional Kuwaiti government installed by Iraq, which declared that it wanted "the hero Saddam Hussein to be our leader and protector." The prime minister, Alaa Hussein Ali, believed to be an Iraqi officer, was named a deputy prime minister of Iraq. Responding to the Western buildup, the ruling council declared that "All the navy fleets and squadrons . . . will not shake us."

Episode/Cross-ref(s)	Iraq invades Kuwait/Gulf War (ep100)
Actor(s)	Iraq (645)
Target(s)	Kuwait (690)
Other(s) Affected	USA (002)
	Saudi Arabia (670)
Location	Iraq (645)
Issue Type(s)	Milit.-Strategic; Political-Legal (3;7)
Verbal/Substantive	Substantive (1)
Event Category	Annex territory by force (m23)
Casualties (k/w)	/
Source	Reuters World Service (094)
Reference/Event No.	8 Aug 1990 Nicosia w724 a342 #1
Alt. Source/Cross-Ref	
Coder/Affil	Beata Rybczynski, CIDCM, 1990
Coding Date	15 Aug 1990
Editor/Affil	Steven Kurth, CIDCM, 1989
Edit Date	20 Sep 1990

Symbols used to flag additional information within the summary field are:

- \# Actor(s)/sub-actor(s)
- ~ Action defining the event
- * Target(s)/sub-target(s)
- ^ Location details
- <> Institutional context
- " Direct quotes from participants
- [] Casualty figures (not needed in the above example)

The reference field for a news wire report gives the dateline (when and where the report was submitted), word count, article number (for that day), and event number (for that article). If the same event is coded from another source, that event record will be cross-referenced in the next field.

In addition, the GEDS record will incorporate as far as practicable specialized COPDAB, WEIS, BCOW and WHPSI codings for the event as these become available to us. COPDAB scale values — international scale 13 in the above example — are being generated and incorporated concurrently.

Advances achieved through the GEDS system include the following.

1. Event Summaries: Providing Adequate Descriptive Detail, Including Context and Multiple Perspectives

The core of each GEDS event record is a variable length narrative summary, typically from 8 to 16 lines in length, but with no length limit (in contrast, for example, to the single line, 76 character limit imposed on COPDAB records using the old mainframe procedures). These narratives are structured to balance the need for conciseness with that for preserving the key elements of each event, retaining as far as possible the natural language expressions used in the original report.

In general, each summary is crafted to reflect the general characterization of the event conveyed by the source article. This is achieved in large part by retaining as much as possible the actual language the article uses to describe the actions, motives, perspectives, etc. of the parties, *including all direct quotes by participants*. Within the summary, the verbal or non-verbal action-phrase defining the event, and the relevant actors, targets, etc., are specifically flagged to distinguish them from other actions and participants which may be mentioned in providing context (as in the above sample record).

Information reported as to expectations, goals, strategies, investments, identifications, or reasons for each action are included in the summary, at least to the extent they are offered by, or attributed by the source to, the participants, and to the extent they can be systematically identified through computer-assisted coding. Explicit references to recent or historical events or precedents as context for present action, are included; and as far as practicable related events, such as those forming part of the same episode, will be cross-referenced. The combined GEDS summaries thus provide a basis for subsequent analyses along Lasswellian lines, for example, allowing maximum flexibility for the development of typologies and coding schemes addressing the dynamic context and differing perspectives of the parties. Development of such an interpretive analytical scheme for GEDS summaries is currently being undertaken by Hayward Alker and colleagues at MIT.

Separate event records will be maintained when the same event is reported by separate sources. These will be uniquely cross-referenced to allow default/ selection of a single record per event, with priority to, or exclusive use of, certain source(s) as desired by the user. However, separate records also allow preservation of information on the diverse perspectives that different parties or communities may have on a given event (as far as they may be reflected in different news sources), avoiding the dubious step of attempting to construct a single "objective" account of each event from conflicting reports (see Hermann, 1989). Each user may decide which source(s) are to be relied upon, or compared, for a given purpose.

GEDS thus avoids collapsing diverse narrative accounts into one, or into categorical or quantitative coding to be used without benefit of sufficient contextual detail to allow the possibility of checking or improving on the accuracy or appropriateness of the coding. Narrative information is maintained, along with analytic data which allow identification and quantitative analysis of patterns of change. The analytic data also provide efficient indexing, management and user access and manipulation of the qualitative data; and ensures that adequate information is being included in the summaries to support more specialized coding schemes (COPDAB, WEIS, etc.). At the same time, retaining the information from which these codes are derived in the summaries allows coding accuracy to be easily checked by editors and users, and also allows for the generation and comparison of alternative or more detailed coding schemes without the prohibitive cost and duplication of effort involved in going back to the original sources.

Two aspects of the contextual detail for each event that are specifically coded in GEDS are location and institutional context. As with actors and targets, the place of occurrence of each event is coded on two levels: first, according to state or region (3-character code as used for actors — see appendix 2.3 — following a similar convention as for BCOW), and second, details of the location (e.g., city) are flagged within the summary.

Institutional context refers to the setting in which the event occurred (e.g., summit meeting, UN General Assembly, US Senate, press conference) and can be essential in defining the significance of verbal events. Relevant information is flagged within the summary to facilitate more detailed analysis by the user.

2. Source Coverage: Improving Density and Evenness of the Data

Given the economies of computer-assisted, partially automated coding from on-line sources, it has become possible to expand from traditional hard-copy news sources such as the *New York Times* and archives such as *Facts on File*, to the much denser and more detailed coverage of world events offered by the international news wire services. Of these, Reuters, whose Library Report yields about 200-300 news reports per day (after excluding non-codable administrative reports, coverage of sports and cultural events, weather and statistical reports, features, and subsequently revised reports) is used as the primary GEDS source.

This choice is based on Reuters' policy of even coverage of all world regions, with journalists based in all major population centers of the world. These journalists are typically recruited from among local reporters who also write for local news sources in the region — foreign language articles being translated into English by Reuters staff. Thus distortion of information by foreign reporters unfamiliar with local cultural and political perspectives is minimized. Also, when media attention shifts to new priorities (such as democratization in Eastern Europe, or the Gulf War) continuing coverage of other issues and regions is not squeezed out by limited space or resources, as happens with newspaper sources. This evenness of coverage is uniquely reflected in the World Service, which, unlike the other Reuters wires, does not slant the density of its coverage relative to the location of the user.

COPDAB, which, more than any of the other existing data banks, attempts to achieve the same thoroughness and evenness of coverage through drawing on multiple (70) international and regional news sources, has had limited success in this regard. Inevitably, given limited resources for coding from foreign language sources, sources are not evenly drawn from all world regions, the same sources are not consistently used throughout, and all together they generally yield an average of only 30-40 events per day (the other world datasets report less than this). Thus, even relying on Reuters alone and with one or two events typically being coded per report (yielding 300-400 events per day), GEDS will allow a considerable gain in both density (by a factor of 10) and evenness of coverage.

While the project focuses on coding events from Reuters as the primary source, we anticipate that once the coding programs and procedures have been sufficiently developed, it will be possible to add and compare other subsidiary sources, at least in collaboration with other research groups. For example, the *Foreign Broadcast Information Service* (FBIS), which provides translations of (unevenly selected) foreign language news broadcasts world-wide, is expected to be made publicly available on magnetic tape soon; the *New York Times* and other sources used for COPDAB, WEIS, WHPSI and other datasets are already available on-line; and GEDS coding can also be done (more slowly) from local off-line sources. Some coding from other sources is already being undertaken (both at the University of Maryland and at the American Graduate School of International Management) to allow assessment of differences in adequacy of source coverage (see Howell and Barnes, chapter 3).

Data from other news or archival source(s) will be integrated with that from Reuters for optional access by users. Users can then conveniently select or exclude data from each source as required. This was not possible with COPDAB, which only cites one source for each coded event, and without referencing the specific article or date of publication.

A key advantage of the greater density and evenness of GEDS data is that it will allow the possibility of more precise tracking and more finely-grained dynamic analyses: i.e., focusing on smaller countries, groups or regions of interest, and using weekly or even daily data aggregations (as distinct from the monthly aggregations recommended for COPDAB). In contrast to Reuters, many of the sources used for COPDAB and other existing datasets are brief news index or archival reports such as the *New York Times Index* or the *Middle East Journal*, which do not report precise event dates, and thus cannot yield accurate daily time-series.

If the precise day of occurrence is not available from the report, for GEDS it is coded by week and/or month (these events can be readily excluded by users focusing on daily time series). Events which continue for more than a day (such as meetings, blockades, etc.) are coded for days on which they are specifically reported as beginning, ending, escalating, de-escalating, or continuing. Each event record will thus be coded as discrete or as reflecting one phase of a continuous event, similar to the coding system now used in BCOW and revised WHPSI coding schemes, and as needed to facilitate SHERFACS coding.

3. Coding the Actors: Recognizing the Major Non-State Entities

The list of recognized actors has expanded dramatically beyond those in earlier systems. Events involving all nation-states (including small states overlooked by other datasets), and major international organizations (such as the UN, EC, OAS, OAU, OPEC, NATO, and INGOs such as the International Red Cross or Amnesty International) are coded, expanding the roughly standardized list of 3-digit and 3-letter actor codes used in earlier datasets.

In addition, and more significantly for meeting current research and policy needs, the world's major non-state communities and identity groups are coded and tracked as distinct actors. These include groups that are key actors in more than 70 ongoing protracted social conflicts (such as those in Yugoslavia, Lebanon, Sri Lanka, Israel, the former USSR, Iraq, South Africa, Northern Ireland, and Ethiopia). Typically these groups are ascriptively defined by ethnic, cultural, religious, and/or linguistic characteristics which contrast with those of neighboring groups (e.g., Azar, 1990).

Research interest in such groups has increased enormously in the data-oriented research community. At one level, this is due to a paradigm shift away from the traditional focus on nation-states as the only significant international actors. At the policy level, this follows from recognition by diverse elites — national security managers, human rights advocates, conflict management specialists, administrators of refugee programs — that communal groups have become principal protagonists and targets in the local and regional conflicts of the late 20th century.

Such identification and coding of communal groups as actors has become an essential step in generating data for empirical research on the dynamics of contemporary conflicts and processes of conflict management. The most significant of these groups (politically and numerically) have been identified and systematically profiled in Phase 1 of Ted Robert Gurr's Minorities at Risk Project (Gurr and Scarritt, 1989), which is now housed at this Center, and have been added to the list of GEDS actors, with some additions (e.g., dominant ethnic groups such as the Sinhalese in Sri Lanka, or significant ethnic groups in small countries, such as Indians in Fiji, or in newly independent states such as Russians in Ukraine).

Along with these communal groups (numbering over 250), the nation-states and the major international organizations, other entities coded as primary actors in GEDS are: external territories administered by a nation-state (e.g., Puerto Rico, Hong Kong, French Guiana); durable political/military organizations which do not represent communal groups, but do control substantial territory (e.g., the Khmer Rouge); and political organizations which have otherwise gained status in the international system (e.g., the PLO). In contrast, multi-national corporations (e.g., Exxon) are only codable when they interact with one of the primary actors, as either co-actor or target. A current list of actors (subject to revision) is included in appendix 2.

The standard list of codes for states and international organizations has been augmented, so that each domestic non-state actor is identified by a 2-digit code in addition to the 3-digit code for the nation-state(s) governing its territory. Data users may thus choose to treat communal actors either separately (as a distinct minority in each state), or as an aggregate ethnic group spread across nation-state borders (e.g., the Kurds, Jews, or Palestinians). Alternatively, a researcher may aggregate data for all groups living within the boundaries of a given nation-state or region, depending on the nature of the desired analysis.

The (state or non-state) parties involved in each event are coded as to who is acting ("actor"), who is acted upon or most directly affected ("target"), and who else is explicitly referred to as being involved or affected ("others affected"). In this respect, GEDS introduces three further innovations:

i. *Multiple actors* and/or targets, if they are reported to be acting or affected identically, may be coded within a single event record. This avoids the distortion in time-series data of the apparent number of events per time period resulting from the old practice of generating separate records for each actor-target pair. At the same time, users retain the option to select only events involving specified parties, or to differentially weight multi-actor events;

ii. *Other parties* referred to as being involved or affected (differently from the primary actors and targets) are also coded as such, to facilitate identification of all events involving any party of interest and vice-versa; and

iii. *Reciprocal actions* (agreements, meetings, etc.) affecting only the actors themselves are coded as such, avoiding the artificial assignation of mutual actors to target status.

The current conventional procedures for coding domestic events (i.e., when actors and targets do not have separate codes), unidentified targets, etc. are retained.

To allow differentiation of the diverse roles played by different participants in both international and domestic events, the specific *individuals, bodies or groups representing each state or non-state actor and target* — including their names, positions, roles — are flagged as *sub-actors* and *sub-targets* within each summary, as in the sample given above. This preserves the information as required, for example, in SHERFACS or domestic WEIS coding, and allows systematic selection, tracking and analysis of events in terms of specific subnational groups or participants of interest to the user. Even the actions of those who do not officially represent any of the codable actors (see appendix 2) can be tracked to the extent that they are codable as domestic events of national interest.

4. Specifying the Issues: Coding Issue Types and Episodes

To allow users to investigate distinct patterns or themes of interaction specific to a single dimension, crisis, etc., GEDS includes coding for each event according to issue type(s) and episode. The existing COPDAB classification of international and domestic events into the eight issue types listed below has been incorporated in GEDS coding (retaining the detailed definitions as used in COPDAB):

symbolic
economic
military/strategic
cultural/scientific
environmental/ecological/natural resource
minorities/human rights/health
political/legal
other

As with all GEDS coding (except event date and coder and editor identification), the information on which the issue type codes are based is also retained in the summary, allowing users to check them or to develop and compare alternative or more refined coding schemes.

In addition, it is intended that each event summary will be cross-referenced as far as possible to records of related events through identifying the specific episode(s) of which the event is a part (such as the invasion of Kuwait and Gulf War in the above sample event record). This step, which will be undertaken in coordination with coding projects for SHERFACS, BCOW, and other episodic datasets, helps to place each event in its immediate context, and allows more focused differentiation among issues than is possible through issue-type coding alone.

Detailed summaries and user software will provide each user with a basis for still more focused differentiation of issues within each type or episode, with summaries frequently cross-referring to specific related events; and cross-referencing procedures also allowing the user to identify which events were reported together in the same article.

5. Supporting Analysis of Verbal Events

An area where there is particular interest in comparing and further developing coding schemes is in the analysis of verbal events. Verbal behavior such as praise, promises of support, criticisms, requests, or threats — as opposed to "substantive" actions with immediate physical or legal impact — is of particular interest in the analysis of diplomatic and conflict management strategies. For such purposes, the precise form of a verbal statement or exchange can be critical in understanding its significance. GEDS coding therefore distinguishes between verbal and substantive events, and where they are available, *direct quotes by participants are included in the summary*.

Detailed analysis of verbal exchanges has been a particular emphasis of the BCOW project. In structuring the GEDS summaries to ensure that information required for subsequent BCOW analysis is included, it is convenient to code verbal events into six categories, broadly defined (following BCOW) so as to be mutually exclusive and exhaustive:

comment   — on past event(s)
             — on future
request   — conditional
             — unconditional
statement of intention
             — conditional
             — unconditional

Specific details of any conditions are included in the summary, and cross-referencing will be provided as far as possible to records of past events commented on. Also, where a verbal event refers to *inaction* (e.g., an actor may comment on his own or another's failure to act, request another not to act, or express an intention to refrain from acting under certain circumstances), sufficient detail of such utterances will be given to allow subsequent coding of the inaction under the BCOW coding scheme.

There are, of course, several possible alternative schemes for generating typologies for verbal events, whose relative merits are the subject of ongoing discussion amongst DDIR participants and others. Our approach is to support BCOW's existing scheme, and in doing so ensure that a firm basis is provided for the development, evaluation and comparison of new and existing schemes, thus facilitating both the cumulation and progression of scientific knowledge.

6. Providing a Common Basis for Updating Existing Data Banks; and Comparing/Developing Existing and Potential Coding Schemes

A primary concern in developing GEDS is to provide an open resource that is accessible and useful for researchers working within (or interested in comparing) a range of different theoretical perspectives, rather than being tied to whatever framework was adopted by the original developers of a dataset. Thus, the core of the GEDS data is made up of detailed event summaries, containing enough information for the user to check, adopt, ignore, or improve on the specific coding that is also provided along with the summaries. The summaries themselves can also be checked and augmented as needed, by accessing the original, fully referenced source articles on-line for more detail.

An immediate advantage of establishing a common, expanded event-data stream from which existing datasets can be updated — beyond the obvious economy of time and effort — is that it becomes possible to assess the interrelationships among the various coding schemes, and how the theoretical assumptions and practices involved in each one may give a different slant or perspective in analysis of the same international and domestic behaviors.

To this end, a detailed list of several hundred GEDS "event categories" is currently in the very early stages of development (see sample event record) as a basis for fully or partially automated generation of specialized codes for the broader (and partially overlapping) WEIS, BCOW, and WHPSI event categories, the COPDAB cooperation-conflict scale values, and future alternative scales. The task of generating the specialized codes from the GEDS event records is being undertaken primarily by other research groups collaborating with us through DDIR. The GEDS event category list is a contribution toward this collaborative programming effort, and will also serve as an index to guide human coders and editors in checking and editing the specialized coding from the (partially) automated coding programs.

But in addition to facilitating the development of programs for coding under the more specialized coding schemes — and testing the adequacy of the GEDS summaries for the purpose — the list will serve as a common index to help clarify the relationships between the different coding schemes, facilitating assessment of their relative strengths and suitability for diverse analytical tasks.

One disadvantage in adopting GEDS as a common event-data stream for updating and interfacing existing data banks, is that a new discontinuity is created in the switch to Reuters as the primary news source. Even though the discontinuity is in the direction of greater density, detail, accuracy, consistency over time, and evenness in coverage across different regions, it presents a potentially significant problem for some long-range quantitative analyses spanning the years before and after 1979, at least for the non-episodic datasets.

However, it should be remembered that such a discontinuity in sources is not unique. Similar problems have been encountered with COPDAB every time a new source is added, or an existing source becomes unavailable. For example, with the addition of data coded from the African Research Bulletin, which became available only in the early 1960s, the density of COPDAB data for most sub-Saharan African countries increased several-fold. As with Reuters, which is only available from early 1979, it is not possible to resolve the problem by going back and coding the earlier years from the new source.

One approach to this difficulty is to compare the GEDS data from Reuters with data similarly coded from other source(s) (used prior to 1979) for the same period. This is already being done to some extent for the *New York Times* and some other regional sources in collaboration with Llewellyn Howell (see chapter 3). Change in density of coverage can then be assessed (either globally or in relation to specific regions or issues of interest) and factored in to adjust time-series data for the impact of the change of sources.

Another approach is to add other sources to supplement Reuters from 1979. This allows the user to achieve full continuity where this is the priority, by excluding sources not used for the entire period of interest in any particular study. When it is more important to have the advantages of fuller coverage from 1979, the expanded source(s) can be retained and discontinuities adjusted for. Thus GEDS is being developed as an open-ended data system, rather than a dataset: new sources will be added (in collaboration with research groups on other campuses) as demand and resources dictate. User software then provides several convenient options as to how data can be selected (by source, period, location, participants, etc.) and manipulated as required for the desired analysis.

Other discontinuities created in the transition to reliance on GEDS for updating existing datasets reflect the greater descriptive and analytic detail provided for each event record. For example, the actor list has been greatly expanded to include many non-state actors. Again, however, GEDS user software can readily be used to exclude events or information that would not have been included under the earlier coding scheme being updated.

On the other hand, the user can choose to take advantage of the GEDS enhancements, allowing for the shift in 1979. Some adjustments will need to be made in current specialized coding schemes to allow them to be fully utilized in the context of the expanded GEDS data. In particular, the 15-point International and Domestic COPDAB Scales for assessing the level of cooperation or conflict in each event now need to be supplemented with a third, parallel, *Non-State Actors Scale*.

The new scale is modeled on the present International Scale, but acknowledges the different repertoire of behaviors available to non-state actors. It will thus add a third "layer" of COPDAB coding from GEDS event-data, focusing on the activities of non-state actors, while substantially preserving the continuity of the existing international and domestic coding beyond 1979 (in some cases both the Non-State Scale and one of the original scales can be used to provide alternative values for the same event).

To allow the three different "layers" of data to be used in combination for generating aggregate periodic (daily, monthly, etc.) cooperation and conflict levels for any group, state, dyad or region of interest, a new set of weights is being derived using a single standard across the three scales simultaneously. This is being done following similar procedures as those established by Azar and Havener (1976) for the earlier COPDAB scales. The new weights will retain the advantage of allowing interval scaling, treating "neutral" events (level 8) as having zero intensity. They will also reflect more contemporary judgements as to the relative intensity of scale levels, and overcome the present limitation that even international and domestic events cannot be aggregated together.

Other innovations within existing datasets that will be made to take advantage of the expanded GEDS event data include the expansion of SHERFACS data to cover domestic as well as international disputes; and the further automation of coding procedures for WEIS and BCOW.

As partially-automated coding from GEDS summaries of the COPDAB scales, the WEIS, WHPSI and BCOW categories, and other specialized coding schemes (including SHERFACS) is developed and adequately validated, the additional data will as far as possible be integrated with the GEDS archive in coordination with the DDIR project at the University of Illinois at Urbana-Champaign.

7. Reporting Casualty Data

Casualty figures reported in relation to any event are included and flagged in the summary, and the number of any deaths and injuries specifically resulting from the current event are separately coded, providing relatively reliable indices, so far unavailable in international event-datasets, for the analysis of conflict processes.

This is the one area where quantitative data are consistently reported by the news media, and more adequate figures are not obtainable (at least for most countries) from other sources. The effort involved in scanning the media for such reports over long periods is typically prohibitive for researchers, but if done concurrently with generation of event records (as has been done for domestic political events only by WHPSI) does not add significantly to the coding effort required. Reports of total deaths and injuries occurring over several days' events are also flagged in the summary (as context) to one or more of the events, allowing users to integrate these figures if and as desired into weekly or monthly time-series data.

8. Source Referencing and On-Line Access to Source Articles

Each event record includes detailed source references (alternate records are kept and cross-referenced where different sources report the same event). For newspaper sources, for example, publication date and page number is given (rather than just the name of the source as currently given in COPDAB and other data banks). For newswire reports such as Reuters, the city from which the article was filed, the length and number of the article are also given. To the extent feasible, back pointers will be developed to facilitate on-line user access (through normal channels such as the Reuters and Lexis-Nexis information services) to the full text of the source article(s) for each event. This will allow GEDS to be used as an index for accessing more detailed discussion on events of particular interest, beyond what is available in the summaries.

9. Coder and Editor Identification

To allow users to be able to further evaluate the reliability of event records, information is provided not only as to source(s), but also on who coded each event, where and when they were trained and supervised, and when (how soon after the event) the coding and editing was done. This information also facilitates internal procedures for editing, monitoring of inter-coder reliability, and efforts to improve reliability through optimizing the level of automation in coding and through coordination across different campuses collaborating with us in the coding process.

10. The Potential for Near-Real-Time Coding

Utilization of partially automated procedures for event identification, abstracting and coding, and cross-project collaboration through DDIR, maximize an economy of effort which should (based on current projections) allow an ongoing process of near-real-time updating to be instituted, once the development and testing phase of the project is complete. Minimizing the lag between current events and coded data allow the data (and research employing it) to be of much greater usefulness to policy professionals dealing with current problems and wishing to anticipate future developments.

11. User Access and Software Support

User software (initially being developed for an IBM/Windows environment, but to be adapted also for the Macintosh and possibly UNIX environments as resources allow) will include menu-driven programs for easy browsing, data selection (by reference to any combination of the variables coded), temporal (time-series) and spatial data aggregation, transformation, graphic display, and interface with full-text sources and with statistical and interpretive software packages. Distribution of data and user software will be possible via email or using high density floppy or optical disks, avoiding sole reliance on the cumbersome mainframe tapes and procedures currently used in distributing major event-datasets.

APPENDIX 1: SOURCE ARTICLE FOR SAMPLE EVENT RECORD

(Note that several events are separately codable from this report; and that other Reuter World Report articles provide more detail on each of these events. The format is that of the Lexis-Nexis Information Services, through which this article was retrieved.)

LENGTH: 724 words
HEADLINE: U.S. TROOPS REACH SAUDI ARABIA; BAGHDAD
ANNEXES KUWAIT
BYLINE: By John Baggaley
DATELINE: NICOSIA, Aug 8
KEYWORD: GULF
BODY:

Iraq annexed Kuwait on Wednesday despite the deployment of U.S. combat troops in Saudi Arabia and growing military and economic pressure on Baghdad.

Denouncing Iraq's Saddam Hussein as an aggressive dictator, President George Bush told Americans that Baghdad "has massed an enormous war machine on the Saudi border" and was able to start hostilities at a moment's notice.

There could be "no appeasement," Bush said.

Arab leaders — most of them now committed to opposing last Thursday's Iraqi invasion of Kuwait — called a summit meeting in Cairo for Thursday to discuss the explosive crisis on their doorsteps.

Egyptian President Hosni Mubarak urged President Saddam to attend, saying Iraq faced a "horrible and destructive" strike if the crisis were not resolved. There was no indication whether Saddam would go.

King Hussein of Jordan, a close ally of Saddam who had disappointed Western governments by his reluctance to condemn the invasion, told reporters in Amman on Wednesday evening he rejected Iraq's annexation of Kuwait and continued to regard the exiled Emir as the legitimate ruler.

The U.S. State Department called the annexation "a feeble attempt by an international outlaw to try to justify or legitimize his actions."

Iraq issued a fresh denial of "unfounded American allegations" that it planned to attack Saudi Arabia.

"What happened in Kuwait is completely different since it is part of Iraq," said a spokesman for the ruling Revolution Command Council in Baghdad.

A senior Middle East diplomat, forecasting conflict, asked: "What happens when Saddam runs out of economic breath? He could just decide to shoot it out...."

A Bush administration official said Saddam was now in a corner and "that makes military action more likely."

Bush said that Iraq had a 100,000-strong force facing Saudi Arabia across the desert frontier. The first wave of U.S. troops flown to Saudi Arabia numbered 4,000. U.S. defence officials said the force could swell to 40,000.

The United States told NATO allies that Iraq was deploying chemical weapons. Iraq used chemical weapons with devastating effect during its 1980-88 with Iran.

In Baghdad Saddam was widely cheered by the national assembly after the ruling council announced it was annexing Kuwait.

"Thank God we are now one people, one state that will be the paradise of the Arabs," Saddam said.

A nine-man provisional government which Iraq had installed in Kuwait was said to have endorsed the annexation, declaring that it wanted "the hero Saddam Hussein to be our leader and protector." The prime minister, Alaa Hussein Ali, believed to be an Iraqi officer, was named a deputy prime minister of Iraq.

Responding to the Western buildup, Iraq's ruling council declared that "All the navy fleets and squadrons... will not shake us."

Some 50 warships from the United States, France, Britain and the Soviet Union are now patrolling the Gulf or converging on the region.

Gulf oil traders said on Wednesday all Iraqi oil exports — outlawed by the U.N. Security Council along with arms sales to Baghdad and other trade — had stopped.

Bush said he was asking oil producers to increase output to make up Baghdad's quota. Several OPEC nations indicated they were ready to do so and prices, which hit nearly 30 dollars a barrel on Monday, fell back to 26.5 dollars on Wednesday.

The armada converging in the Middle East includes three U.S. aircraft carriers and a battleship. Bush described the American role as "wholly defensive" and said U.S. forces would not initiate hostilities.

"But they will defend themselves, the Kingdom of Saudi Arabia and other friends in the Gulf...America will stand by her friends," he added.

Britain announced it would contribute naval and air units to a multi-national force to defend Saudi Arabia.

Huge Saudi army reinforcements headed through the intense heat in the Gulf region on Wednesday towards the Kuwait border where Iraqi troops have been massing since they overran Kuwait last Thursday.

One resident near Dhahran, on the Gulf coast, where U.S. troops were landing, saw a Saudi convoy stretching about 30 kms (20 miles), heading north.

Jittery residents in the region were stocking up on food and water. The Netherlands advised Dutch families living in the Saudi oil province bordering Kuwait to leave immediately.
SUBJECT: WARFARE

APPENDIX 2

1. **Actor Codes**

North and Central America

002> USA; 00201> Blacks/African-Americans; 00202> Hispanics; 00203> Native Americans/Indians; 00204> Puerto Rico; U.S. Virgin Islands; 00205> U.S. Pacific Island Territories; 020> Canada; 02001> French Canadians/Quebec; 02002> Inuit; 02003> Native Indians (exc. Inuit); 035> Bahamas; 040> Cuba; 041> Haiti; 042> Dominican Republic; 04201> Blacks; 050> Dominica; 051> Jamaica; 052> Trinidad & Tobago; 053> Barbados; 054> Grenada; 055> Antigua & Barbuda; 056> Saint Lucia; 057> Saint Kitts and Nevis; 058> Saint Vincent and the Grenadines; 070> Mexico; 07001> Native Indians; 080> Belize; 090> Guatemala; 09002> Native Indians; 091> Honduras; 09101> Native Indians; 09102> Blacks/Carib Indians; 092> El Salvador; 09201> Native Indians; 09202> FMLN; 093> Nicaragua; 09301> Blacks; 09302> Native Indians; 09303> Contra rebels (to 1990); 094> Costa Rica; 09401> Blacks; 09402> Native Indians; 095> Panama;

09501> Blacks; 09502> Native Indians; 096> Caribbean Community; 099> Inter-American Development Bank;

South America

100>Colombia; 10001>Blacks; 10002>Native Highlanders; 10003>Native Lowlanders; 101>Venezuela; 10101>Blacks; 10102>Native Indians; 110>Guyana; 111>Suriname; 130>Ecuador; 13001>Blacks; 13002>Native Highlanders; 13003>Native Lowlanders; 135>Peru; 13501> Blacks; 13502> Native Highlanders; 13503> Native Lowlanders; 13504> Sendero Luminoso; 140> Brazil; 14001> Blacks; 14002> Native Indians; 145> Bolivia; 14501> Native Highlanders; 14502> Native Lowlanders; 150> Paraguay; 15002> Native Indians; 155> Chile; 15501> Native Indians; 160> Argentina; 16001> Jews; 16002> Native Indians; 165> Uruguay; 195> Andean Pact Nations; 196> Central American Common Market; 197> Latin American Integration (Free Trade) Assn; 198> Alliance For Progress (to 1980); 199> Organization of American States;

Europe (Western and Northern)

200> U.K.; 20001> South and East Asians; 20002> Blacks/Afro-Caribbeans; 20003> N.Ireland Catholics/I.R.A.; 20004> Hong Kong; 20005> Other Overseas Dependencies/ Territories; 20006> N. Ireland Protestants/U.D.F.; 20007> Scots/Scotland; 20008> Welsh/Wales; 205> Ireland; 210> Netherlands; 21001> Netherlands Antilles; Aruba; 211> Belgium; 21101> Waloons; 21102> Flemish; 212> Luxembourg; 220> France; 22002>Basques; 22003>Bretons/Brittany; 22004>Corsicans/Corsica; 22005>Immigrant Workers/Maghrebis; 22006>Roma (Gypsies); 22007>Overseas Departments/Territories; 221> Monaco; 223> Liechtenstein; 225> Switzerland; 22501> Jurassiens; 22502> Immigrant Workers; 230> Spain; 23001> Basques; 23002> Catalans; 23003> Roma; 232> Andorra; 235> Portugal; 23501> Roma; 23502> Macao; 260> Germany (FRG); 26001>Turks; 26002>West Berlin (to 1990); 265>East Germany (GDR: to 1990); 290> Poland; 294> Conf. on Security & Coop. in Europe (CSCE); 295> Council of Europe; 296> NATO; 297> European Communities/EEC; 298> European Free Trade Assn.;

Europe (Eastern, Southern, and Nordic)

305> Austria; 310> Hungary; 31001> Roma; 315> Czech & Slovak Republic; 31501> Hungarians; 31502> Roma; 31503> Slovaks; 325> Italy; 32501> Germans/Tyrolians; 32502> Roma; 32503> Sardinians /Sardinia; 328> Vatican; 331> San Marino; 338> Malta; 339> Albania; 33901> Greeks; 345> Yugoslavia (to 27 April 92); 34501> Albanians/Kosovo; 34502> Croats/Croatia; 34503> Roma; 34504> Slovenes/Slovenia; 34505> Serbs/Serbia; 34506> Moslems (exec. Albanians); 34507> Macedonians/ Macedonia; 34508> Montenegrins/Montenegro; 34509> Hungarians; 34510> Bosnia-Hercegovina; 350> Greece; 35001> Muslims; 35002> Roma; 352> Cyprus; 35201> Greek Cypriots; 35202>Turkish Cypriots /Turkish Rep. N. Cyp.; 355> Bulgaria; 35501> Turks; 35502> Roma; 360> Romania; 36001> Germans; 36002> Hungarians; 36003> Roma; 365> USSR (to 26 Dec. 91); 36501> Armenians/Armenia; 36502> Azerbaijanis /Azerbaijan; 36503> Karachai & Balkars; 36504> Chechen & Ingush; 36505> Crimean Tatars; 36506> Estonians/Estonia; 36507> Georgians /Georgia; 36508> Germans; 36510>Jews; 36511> Kazakhs/Kazakhstan; 36512> Kirghiz/Kirghizia; 36513> Kurds; 36514>Latvians/Latvia; 36515>Lithuanians/Lithuania; 36516>Roma; 36517>Tadjiks

/Tadjikistan; 36518> Turkmen/Turkmenistan; 36519> Russians/RSFSR; 36520> Ukrainians/Ukraine; 36521> Uzbeks/Uzbekistan; 36522> Byelorussians/Byelorussia; 36523> Moldavians/Moldavia; 36524> Ossetians/North & South Ossetia; 36525> Tatars (exc. Crimean)/Tatarstan; 36526> Chuvash/Chuvashia; 36527> Bashkir/Bashkiria; 36528> Mordvinians/Mordovia; 36529> Udmurt/Udmurtia; 36530> Mari/Mariel; 36531> Buryat-Mongol/Buryatia; 36532> Kabardin/Kabardino-Balkar; 36533> Yakut/Yakutia; 36534> Komi; 36535> Kalmyk/Kalmykia; 36536> Tuvan/Tuvinia; 36537> Karelians; 372> Latvia (from 5 Sep 91); 37201> Russians; 37202> Byelorussians; 373> Lithuania (from 5 Sep 91); 37301> Russians; 37302> Poles; 374> Estonia (from 5 Sep 91); 37401> Russians; 375> Finland; 37501> Sami; 380> Sweden; 38001> Sami; 385> Norway; 38501> Sami; 390> Denmark; 39001> Greenland; 395> Iceland; 398> Council for Mutual Econ. Assist. (COMECON); 399> Warsaw Pact; (NOTE: Only the codes for the period prior to the final breakup of the USSR and of Yugoslavia, are listed here. Separate codes are used for the newly independent states and their ministries.)

Africa (Western and Central)

403> Sao Tome & Principe; 420> Gambia; 430> Cape Verde; 432> Mali; 43201> Tuareg; 43202> Mande; 433> Senegal; 43301> Diola; 434> Benin; 435> Mauritania; 43501> Kewri; 436> Niger; 43601> Djerma-Songhai; 43602> Hausa; 43603> Tuareg; 437> Ivory Coast; 43701> Europeans; 43702> Lebanese; 438> Guinea; 43801> Fulani; 43802> Malinke; 43803> Susu; 439> Burkina Faso; 440> Equatorial Guinea; 441> Guinea-Bissau; 450> Liberia; 45001> Creoles (American-Africans); 45002> Krahn; 451> Sierra Leone; 45101> Creoles; 45102> Limba; 45103> Mende; 452> Ghana; 45201> Ashanti; 45202> Ewe; 45203> Mossi-Dagomba, 461> Togo; 46101> Ewe; 46102> Kabre; 471> Cameroon; 47101> Kirdi; 47102> Westerners; 47103> Bamileke; 475> Nigeria; 47501> Hausa-Fulani; 47503> Ibo/Biafra; 47504> Yoruba; 481> Gabon; 482> Central African Republic; 483> Chad; 48301> North Chadiens; 48302> South Chadiens; 484> Congo; 48401> Lari (Bakongo); 490> Zaire; 49001> Bakongo; 49003> Luba Kasai (in Katanga); 49004> Lingala (in Katanga); 49005> Lunda /Yeke (in Katanga); 499> Econ. Com'ty of W. African States;

Africa (Eastern and Southern)

500> Uganda; 50001> Acholi; 50002> Konjo/Amba; 50003> Ankole; 50004> Baganda; 50005> Bunyoro; 50006> Kakwa; 50007> Karamajong; 50008> Langi; 50009> Lugbara/ Madi; 50011> Toro; 50012> Nyarwanda; 501> Kenya; 50101> Asians; 50103> Kikuyu; 50104> Luo; 50105> Maasai; 50106> Somalis; 50107> Turkana; 50108> Rendille; 50109> Europeans; 510> Tanzania; 516> Burundi; 51601> Hutu; 51602> Tutsi; 517> Rwanda; 51701> Tutsi; 520> Somalia; 52001> Issaq; 521> Djibouti; 530> Ethiopia; 53001> Afar; 53002> Eritreans /Eritrea; 53003> Nilo-Saharans; 53004> Oromo (Galla); 53005> Somalis; 53006> Tigreans/Tigre; 540> Angola; 54001> Bakongo; 54002> Ovimbundu (incl. UNITA rebels to 1991); 551> Zambia; 55101> Bemba; 55102> Lozi (Barotze); 55103> Tonga; 552> Zimbabwe; 55201> Europeans; 55203> Ndebele; 553> Malawi; 554> Mozambique; 55401> Renamo (RNM) guerillas; 560> South Africa; 56001> Asians (Indians); 56002> Black Africans (incl. ANC; excl. Zulu); 56003> Coloreds; 56004> Europeans/Whites/Afrikaans; 56005> Namibia/ns /SWAPO rebels (to 1990); 56006> Zulu/Nkatha; 561> Namibia (from 1990); 56101> Europeans; 56102>

San (Bushmen); 570> Lesotho; 571> Botswana; 57101> San; 572> Swaziland; 580> Madagascar (Malagasy Republic); 58001> Asians; 58002> Merina; 581> Comoros; 585> Seychelles; 590> Mauritius; 599> Organization of African Unity;

North Africa and The Middle East

600> Morocco; 60001> Berbers; 60003> Saharawis/Western Sahara; 615> Algeria; 61501> Berbers; 616> Tunisia; 620> Libya; 625> Sudan; 62501> South Sudanese; 630> Iran; 63002> Azerbaijanis; 63003> Bah'ais; 63004> Bakhtiari; 63005> Baluchi; 63007> Kurds; 63008> Turkmens; 63009> Arabs; 632> Qatar; 640> Turkey; 64001> Armenians; 64005> Kurds; 64006> Roma; 645> Iraq; 64504> Kurds; 64505> Turkmens; 64506> Shi'ites; 651> Egypt; 65101> Copts (Christians); 652> Syria; 65201> Alawis; 65203> Kurds; 655> Lebanon; 65501> Druze/PSP; 65502> Maronites/Christians (inc. Leb Front, SLA); 65503> Palestinians; 65504> Shi'ites (incl. Amal, Hezbollah); 65505> Sunnis (incl. Murabitoun); 65506> Moslems (unspecified /other); 65599> Unidentified guerilla groups; 663> Jordan; 66302> Palestinians; 664> PLO (and affil. orgns.); 665> Israel; 66501> Palestinians/Arabs (excl. occ. terr.); 66502> Sephardim; 66503> Palestinians in/ occupied territories; 66504> Jews (incl. Eur. & Russian; exc. Seph.); 670> Saudi Arabia; 67002> Shi'ites; 672> Bahrain; 675> United Arab Emirates; 678> Yemen (North/ United); 680> Yemen (PDRY: to 1990); 690> Kuwait; 691> Gulf Cooperation Council; 698> Oman; 699> Arab League;

Asia (East, Central, and South)

700> Afghanistan; 70001> Baluchi; 70002> Mujaheddin rebels; 710> China (PRC); 71002> Hui Hui (Muslims); 71003> Kazakhs; 71004> Mongols/Inner Mongolia; 71005> Tibetans/Tibet; 71006> Uighurs; 712> Mongolia; 713> Taiwan (ROC); 71301> Aboriginal Taiwanese; 71302> Taiwanese; 71303> Mainlanders (Nationalists); 731> N. Korea; 732> S. Korea; 740> Japan; 74003> Koreans; 750> India; 75001> Assamese/Assam; 75006> Gurkhas; 75008> Muslims (other/unspecified); 75009> Nagas/Nagaland; 75010> Santhals; 75011> Meiteis/Manipur; 75012> Sikhs/Punjab; 75013> Tripuras/Tripura; 75014> Kashmiri Muslims/Kashmir; 75015> Misos/Misoram; 75016> Hindus (other/ unspecified); 751> Bhutan; 770> Pakistan; 77001> Ahmadis; 77002> Baluchi; 77004> Hindus; 77005> Pushtuns; 77006> Sindhis; 771> Bangladesh; 77101> Chittagong Hill Tribes (Chakmas etc); 77102> Hindus; 775> Myanmar (Burma); 77501> Arakanese (Muslims); 77502> Chins; 77503> Kachin; 77504> Karen; 77505> Mons; 77506> Nagas; 77507> Shan; 77508> Mountain Tribals; 780> Sri Lanka; 78001> Indian Tamils; 78002> Sri Lankan Tamils; 78003> Moslems; 78004> Sinhalese; 781> Maldive Islands; 790> Nepal; 795> Asian Development Bank;

South-East Asia

800> Thailand; 80001> Chinese; 80002> Malay Muslims; 80003> Northern Hill Tribes; 811> Kampuchea (Cambodia); 81102> Vietnamese; 81103> Chams (Muslims); 81104> Rebel Coaln Govt /Forces (exc Khmer Rouge); 81105> Khmer Rouge; 812> Laos; 81201> Hmong (Meo); 816> Vietnam (North/United); 81601> Catholics; 81602> Chinese; 81603> Khmers; 81604> Montagnards (Mountain Chams); 817> Vietnam (South: to 1976); 820> Malaysia; 82001> Chinese; 82002> Ibans/Sarawak Dayaks; 82003> East Indians; 82004> Kadazans/Sabah Dayaks; 82005> Orang Asli/Other

Aboriginal Peoples; 82006> Malays; 825> Brunei; 830> Singapore; 83001> Malays; 840>Philippines; 84001>Chinese; 84002>Cordillera Peoples; 84003>Moros (Muslims); 84004> New Peoples Army; 850> Indonesia; 85001> Aceh; 85002> Ambonese; 85003> Chinese; 85004> East Timorese/East Timor; 85005> Papuans/Irian Jaya; 890> Assoc. of South East Asian Nations (ASEAN);

The Pacific

900> Australia; 90001> Aborigines; 910> Papua New Guinea; 91001> Bougainvilleans/ Bougainville; 915> Kiribati; 920> New Zealand; 92001> Maoris; 921> Nauru; 930> Fiji; 93001> Indians; 93002> Fijians; 935> Tonga; 940> Solomon Islands; 945> Western Samoa; 950> Vanuatu; 955> Marshall Islands; 956> Micronesia (Fed. States of) 960> Tuvalu;

Non-Regional Organizations, Other

985> British Commonwealth Secretariat; 986> Non-Aligned Countries Coordinating Bureau; 991> International Monetary Fund/World Bank; 992> Orgn. for Economic Coop. and Development (OECD); 993> OPEC; 995> Internat'l Non-Govt Organizations (INGO's); 996> United Nations Org'n (exc. IMF & World Bank); 997> Orgn. of the Islamic Conference; 998> Other Multi-Lateral Govt. Organizations; 999> Not stated, not determinable.

2. Additional Target Codes

000> No target (reciprocal behavior among actors); 001> Domestic target (parties not separately listed); 994> Multinational Corporations.

3. Regional Codes

030> North American Region; 097> Central American/Caribbean Region; 098> Atlantic Ocean; 190> South American Region; 299> European Region; 396> Arctic Ocean (incl. North, Baltic, Bering Seas); 397> Mediterranean, Black, Red, and Caspian Seas; 598> Sub-Saharan African Region; 691>Persian Gulf Region; 695> Middle East Region; 696> North African Region; 797> Indian Ocean; 798> East Asian Region; 799> South Asian Region; 899> South East Asian Region; 970> Antarctic Region; 980> Pacific Ocean Region.

NOTE

The major part of this chapter is drawn from a paper accepted for publication in an upcoming special issue of International Interactions focusing on current issues in international event data, with permission from the publishers.

REFERENCES

Alker, H. R., Jr. 1975. "Polimetrics: Its Descriptive Foundations." In Vol. 7 of *Handbook of Political Science*. Eds. Greenstein, F. and N. Polsby. 139-210. Reading, MA: Addison-Wesley.

Alker, H. R., Jr. and F. L. Sherman. 1982. "Collective Security-Seeking Practices Since 1945." In *Managing International Crises*. Ed. Frei, D. 113-145. Beverly Hills, CA and London: Sage Publications.

Azar, E. E. 1975. "Ten Issues in Events Research." In *Theory and Practice of Events Research: Studies in International Actions and Interactions*. Eds. Azar, E. E. and T. D. Ben-Dak. 1-17. New York: Gordon and Breach.

___. 1980. "The Conflict and Peace Data Bank (COPDAB)." *Journal of Conflict Resolution* 24, 1 (March): 143-152.

___. 1982. *The Codebook of the Conflict and Peace Data Bank (COPDAB)*. College Park, MD: University of Maryland, Center for International Development and Conflict Management.

___. 1990. *The Management of Protracted Social Conflict: Theory and Cases*. Aldershot, UK: Dartmouth.

Azar, E. E. and T. Havener. 1976. "Discontinuities in the Symbolic Environment: A Problem in Scaling." *International Interactions* 2, 4: 231-246.

Azar, E. E. and S. Lerner. 1981. "The Use of Semantic Dimensions in the Scaling of International Events." *International Interactions* 7, 4: 361-378.

Azar, E. E. and T. J. Sloan. 1975. *Dimensions of Interaction: A Sourcebook for the Study of the Behavior of 31 Nations from 1948 through 1973*, Occasional Paper #8. Pittsburgh, PA: International Studies Association.

Davies, J. L. and C. K. McDaniel. Forthcoming. "A New Generation of International Event-Data." *International Interactions*.

Farris, L., H. R. Alker, Jr., K. Carley and F. L. Sherman. 1980. "Phase/Actor Disaggregated Butterworth-Scranton Codebook." Cambridge, MA: The Massachusetts Institute of Technology, Center for International Studies. Working paper.

Gurr, T. R. and J. R. Scarritt. August 1989. "Minorities' Rights at Risk: A Global Survey." *Human Rights Quarterly* 11, 3 (August): 375-405.

Hermann, C. F. 1982. "Foreword." In Describing Foreign Policy Behavior. Eds. Callahan, P., L. P. Brady and M. G. Herman. 7-10. Beverly Hills, CA and London: Sage Publications.

___. 1989. "Two Kinds of Event Data." *DDIR Update* 3, 2 (January): 1-2.

Leng, R. J. and J. David Singer. 1988. "Militarized Interstate Crisis: The BCOW Typology and Its Applications." *International Studies Quarterly* 32, 2 (June): 155-173.

Mansbach, R. W. and J. A. Vasquez. 1981. "The Effect of Actor and Issue Classifications on the Analysis of Global Conflict-Cooperation." *The Journal of Politics* 43, 3 (August): 861-874.

McClelland, C. A., R. G. Tomlinson, R. G. Sherwin, G. A. Hill, H. A. Calhoun, P. H. Fenn and J. D. Martin. 1971. "The Management and Analysis of International Event Data: A Computerized System for Monitoring and Projecting Event Flows." Report in support of ARPA/ONR Contract #N00014-67-A-0269-0004 for Short-Term Conflict Prediction. Los Angeles, CA: University of Southern California, School of International Relations. Mimeograph.

McDaniel, C. K. and J. L. Davies. 1991. "A Speech Act Perspective for Event-Data Research." Paper presented at the International Conference: Vancouver, BC.

McGowan, P., H. Starr, G. Hower, R. L. Merritt and D. A. Zinnes. 1988. "International Data as a National Resource." *International Interactions* 14, 2: 101-113.

Sherman, F. L. 1987. "Partway to Peace: The United Nations and the Road to Nowhere." Ph.D. dissertation. State College, PA: The Pennsylvania State University.

Taylor, C. L. and D. A. Jodice. 1983. *World Handbook of Political and Social Indicators*, 3d ed. New Haven: Yale University Press.

VanBeers, L. and R. G. Sherwin. 1977. World Event/Interaction Survey Handbook and Codebook. Monterey, CA: Department of National Security Affairs, Naval Postgraduate School. Mimeograph.

CHAPTER 3

Event Data for Region-Specific Interactions:
A Research Note on Source Coverage

Llewellyn D. Howell and Gillian Barnes

Abstract

Event data have considerable potential for use by policy makers and by analysts who focus on the Third World or on smaller states. Such use has been limited by source selection. In a study focussing on Malaysian foreign policy, five sources — including the broadly international and regional news sources — are used for data creation and the data are compared. The *New York Times Index* and *London Times Index* provide the lowest frequencies of Malaysian events in 1989-90. The regional sources and Reuters include a higher frequency of events but the balance between cooperative and conflictual events varies widely and is dependent on the source selected. The study discusses the nature of this imbalance and the ultimate effects of source choice on analytical outcomes.

Event data have a long and somewhat checkered history as a basis for the study of foreign policy and international relations. The Global Event Data System Project has brought together not only a number of scholars but also a number of approaches to the creation and application of the data. To justify the significant and appropriate support being sought for the study of event data through this project, several amendments need to be made to the previous approaches to gathering event data.

Event Data for the Study of Third World Foreign Policy

Among these amendments are two that will be addressed in this study. The first is that event data can and should be made usable for those involved in policy studies and applications. A question is continually raised by both practitioners and more traditional political scientists regarding the importance or utility of event data studies if the data used do not reflect the reality seen by policy makers. Daly and Andriole (1980), Andriole (1984), and Laurance (1990) have all conducted examinations of previous attempts to bring event data into such analysis. While a variety of problems enter into the non-usability equation, one major problem has always been the apparent superficiality of the data. Greater data density is clearly required over what is provided by the Conflict and Peace Data Bank (COPDAB) or the World Event Interaction Survey (WEIS). While both of these major datasets have their qualities, each also has some deficiencies. COPDAB has great strength in the inclusion of Middle East events but is inconsistent and sometimes thin in the coverage of other regions. WEIS relies solely on the *New York Times* and is thereby strong on U.S. and East-West coverage but contains little on the Third World except in cases of major conflicts (such as the Vietnam War).

The second significant problem is that event data have previously been used almost exclusively for the study of major power interactions. While it might be argued that there is some reasonable representation of U.S. or Soviet behavior in the event datasets, the heavy reliance on Western news sources, and the *New York Times* in particular, have colored the characterization of that behavior. Datasets have also been inconsistent with each other (see Howell, 1983; Vincent, 1983), even when the major actors are the focus of the study. This suggests some inconsistency in coding practice between datasets, and perhaps within datasets, apart from the matter of source inclusion since both COPDAB and WEIS use the *New York Times* as a source.

The most serious difficulty is that the reliance on one or a few sources, especially newspapers, has introduced an imbalance in the datasets that is unfavorable to smaller nations and to those who study them. Area studies specialists who focus on regions other than North America and Europe have had difficulty in finding anything useful in event data or analyses of such data. COPDAB tried to address this problem, especially for the Middle East, but even attention across regions and regional sources is both expensive and difficult to manage administratively.

Our purpose here is to focus on the data that is being generated for a relatively small state (Malaysia), with the objective being to examine how data being generated by the GEDS Project might be received by the area specialists and policy makers who have declined use of event data in the past. The study is exploratory, as well as preliminary, and is intended to propose directions for GEDS and research on the Third World more than to present analyses of the current situation.

An Examination of Five Sources

In this study we have chosen to examine the event data that have been generated for Malaysia from five commonly used sources. These include the *New York Times*, the *London Times*, the *Far Eastern Economic Review*, the *Straits Times* of Singapore, and the Reuters news service. The *New York Times* and the *London Times* are widely known and little needs to be said about them here other than the fact that the indexes for both were used as the source of Malaysia citations for this study.

The *Far Eastern Economic Review* is a weekly magazine published in Hong Kong that is read extensively throughout Asia and elsewhere. It covers both political and economic events in detail, but tends to focus on domestic rather than international matters. The *Straits Times* is a daily Singapore publication that is controlled and closely monitored by the Singapore government. However, its international coverage is extensive and tends to be less restricted than that which focuses on Singapore itself. Its "Across the Causeway" section deals specifically with Malaysian matters and appears in every issue.

The Reuters news service is also well known. Our access is off the service wire (rather than through a newspaper's edited version) with both the problems and advantages that that entails. Reuters has been selected as the primary source (at least initially) for the GEDS Project and its utility is of particular interest to us for that reason.

Frequency Comparisons for 1989-90

In this preliminary project, data has been gathered for a 24 month period for four of the sources: Reuters, the *Far Eastern Economic Review* (known as *FEER*), the *New York Times Index* (*NYTI*), and the *London Times Index (LTI)*. Data were coded using the Conflict and Peace Data Bank (COPDAB) method as amended for the GEDS project. For our study, we are simply focussing on the frequency of events, whether the event was cooperative or conflictual, and whether Malaysia was the Actor or the Target in the interaction.

As figure 3.1 indicates, the numbers of events involving Malaysia that were reported by either the *New York Times Index* or the *London Times Index* were minimal, almost to the point of non-existence. In their early work on global versus regional data sources, Doran, Pendley, and Antunes (1973) correlated the data patterns to determine whether the more accessible global news sources could represent the more complete regional news source characterization of events. Using *Deadline Data* and the *Yearbooks of the Encyclopedia Britannica* as their global sources and Latin American regional sources, they found that the global sources reported far fewer events than the regional sources, as expected, but also that the patterns did not coincide (p. 181). Here, the numbers of reported events from the *New York Times* and *London Times* are so low that a correlation cannot be appropriately computed.

Reuters, however, can also be considered a global source. In figure 3.1, we compare event frequencies for all international events involving Malaysia as actor or target for 1989 and 1990 for the *New York Times Index*, the *London Times Index*, Reuters, and *FEER*. Both the *FEER* and Reuters show considerably more events than do the *NYTI* and *LTI*, but it is interesting to note that the global source, Reuters, has considerably more Malaysian events than does the regional source, the *Far Eastern Economic Review* (see figure 3.2). This will be partly accounted for by virtue of the fact that *FEER* is a weekly while Reuters reports events on a daily basis. But a perusal of the weekly also seems to indicate that it gives considerably more emphasis to domestic events, as well as economic activity,

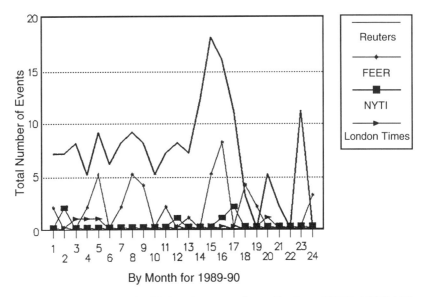

Fig. 3.1. Frequencies for Malaysia events from Reuters, FEER, NYTI, LTI

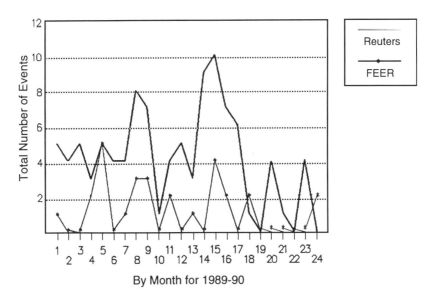

Fig. 3.2. Malaysia foreign policy events frequencies from Reuters, FEER

which may show up more systematically when an examination of domestic events is undertaken. In the meantime, Reuters shows considerable promise as an easily accessible source (assuming commercial access, of course).

Figures 3.3 and 3.4 present comparisons of the two regional sources, the *Straits Times* of Singapore, a daily, and *FEER*, a weekly, with the daily global coverage of Reuters. The seven units of coverage (weekly aggregations) are insufficient to assess whether Reuters can appropriately represent the in-depth coverage of the *Straits Times* but figure 3.4 in particular (Malaysia as an Actor) would seem to indicate that this would be so.

The *Far Eastern Economic Review*, although widely read and respected, provides several problems for event data researchers. It concentrates so specifically on internal events that it often reports *no* foreign policy events in an issue for any particular country. If the week is the unit of analysis, there will often be zeros as data points in the study, making mathematical manipulation difficult in many instances. This is seldom the case for Reuters, which has a high enough frequency that policy analysts can find that it reflects well the information that they otherwise might have available to them about foreign policy activity. This bridges one of the gaps that has previously presented a credibility problem for event data and those that work with it.

Doran et al. (1973) correlated patterns of events to test adequacy of available but lower reporting sources in representing the regional source. We have similarly correlated Reuters and *FEER* data over the 24 month period for which data has thus far been coded using Pearson product-moment correlation. The results are no more promising than those reported by Doran et al. (1973). Total events from the two sources (Malaysia as either actor or target) correlate at only R = .39, hardly an indication that the patterns match. Events with Malaysia as the originator of the action show a slightly lower correlation at R = .38. Figure 3.5 shows visually that event proportions also do not match between the two sources. While the sources might ultimately supplement each other, they cannot be substituted for each other.

The *Straits Times* clearly will generate more events for Singapore's neighbor, Malaysia, as is indicated in figures 3.6 and 3.7. But even though this might seem a valuable resource on that basis, it too has problems. One is that many of Malaysia's foreign policy actions involve Singapore, and many of them fall into the low end of the conflict range on the COPDAB scale. Will a Singapore-controlled newspaper report these events in an even-handed way? Since there is no yardstick to determine what constitutes "even-handed" (Is the Western-oriented Reuters even-handed?), this will be difficult to determine. However, the circumstances may still make one suspect the worst.

Access to the *Straits Times* also constitutes a practical problem for a dataset that is intended to approach real time. At best the *Straits Times* is delivered to the U.S. several weeks after publication. It is available in very few libraries in the U.S. At this stage it would be prohibitively expensive to try to set up a coder

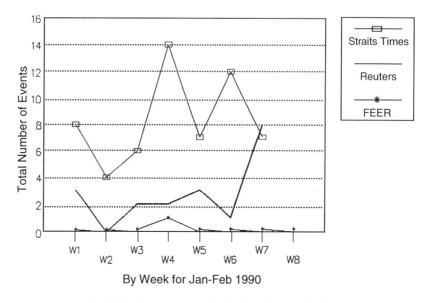

Fig. 3.3. Frequencies for Malaysia events from
Straits Times, Reuters, FEER

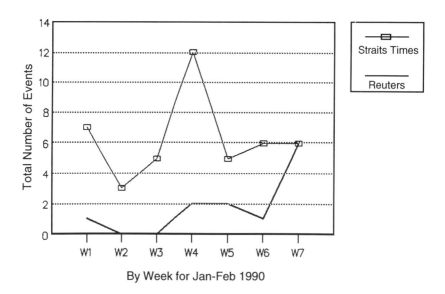

Fig. 3.4. Malaysian foreign policy events
(Straits Times vs. Reuters)

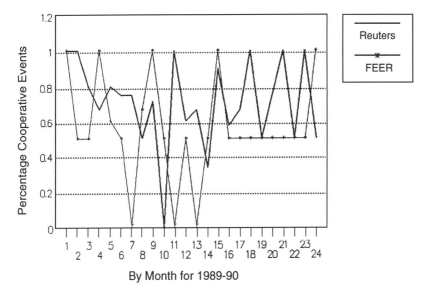

By Month for 1989-90

**Fig. 3.5. Malaysian foreign policy ratios coop/total events,
Reuters vs. FEER**

in Singapore to code daily as Charles McClelland once did in the U.S. with WEIS data. Other matters intervene as well. At the Library of Congress, where we have obtained our access to the *Straits Times*, numerous issues are missing for one reason or another. For January of 1990, for example, one of two months coded in this pilot study, there were only 23 issues available out of 31 days. For February, there were only 16 issues available covering 28 days. Such gaps can be filled in when the microfilm version of the newspaper becomes available but the real time intentions of the GEDS Project would have to be sacrificed. The availability of Reuters from the wire is an advantage that paper copy does not have.

Even for the available issues of the *Straits Times*, the number of reported events far exceeds that of Reuters. For January and February of 1990, the *Straits Times* reports 33 cooperative events and ten conflictual events toward any target, for a total of 43. Reuters reports, for the same period, seven cooperative events and six conflictual events, for a total of thirteen. For Malaysia as a target during the same months, the *Straits Times* reports sixteen cooperative events and six conflictual events, a total of 22, while Reuters presents only two cooperative events and three conflictual events, totalling five. For Malaysia as an actor, the *Straits Times* is reporting roughly three times the number of events for Malaysia as Reuters. In the target category, the *Straits Times* has reported more than four times the events of Reuters.

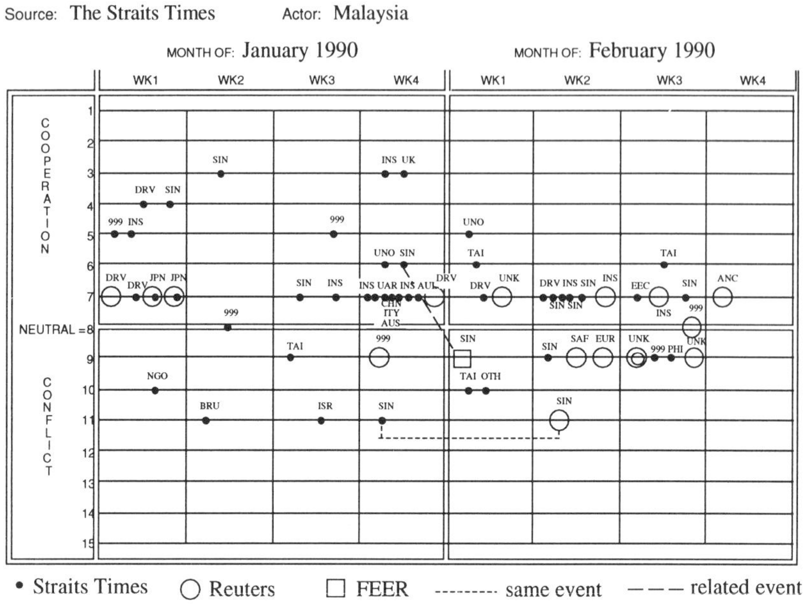

Source: The Straits Times
Actor: Malaysia
MONTH OF: January 1990
MONTH OF: February 1990
WK1 WK2 WK3 WK4 WK1 WK2 WK3 WK4
COOPERATION
NEUTRAL = 8
CONFLICT
• Straits Times
○ Reuters
□ FEER
--------- same event
— — — related event

Fig. 3.6

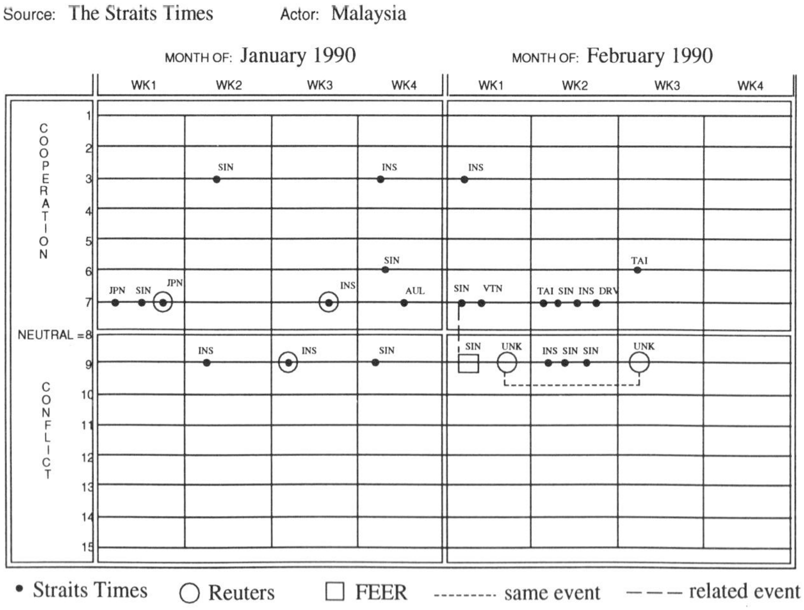

Source: The Straits Times
Actor: Malaysia
MONTH OF: January 1990
MONTH OF: February 1990
WK1 WK2 WK3 WK4 WK1 WK2 WK3 WK4
COOPERATION
NEUTRAL = 8
CONFLICT
• Straits Times
○ Reuters
□ FEER
--------- same event
— — — related event

Fig. 3.7

While the local source would be expected to report more events than a global source, the balance between cooperative and conflictual events as provided by the two sources is much more troubling. In both the actor and target categories, the *Straits Times* reports approximately three times the number of cooperative events as conflictual events. Reuters indicates a 50-50 split between cooperation and conflict. That is, the *Straits Times* is reporting that Malaysia is a relatively cooperative country in the international system, while Reuters is reporting that it is equally cooperative and conflictual or, that it is relatively much more conflictual than the Malaysia portrayed in the *Straits Times*.

While a number of possible explanations can be generated for this disparity, it is unlikely that the *Straits Times* is over-reporting cooperative events or under-reporting conflictual events from its neighboring arch-rival. More likely, but still speculative, is the possibility that Reuters has under-reported the low level cooperative events (see scale category seven in figure 3.6) that are probably not going to be of much interest in the larger global context. The "good news" of cross-national greetings and praise is not the material from which newspaper sales are made.

This inconsistency in balance is a problem when looking at the nature of a single country's foreign policy (e.g., see Kegley and Wittkopf, 1987: 57) since it may make a single country appear to be more conflictual than it really is. But it will be less of a problem when the analyst's goal is comparison. If cooperative events are evenly underreported, the *relative* levels of cooperation and conflict can still tell us something about a country's behavior in the context of the behavior of others.

Despite this possible drawback, Reuters clearly represents a credible "global" and readily accessible source in our preliminary study. While this may be no surprise in many other contexts, including that of earlier event data studies, it is important to note here that it shows credibility with respect to a study of Malaysia. Since Malaysia is out of the American and Western eye, most academicians give it little attention and have not created globally-inclusive datasets in which characterizations of Malaysian (or other Third World) foreign policy behavior are at all credible. The use of Reuters instead of or as a preliminary for other, more commonly used news sources has the possibility of bringing credibility to a renewed use of event data in the study of international relations.

NOTE

This chapter represents preliminary source and coding work in the Global Event Data System (GEDS) project under the auspices of the Data Development for International Research (DDIR) project.

REFERENCES

Andriole, S. J. 1984. "Detente: A Quantitative Analysis." *International Interactions* 11, 3-4: 381-395.

Daly, J. A. and S. Andriole. 1980. "The Use of Events/Interaction Research by the Intelligence Community." *Policy Sciences* 12, 2 (August): 215-236.

Doran, C. F., R. E. Pendley and G. E. Antunes. 1973. "A Test of Cross-National Event Reliability: Global Versus Regional Data Sources." *International Studies Quarterly* 17, 2: 175-201.

Howell, L. D. 1983. "A Comparative Study of the WEIS and COPDAB Data Sets." *International Studies Quarterly* 27, 2: 149-159.

Kegley, C. W., Jr. and E. R. Wittkopf. 1987. *American Foreign Policy: Pattern and Process*. 3d ed. New York: St. Martin's Press.

Laurance, E. J. 1990. "Events Data and Policy Analysis: Improving the Potential for Applying Academic Research to Foreign and Defense Policy Problems." *Policy Sciences* 23, 2 (May): 111-132.

McClelland, C. A. 1983. "Let the User Beware." *International Studies Quarterly* 27, 2 (June): 169-177.

Vincent, J. E. 1983. "WEIS vs. COPDAB: Correspondence Problems." *International Studies Quarterly* 27, 2 (June): 160-168.

CHAPTER 4

Monitoring WEIS Event Data in Three Dimensions

Rodney G. Tomlinson

Abstract

This paper demonstrates the use of World Event/Interaction Survey event scales and exponential smoothing for three cases: (1) U.S.-USSR, (2) USSR-Czechoslovakia, and, (3) U.S.-United Kingdom. The WEIS project of Charles McClelland invented the scales and experimented with exponential smoothing for event flow monitoring in 1971. The events were found to contain nine perceptual constructs in varying amounts, headed by power and evaluation (morality). In 1977 a second study using professional diplomats as judges refined the values and multidimensional findings. It is argued here that conventional conflict-cooperation continua are simplistic and suggests an alternative constructive-deconstructive conflict-terminology to convey the notion of complex events. Event flows are plotted in two dimensions using vector algebraic composite values of the power and evaluative constructs for each event and in three dimensions using the actual values of the power and evaluative constructs. The latter resembles Quincy Wright's (1955) capability fields. The relative positions of the plots, most notably the distances between them, illustrate the states of affairs. Small distances and positive evaluative values appear during 'constructive' periods while greater distances and higher values for power during unstable, 'deconstructive' periods. Constructive relationships (i.e., U.S.-United Kingdom) plot near the origin. The graphs lend support to notions of reciprocity and dispute resolution advanced by Martin Patchen (1990) and Joshua Goldstein and John Freeman (1990). Further case study and experimentation are proposed.

Event Scaling at the WEIS Project

In this paper I wish to reintroduce two ideas developed at the WEIS project under Charles McClelland, WEIS event scaling and exponential smoothing (McClelland et al., 1971). They are lesser known research efforts, but ones that could, in my judgment, prove helpful in our current research environment. Today, desktop computers and their graphics facilities outshine the best tools of just a decade ago. Prudently used, in my view, microcomputer graphics enables the pattern detection power of the eye to see structures and processes overlooked by conventional statistical approaches.

It's been three decades since McClelland introduced "event/interaction" analysis while this year marks the twenty-sixth data-birthday of the World Event Interaction Survey (WEIS). Two decades have elapsed since McClelland commissioned Herbert L. Calhoun, one of the first WEIS research associates, to examine the scaling issues as they might relate to WEIS.

In my view the work done then has relevance now, most usefully, perhaps, in illustrating event flows using these new graphics. There had always been a strong feeling among WEIS researchers that some aspects of system description might better be conveyed visually than statistically. We suggest monitoring event flows by recasting WEIS events into metric dimensions and plotting these on a time line by use of exponential smoothing, a variant of the weighted moving average.

McClelland cared little for event scaling, especially when it embraced without question the cooperation-conflict (friendship-hostility) continuum. He felt WEIS event categories were more complex than indicated by arbitrary scales and marks on a line. To be candid, some scaling approaches of the time gave him heartburn. McClelland did, however, commission staff inquiries in the interest of academic thoroughness (Young and Martin, 1968; Calhoun, 1971). Calhoun, a mathematician by profession, undertook the primary effort of looking into the 'meaning' of WEIS events as related to scaled values.

The First Event Scales 1968-1971

Background and Charter

When this writer joined the WEIS project in 1969 Calhoun had just begun his work. Scaling seemed to fit well into the overall WEIS schema. It held hope of attaching "meaning by measurement" (not raw quantification) to the popular WEIS indicators of volume (Z-scores) and variety (HREL). Other indicators including triadic structural balance, probability density functions, auto-correlation, power spectral density, cross-correlation and its functions, and other notions related to systemic structure and process seemed likely beneficiaries. Keep in mind that McClelland has always been dedicated to process analysis and its meaning. Quantification without meaning meant nothing in his view.

Meaning had always been central to Calhoun's formulation due largely to McClelland's insistence that all avenues, schemes, and ideas be explored thoroughly. If WEIS were to be scaled,WEIS would have the best method (Calhoun, 1977: 3). Referring to other event scaling activities, Calhoun observed:

> A number of insights from these attempts at scaling event data have been instrumental in guiding the present approach. Among these is the recognition of the necessity to scale events along more than a single dimension (mode): to introduce modes other than the traditional good-bad modes (or their semantic equivalents);

there were strong indicators to suggest this necessity (see for example Walter Corson, Edward Azar, Moses-Holsti-Brody writings on scaling of event data), and the recognition that meaning and measurement correspond closely. Most of these scholars were not careful in identifying specific qualities to be measured nor concerned with the precise description of these qualities. (Calhoun, 1971: 5)

McClelland granted Calhoun "intellectual *carte blanche*" with a view to contribute "meaningfully" to the WEIS enterprise and knowledge about the event flow (Calhoun, 1977: 3). The first findings appeared in 1971. A second report followed in 1972, and the final event scales, with validation of the original findings, appeared in 1977. To the present writer Calhoun established the conceptual foundations for an important event flow indicator to join HREL and Z-scores. This was not universally acknowledged.

The potential utility of the scaling effort went largely unnoticed. It occupied but six pages of the 1971 WEIS report and seemed at the time too avant-garde. Scaling seemed an inappropriate leap, perhaps too long, at a time when so little was known about event streams. Categorizing and counting looked adequate and promising and so much remained to be done there. In addition, major concerns about data validity and completeness heightened WEIS project reticence to advocate moves toward "universal scaled" values.

Developing the 1971 Scales

After surveying alternative techniques, Calhoun, with McClelland's concurrence, selected the semantic differential as the preferred tool to identify meanings in the WEIS combined events (contracted to "combevnt," see table 4.1). In this method one postulates a semantic space of unknown dimensions, which is "defined by a set of empirical 'constructs [of meaning]' which are seen to span it" (Calhoun, 1971: 8). The WEIS combevnts occupy points within this space. The values on the constructs determine their positions in semantic space.

Identifying and building these constructs involve evaluating combevnts with a set of bipolar adjectival attribute scales thought to exhaustively encompass the underlying "essence" of the combevnts. Adjectival attributes refer to "any meaningful and distinguishable qualitative characteristics" inherent to the combevnts. Scales show the perceived degree to which these attributes characterize them (Calhoun, 1971: 6; Calhoun, 1977: 95). Therefore combevnts with similar perceived meanings should receive similar ratings on the same attributes. This should not occur, for WEIS combevnts were designed to represent different kinds of behavior. Therefore they should all be rated differently on the attributes.

The semantic differential builds a "geometry of meaning" by using the varimax output of a factor analysis as the mathematical basis for constructing a vector space and for assigning meaning. It is called a "semantic space." This multi-dimensional space allows for the precise identification and positioning of each combevnt on the orthogonal axes that make it up. The semantic space is a metric in the strict sense. Values along any of its axes by definition are scales. Distances along these axes measure qualitative meaning. The process of developing scales in this way is summarized as follows:

1. Select a universe of scales.
2. Construct and administer a questionnaire designed to elicit meanings from the universe of scales for each combevnt.
3. Factor analyze the questionnaire data using a factoring technique that includes an orthogonal rotation.
4. Compute coordinates, distances, and angles to adequately describe elements (constructs) of the semantic space.
5. Use the newly developed space as an instrument for assigning meaning and numerical values to the combevnts. (Calhoun, 1977: 94)

The 1971 study employed forty-one bipolar adjectival scales based on the work of Charles E. Osgood (1957). I will avoid commentary on the reasoning for their selection, the relevance of the method, its nuances, and weaknesses, for Calhoun was his own toughest critic. He has, over the course of two decades,

TABLE 4.1. Summary of WEIS Combined Events

Num	Alpha	Combevnts	Keywords
01	YLD	Yield	Surrender, retreat
02	COM	Comment	Pessimistic, optimistic
03	CNS	Consult	Visit, host, meet
04	APP	Approve	Praise, hail, endorse
05	PRM	Promise	Assure/reassure
06	GRA	Grant	Release, return, truce
07	RWD	Reward	Extend, give
08	AGR	Agree	Substantive agreement
09	REQ	Request	Ask for, call for
10	PPS	Propose	Offer, urge, suggest
11	REJ	Reject	Turn down, refuse
12	ACC	Accuse	Charge, criticize
13	PTT	Protest	Complain
14	DNY	Deny	Deny action/role
15	DMD	Demand	Insist, issue order
16	WRN	Warning	Give warning
17	THR	Threaten	Ultimatum
18	DEM	Demonstrate	Mobilize, boycott,
19	RDC	RdcRltns	Cancel, postpone, halt
20	EXP	Expel	Deport, order out
21	SZE	Seize	Detain, arrest, seize
22	FOR	Force	Engage

insistently reassured this writer of the validity of his operationalization, analysis, and findings. After fifteen years in international diplomacy, he remains firmly committed to the 1977 scales and the constructs they represent. I will review his findings, note my concerns and refer the skeptical reader to Calhoun's original work.

Calhoun performed three semantic studies on WEIS combevnts, one in 1970 and two in 1976. The first, reported in 1971, involved sixty-seven international relations students and faculty of the University of Southern California (USC). I focus on it. The 1976 studies were methodological replications of 1971, but the subjects were diplomats, an important matter to be discussed later.

The subjects judged each of the WEIS combevnts plus five related concepts on forty-one semantic scales, like "good-bad," "proud-humble," "strong-weak" and so on. Nine boxes separated the left and right ends of the scales, with the middle box representing neutrality or zero. The non-WEIS concepts of "cooperate," "conflict," "bargain," "participate," and "negotiate" were added for context and later proved useful in showing perspective.

Calhoun considers the findings from his first study meaningful but not conclusive. The factor analysis revealed nine constructs (clusters, that then define axes) for his semantic space, accounting for 61.51 percent of the total variance (table 4.2). "The WEIS [combevnts] can thus be viewed as vector-points in a nine-dimensional semantic space." (Calhoun, 1971: 13)

These many constructs suggest that the WEIS combevnts are as complex as McClelland suspected, and thus should moderate our enthusiasm for setting them into one dimensional continua like cooperation-conflict. In addition this means each combevnt contains these constructs as weighted "submessages" or "packets." Thus each combevnt could be perceived, theoretically, up to thirty-six different ways, depending on a participant's perceptual calculus (Calhoun, 1971: 21).

McClelland leaped on this before Calhoun's ink was barely dry, noting:

TABLE 4.2. Variance Accounted For (1971)

Evaluative	11.96%
Strength	12.25
Definitiveness	5.40
Stability	5.59
Complexity	6.72
Scope	3.82
Flexibility	5.54
Activity	6.48
Style	3.75
Total Variance	61.51%

It is interesting that none of the revealed dimensions is for conflict or cooperation. The scale that Calhoun finally recommended as most satisfactory for the WEIS processor is a COMPOSITE. It is a merging of the strength and evaluative dimensions and approaches as close as we can come to a reflection of the actions of "friendly" relations at the high end and "hostile" relations at the low end. The existing WEIS data collection does not have to be recoded to accomplish the scaling. Instead, the conversion to scaling is merely a matter of rearranging the category order and attaching weights which, through later computer executions, affect the values of frequency of occurrence counting. (McClelland, 1971: 129)

Table 4.3 summarizes the coordinates of WEIS combevnts in semantic space. From it we see that events constructive to system maintenance and stability [positive on evaluative construct] also tend to be complex, while

TABLE 4.3. Values of WEIS Combevnts in Semantic Space

Concept	Evaluative	Potency	*Definitiveness	Stability	Complexity
ACCUSE	-1.55	1.53	0.63	-0.10	-0.34
AGREE	1.60	-0.72	-0.33	0.47	0.88
APPROVE	1.62	-0.21	0.03	0.52	0.63
BARGAIN	1.62	0.41	0.08	0.25	1.19
COMMENT	0.37	0.24	0.37	0.18	0.46
COOPERATE	2.48	-0.10	-0.31	0.67	2.04
CONFLICT	-1.03	1.80	-1.33	-0.53	-0.37
CONSULT	1.56	-0.16	0.15	0.41	1.03
DEMAND	-0.49	2.03	0.30	-0.15	-0.04
DEMONSTRATE	0.44	1.03	-0.32	-0.22	0.50
DENY	-1.05	0.94	0.41	-0.75	-0.21
EXPEL	-1.01	1.67	-0.61	-0.21	-0.38
FORCE	-1.34	2.32	-0.44	-0.27	-0.49
GRANT	1.60	-0.39	-0.43	0.33	0.81
NEGOTIATE	1.66	-0.02	0.31	-0.36	1.31
PARTICIPATE	1.12	0.31	0.10	0.38	0.99
PROMISE	1.10	-0.11	0.17	0.30	0.69
PROPOSE	1.24	0.16	0.20	0.41	1.22
PROTEST	-0.06	1.19	0.31	-0.19	0.38
REQUEST	-1.02	-0.42	0.18	0.32	0.62
REWARD	2.21	0.12	-0.59	0.39	0.62
REDUCE	-0.65	0.63	-0.39	-0.44	-0.17
REJECT	-0.90	1.48	0.05	-0.08	-0.29
SEIZE	-1.31	1.97	-0.53	-0.47	-0.46
THREAT	-1.36	1.93	0.43	-0.56	-0.47
WARN	-0.25	1.21	0.50	0.30	0.10
YIELD	0.24	-1.80	-0.31	-0.31	0.05

TABLE 4.3. Continued

Concept	Flexibility	Scope	Activity	*Style
ACCUSE	0.14	-0.75	0.88	0.74
AGREE	0.11	1.10	-0.46	-0.51
APPROVE	0.39	0.59	0.70	-0.49
BARGAIN	0.57	1.41	0.41	-0.37
COMMENT	0.22	0.43	0.29	0.11
COOPERATE	1.13	1.76	0.40	-1.41
CONFLICT	1.16	-0.70	0.74	1.09
CONSULT	0.27	1.00	0.17	0.74
DEMAND	0.27	-0.64	0.99	0.85
DEMONSTRATE	0.87	0.67	0.82	0.11
DENY	-0.00	-0.61	0.19	1.19
EXPEL	0.45	1.11	0.84	0.95
FORCE	0.93	-0.94	1.06	1.17
GRANT	0.30	0.80	0.21	-0.35
NEGOTIATE	0.54	1.22	0.05	-0.48
PARTICIPATE	0.59	1.12	0.52	-0.27
PROMISE	-0.17	0.14	0.29	0.11
PROPOSE	0.54	0.35	0.32	-0.50
PROTEST	0.76	0.53	0.86	-0.42
REQUEST	-0.01	0.71	-0.06	-0.09
REWARD	-0.02	1.00	0.49	-0.53
REDUCE	0.18	-0.40	-0.07	0.84
REJECT	0.69	-1.81	0.24	0.76
SEIZE	0.53	-0.56	1.08	1.06
THREAT	0.86	-0.42	0.92	1.03
WARN	0.38	-0.17	0.69	0.52
YIELD	0.30	0.70	-0.86	0.47

*Reverse polarity on scales

deconstructive activities are simpler. Perhaps, depending on the situation, some combevnts might be preferable to others in redirecting interaction sequences. This area of study seems largely unexplored. At this point we acknowledge McClelland's suspicions and proceed with caution.

But as a practical matter we must attach meaning to this nine-scale constellation if it is to do us any good. It won't do to define REWARD as the occupier of coordinates (2.21, 0.12, -0.59, 0.39, 0.62, -0.02, 1.00, 0.49, and -0.53) in WEIS semantic space. What do these values mean? We need to draw some conceptual fields of understanding to relate these coordinates with more familiar concepts.

Conceptual Planes of Morality and Power

Quite fortunately, the two strongest constructs emerging from the study match the central concepts of international politics, namely, morality and power. They relate to something we understand — idealism (moral/evaluation) and realism (power/potency). This sets up conceptual horizons, planes of understanding, with the x and y axes representing evaluation and potency constructs, respectively. Thus we set a framework for understanding the combevnts in terms of meaningful dimensions of morality and power. We exclude the remaining constructs.

Vector algebra determines the composite values for combevnts by using evaluative and potency coordinates. This produces a third scaled value for each combevnt. The three values are: (1) a coordinate value on the evaluative dimension, (2) a coordinate value on the potency dimension, and (3) a composite (perhaps synthesis?) value derived from the first two.

To emphasize, there emerges for each combevnt a set of scaled values derived heuristically from constructs about power and morality. Their values have not been determined arbitrarily, but they occupy a scale about which we know little. We do not know, for example, what value signifies crisis or its resolution, or even if a crisis value holds as a constant. We do not know how these scales relate to HREL and Z-Scores, if they do at all. This must await experimental confirmation.

Table 4.4 shows the WEIS combevnts arranged in rank order by the composite indicator. The coordinates of the evaluative and potency constructs and the nine-dimension composite indicator also appear. Please note the non-WEIS concepts of cooperate, bargain, negotiate, participate, and conflict (indicated with asterics). The sign for the composite value comes from the evaluative construct.

These scales warrant some discussion. First of all the arrangement has considerable face validity. The non-WEIS concepts of *cooperate, bargain, negotiate,* and *participate* align themselves among WEIS concepts usually associated with constructive political behavior. And *conflict* snugs nicely between THREAT and SEIZE. The events range from constructive activities to undertakings very deconstructive to peace and stability. While the combevnts appear strung across a spectrum some would call cooperation/conflict, we can't, in the context of our earlier observations, call it so, and even if we could we would have no consistent and valid way of measuring them. Constructive-deconstructive appears appropriate since combevnt scales might be based on two to nine dimensions.

Except for slightly lower values, the nine-dimensional scales appear similar to their two-dimensional counterparts. A Pearson R of +.944 supports this observation. The evaluative and potency constructs appear to represent discordant concepts ($r = -.770$). We may further generalize on combevnt characteristics in noting that constructive combevnts tend to load less on the potency construct.

The notion of natural divergence of power and morality finds support. In addition, we may uncover clues about the nature of the event flow if it is disaggregated and plotted.

We suspect socially constructive relationships (stabilizing relationships) might be characterized by moderate behavior reminiscent of transaction sequences. Such tendencies would appear graphically as plots near the origin. We could suggest, too, that excesses in any direction may signal destabilizing behavior. That is to say, perturbations by either actor, whether "constructive" (+) or "deconstructive" (-) on either the evaluative or potency constructs may herald changes in the flow.

We now have the essential value sets for plotting WEIS event flows. In review, they are: (1) a composite indicator derived from the evaluative and potency constructs, (2) a composite indicator derived from all nine constructs,

TABLE 4.4. Events Scales (1971)

Combevnt	2Dim	Eval	Ptncy	9Dim
COOPERATE*	4.67	2.48	-0.10	4.17
BARGAIN*	3.53	1.62	0.41	2.63
REWARD	3.39	2.21	0.12	2.70
NEGOTIATE*	3.06	1.66	-0.02	-2.59
CONSULT	2.94	1.56	-0.16	2.32
AGREE	2.78	1.60	-0.72	2.42
PROPOSE	2.57	1.24	0.16	2.39
GRANT	2.52	1.60	-0.39	2.14
APPROVE	2.51	1.62	-0.21	2.14
PARTICIPATE*	2.46	1.12	0.31	2.00
REQUEST	1.24	1.02	-0.42	1.50
PROMISE	1.02	1.10	-0.11	1.40
YIELD	0.72	0.24	-1.80	1.67
COMMENT	0.11	0.37	0.24	0.95
RDCRLTNS	-1.07	-0.65	0.63	-1.45
WARNING	-1.67	-0.25	1.21	-1.67
DEMONSTRATE	-1.81	0.44	1.03	-1.88
DENY	-1.87	-1.05	0.94	-2.14
PROTEST	-1.98	-0.06	1.19	-1.86
ACCUSE	-2.65	-1.55	1.53	-2.68
REJECT	-2.88	-0.90	1.48	-2.74
EXPEL	-3.06	-1.01	1.67	-2.72
DEMAND	-3.18	-0.49	2.03	-2.58
THREATEN	-3.342	-1.36	1.93	-3.02
CONFLICT*	-3.441	-1.03	1.80	-3.17
SEIZE	-3.50	-1.31	1.97	-3.00
FORCE	-4.04	-1.34	2.32	-3.45

*Non-WEIS concepts.

and (3) a set of *x-y* coordinate values on the evaluative and potency axes for the twenty-two combevnts.

Indicators (1) and (2) employ conventional graphing techniques, where time occupies the horizontal axis and the event on the vertical. Corson's (1970) early work using modified WEIS events and Goldstein and Freeman (1990), without the aggregations, typify this approach. Figure 4.1 shows our rendition of Soviet-Czech interaction, with the constructive-destructive spectra occupying the vertical axis.

These plots provide very attractive overviews of event flows, but they could be misrepresenting the actual state of affairs since the plotted values represent composite meanings derived from multiple constructs. Two graphs could look alike but represent different concept mixes. Traditional approaches sort out the problem with "wisdom" and "judgment."

Most of us avoid this inconvenience by selecting general terminology to characterize event indicator axes. Most commonly we use "conflict-cooperation" because everyone understands it. We discard, or at best fold in or ignore associative constructs like complexity, flexibility, stability, style and the like. If we gain acceptance or a consensus supporting our scaling technique, we achieve, in scientific terms, status and validity until someone comes along to propose and/ or demonstrate a better alternative.

The convenience of single axis indicators like conflict-cooperation argues for their retention. Furthermore, they graph easily. So for practical reasons we retain them. It seems to us that conflict-cooperation might be too simplistic now, so we propose the terms "constructive-deconstructive" to label our spectrum. This acknowledges the underlying complexities of the combevnts. Constructive activities have positive values in the evaluative dimension. Deconstructive have negative ones. The degree of impact on system process comes from the potency dimension. The composite value takes the valence of the evaluative and a magnitude based on a vector solution in semantic space along the evaluative and potency axes. We believe constructive behavior indicates activities likely to improve the human condition while deconstructive could indicate either turning points in the event flow or actions dysfunctional to improvement.

The Conceptual Plane of Morality and Power

We just introduced composite indicators, leaving consideration of the evaluative and potency constructs for last. They are, in review, conceptual axes with metric values of meaning in semantic space. As orthogonal axes they define a conceptual plane in terms of morality and power. Calhoun (1977: 155) notes, "the coordinates themselves may be used directly as valid interval scales." On

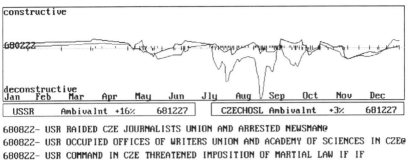

680822- USR RAIDED CZE JOURNALISTS UNION AND ARRESTED NEWSMAN@
680822- USR OCCUPIED OFFICES OF WRITERS UNION AND ACADEMY OF SCIENCES IN CZE@
680822- USR COMMAND IN CZE THREATENED IMPOSITION OF MARTIAL LAW IF IF
DEMONSTRATION PLANNED FOR THIS EVENING TOOK PLACE@
680822- CZE DEMONSTRATION CANCELLED AS RESULT OF USR THREATS@
680910+ CZE PRM CONFERRED WITH THREE PRINCIPAL LEADERS OF USR@
680910+ CZE AND USR AGREEMENT ON EXCHANGE OF GOODS@
680910+ CZE PRM CONFERRED WITH THREE USR LEADERS@
680910+ USR&CZE ISSUED JOINT COMMUNIQUEUF MUTUAL CONVICTION THAT PRACTICAL
STEPS BE TAKEN RESULTING FROM AGREEMENT SIGNED BY USR&CZE ON AUG. 26@
680910+ CZE AND USR AGREEMENT ON EXCHANGE OF GOODS@
681107- CZE DEMONSTRATORS BURN USR FLAGS AND JEEP@

Fig. 4.1. World event/interaction survey scaled event flows

it we overlay Cartesian coordinates and plot WEIS combevnts according to their "*x*" (evaluative) and "*y*" (potency) values. By adding time as the third dimension each event becomes a snapshot, or 'slide,' of a moment in the flow of the event stream. The chronological event sequence resembles a slide show or, perhaps, sliced bread. An end view reveals the event stream meandering in, across, and between the quadrants defined by the "*x*" and "*y*" axes on each slice.

Credit for the conceptual underpinnings for three dimensional illustrations of event streams surely must go to Quincy Wright, his cheese and maggots (Wright, 1955: 546). This formulation shows dyadic systems of action in a manner reminiscent of Wright's "Capability field (b)." We postulate nations creating trails as they munch through successive slices of time. Their absolute and relative positions and trajectories provide clues about event flow state and direction. As we noted before, experimentation must now follow to establish this perspective.

But before plunging into this, we need to nail down the event scale values again and establish them as reasonable parameters for research. We consider now some issues regarding the 1971 findings and then summarize how the 1976 studies resolved them.

1976 Event Scales

Some Issues

An overall issue relates to the applicability of the semantic differential in the first place. If the reader rejects it out of hand, read no farther. Folded four times this chapter should make a fine doorstop on dry days. If doubtful, please examine Calhoun's rationales. They are cogent and persuasive, enough so to nudge McClelland towards neutrality (McClelland et al., 1971:127).

Other objections center on the scale value derivations. To begin, much of the variance explained by nine dimensions (61.5%) was lost in using only the evaluative and potency constructs (24.2%). In addition, one might have misgivings about polling students on complex foreign affairs concepts during the tense and tempestuous Vietnam war. Calhoun had but sixty-seven subjects, probably a minimum for this kind of work.

Calhoun used the 1971 study as the core of his master's thesis. The 1976 studies did the same for his doctoral dissertation. By this time Calhoun had joined the State Department as a scientist and arms negotiator in its Arms Control and Disarmament Agency (ACDA). From this position he was able to replicate his work using foreign affairs professionals drawn from middle and upper ranks of the State Department. Calhoun has reported that at least one questionnaire was completed in the Secretary of State's office perhaps even by the Secretary himself and that this new research environment was "infinitely better" than the first one (Calhoun, 1977: 107; 1991).

The newer research design sought to: (1) employ an enlarged population directly involved, and therefore relevant to international politics, (2) investigate the effect of situations on event perceptions, notably differences between non-threat and high-threat, (3) determine the stability of the combevnt scale values, and (4) reevaluate the scaling methodology to determine if the evaluative-potency dimension dominates across populations (Calhoun, 1977: 11). We focus on these issues here and then proceed to the matter of graphing them using event models based on exponential smoothing.

Design: The Diplomatic Population

Calhoun's access to diplomatic professionals for the second and third surveys was truly fortunate. Whereas the first study used students and academics of all stripes, these surveys used diplomatic practitioners whose judgment, we surmise, really counts in these things. "Bureau heads were explicitly sought out and every effort was made to recruit them for the test" (Calhoun, 1977: 161). If the Bureau heads would not or could not participate, their deputies or ranking assistants were recruited. The final population included representation from fifteen bureaus of the State Department, eight from the Agency for International Development, five from the Arm Control Agency, and seven from the U. S. Information Agency. The final sample for the second survey had 121 cases and, for the third, 100 cases.

A review of the 1971 results found, that after factor-rotation to "simple-structure," both "unique" and "most descriptive" scales remained as high loaders. In the interest of retaining only the most descriptive (universal) scales, Calhoun deleted the unique ones, leaving fifteen scales for use by the diplomats. Therefore the 1971 and 1976 surveys are not precisely comparable.

Design: Situational Effects

Finally comes the question of context or situation. Three contrasting schools of thought emerge on this issue. One holds the event supreme while another favors the situation. A third holds for something in the middle. Calhoun did not address this in 1971 but he did in 1976.

The second survey elicited perceptions for a "non-contextual" (non-threat) situation. The third addressed a "contextual" (high-threat) situation.

The questionnaires were reworded carefully to impose a high threat environment. Each subject assumed the role of a spokesman for nations involved in the interaction.

Findings: The 1977 Scales

As in the 1971 survey, the data from the second and third surveys were factor analyzed to yield two sets of summary statistics. The emerging factors for the non-threat (2nd survey) and high-threat (3rd) situations appear in table 4.5.

Most striking is the re-emergence of the evaluative and potency constructs. The seven remaining 1971 constructs do not reappear, being replaced by four new ones: "Scope," "Competitiveness," "Honor," and "Importance." Scope, third place in the non-threat environment, fades to fifth in high-threat. Importance, fifth place in non-threat moves up to fourth in high-threat. Honor, fourth in non-threat, disappears altogether in high-threat. The construct "Competitiveness"

TABLE 4.5. Variance Account For (1977)

Non-Threat		High-Threat	
Evaluative	20.0%	Evaluative	20.1
Potency	15.0	Potency	13.5
Scope	7.5	Competit.	9.0
Honor	4.6	Importance	9.1
Importance	3.5	Scope	3.4
Total	50.6		55.1

appears in the high-threat situation, an intuitively pleasing observation. These level shifts in loadings, while beyond the purview of this paper, appear interesting and worthy of further study.

The evaluative and potency constructs again dominate the surveys, and by so doing focus Calhoun's attention for scaling. He defers further consideration of "Honor," "Scope," "Competitiveness," and "Importance." With regard to evaluative and potency dominating all three surveys Calhoun observes:

> ... the same clusters of scales describe the two most important factors [evaluative and potency] underlying international behavior. Compressing semantically equivalent scales we have: fair-unfair, strong-weak, stable-unstable, flexible-inflexible, aggressive-non-aggressive, and proud-humble.
>
> This is certainly a surprisingly efficient and economical outcome of three radically different factor analyses, all of which were designed for different reasons using different populations. It is an especially gratifying result considering the large number of degrees of freedom available to each respondent in answering each question.
>
> What conclusions may we draw at this point concerning this analysis? At worst, we may say that there is a "sort-of-universal" meaning attached to verbs of action describing international behavior, a necessary prerequisite for scaling. Further, we may state that two primary factors seem to underlie the description and communication of international interaction: "evaluation and potency." Third, *we may say that the interpretation of these descriptors does not change radically with contextual nuances.* And finally, we may make the further limited claim that with cultural factors remaining constant these descriptors span the space of meaning applied to day-to-day interaction between nations.
>
> It may seem that this last claim stretches the conclusions a bit, given the universe of possibilities; however, it must be remembered that the bipolar scales used in the present study and in the 1971 study represent the distillation of more than 278 bipolar dimensions of discrimination taken from Osgood's original studies. Additionally, it is apropos to point out that Osgood has found the evaluation and potency dimensions, with the same underlying scales as those in this analysis reappearing in several cultural analyses. Thus, it may just be the case that these dimensions hold across cultures as well. (Calhoun, 1977: 147-148)

We now introduce the combevnt scale values derived from the potency and evaluative constructs. Table 4.6 shows these for the non-threat and high-threat situations along with vector positions in semantic space for high threat evaluative and potency. Some of the differences between the two situations include: (1) YIELD is viewed as a deconstructive option in both non-threat and high-threat environments; (2) AGREE, PROPOSE, CONSULT, and APPROVE, important as constructive events in non-threat environments, lose a lot of their impact in high-threat environments; (3) REDUCE RELATIONS, WARNING, and SEIZE, with high deconstructive impact for non-threat situations lose a lot of this in periods of high-threat; (4) ACCUSE increases in deconstructive impact during crises, indicating its dysfunctional nature in all situations; and (5) events of tangible substance REWARD and GRANT retain their constructive impact in both situations while PROMISE slips a bit. This cursory examination may provide useful clues to the direction different behavior alternatives are likely to drive an interaction sequence.

Table 4.7 shows the coordinates in semantic space for the evaluative and potency constructs and the differences between them for non-threat and high-threat environments. The reader should note the two rightmost columns, titled "Diffs Evl" and "Diffs Ptn," derived by subtracting NON-threat values from the HIGH-threat values. The value signs come from the arithmetic and show the direction of change as situation moves from non-threat to high-threat.

Calhoun concluded that situation differences did not significantly change the event scales. We can't see this. From our earlier discussion it seems that the impact of some constructive events decreased in the third (threat) survey. From this perspective crises appear harder to resolve than prevent.

We now proceed to applications to event flows without further discussions of the advisability or inadvisability of using these values. As noted earlier, we assume their development has been sound and we consider them parameters for events research.

TABLE 4.6. Combined Events Ranked by Scale Values

Combevnt	Hi-Thr	Non-Thr	Hi-Thr-Evl	Hi-Thr-Ptn
REWARD	3.02	3.21	3.07	2.97
PROMISE	1.11	1.32	1.24	-0.98
GRANT	0.91	1.02	1.24	0.63
AGREE	0.68	1.50	1.24	0.26
PROPOSE	0.52	2.55	0.23	0.88
REQUEST	0.44	0.34	-0.08	-0.91
APPROVE	0.38	0.91	0.68	-0.14
COMMENT	0.26	0.00	0.23	0.30
CONSULT	0.17	0.66	-0.08	0.26
THREATEN	-0.47	-0.70	-1.05	0.05
RDCRLTNS	-0.59	-2.37	-0.73	0.47
WARNING	-0.63	-2.30	-0.08	-1.45
DEMONSTRATE	-0.69	-0.63	-1.21	-0.30
PROTEST	-1.02	-1.01	-1.55	-0.60
REJECT	-1.18	-1.58	-1.87	0.66
DENY	-1.20	-0.88	-0.73	-1.80
YIELD	-1.79	-2.20	-0.73	-3.50
ACCUSE	-2.24	-1.58	-1.55	3.11
SEIZE	-2.50	-3.77	-1.72	3.50
DEMAND	-2.51	-2.30	-2.42	2.61
EXPEL	-3.49	-3.49	-3.54	3.45
FORCE	-3.76	-4.00	-3.54	4.00

Depicting Event Flows

Exponential Smoothing

The standard monitoring procedures advocated by McClelland had evolved from aggregated tabulations to models with time lines, which means increased focus on single or small aggregations of events. McClelland had adopted a rule of thumb — event aggregations of a week or less were event/interaction analysis; anything greater was comparative studies of political behavior (McClelland, 1991). McClelland preferred other methods to comparative, so by 1971 projects employing event aggregations through the original WEISUM cross-tabulator had largely been abandoned in favor of specialized programs more attune to the notion of dynamic streams of events.

The author modified WEISUM for time aggregations in the rows. Time always appeared in the WEIS event flow models. The automated monitors

TABLE 4.7. Coordinates of WEIS Combevnts in Semantic Space
Comparison of the Contextual, Noncontextual, and Student Populations

Combevnt	Hi-Thr		Non-Thr		Stdnts		Diffs	
	Evl	Ptn	Evl	Ptn	Evl	Ptn	Evl	Ptn
ACCUSE	-1.55	3.11	-2.48	2.79	-1.55	2.53	-0.93	-0.32
AGREE	1.24	0.26	2.57	0.75	1.60	-0.72	1.33	0.49
APPROVE	0.68	-0.14	1.24	0.63	1.62	-0.21	0.56	0.77
COMMENT	0.23	0.30	0.00	0.00	0.37	0.24	-0.23	-0.30
CONSULT	-0.08	0.26	0.68	0.65	1.56	-0.16	0.76	0.39
DEMAND	-1.21	-0.30	-0.78	0.50	-0.49	2.03	0.43	0.80
DMNSTRTE	-2.42	2.61	-2.48	2.14	-2.49	2.03	-0.06	-0.47
DENY	-0.73	-1.80	-0.73	-1.04	-1.05	0.94	0.00	0.76
EXPEL	-3.54	3.45	-3.54	3.45	-3.01	2.67	0.00	0.00
FORCE	-3.54	4.00	-4.00	4.00	-3.34	2.32	-0.46	0.00
GRANT	1.24	0.63	2.57	-0.14	1.60	-0.39	1.33	-0.77
PROMISE	1.24	-0.98	2.25	-0.65	1.10	-0.11	1.01	0.33
PROPOSE	0.23	0.88	2.07	2.09	1.24	0.16	1.84	1.21
PROTEST	-1.55	-0.60	-1.87	-0.41	-0.06	1.19	-0.32	0.19
REDUCE	-0.73	0.47	-2.48	2.27	-0.65	0.63	-1.75	1.80
REJECT	-1.87	0.66	-2.92	0.70	-0.90	1.48	-1.05	0.04
REQUEST	-0.08	-0.91	-0.08	-0.66	1.02	-0.42	0.00	0.25
REWARD	3.07	2.97	3.46	2.97	2.21	2.12	0.39	0.00
SEIZE	-1.72	3.50	-4.00	3.56	-3.31	2.97	-2.28	0.06
THREAT	-1.05	0.05	-1.05	0.41	-1.36	0.93	0.00	0.36
WARN	-0.08	1.45	-0.78	1.00	0.25	1.21	-0.70	-0.45
YIELD	-0.73	-3.50	-1.05	-4.00	0.24	-1.80	-0.32	0.50

HREL (Information Content) and AUTOHOG (Z-scores) provided for time axes and recalculated each time a new event joined the stream.

Event flow projecting techniques received the most attention in the 1971 Report. They fell under general headings of time series and exponential smoothing (ES). The former included nine variants, while the latter had eight. None met with resounding success, but exponential smoothing demonstrated modest degrees of projecting accuracy. While event flow projections do not concern us directly, we are advocating ways to improve our illustration techniques with microcomputer graphics. A strong view from the WEIS studies held that event flow illustration might well be served by techniques like exponential smoothing linked to advanced graphics devices. None existed then. This anchors our interest here, for we believe it premature to suggest event forecasting without extensive experimentation.

After an exhaustive search, Calhoun selected exponential smoothing to demonstrate event flow forecasting with scaled events. Calhoun evaluated eight equations (McClelland et al., 1971: 266-325). Four data sequences derived from WEIS data and typical of event streams tested the equations. The general second order equation, which we discuss below, performed the best (or least worse).

Techniques of Exponential Smoothing

Exponential smoothing resembles weighted moving averages, but with some variants. Whereas a typical weighted moving average takes the form:

(a) $\quad \overline{X}_i = \dfrac{w_i X_i + w_{i-1} X_{i-1} + \ldots + w_{i-n+1} X_{i-n+1}}{\sum w}$

where X defines a family of n elements (or events) with associated weights (w), exponential smoothing takes the general form:

(b) $\quad \overline{X}_i = kX_i + (1 - k)\overline{X}_{i-1}$

with the smoothing constant k analogous to the weights w in the moving average.

But there are differences. First, in ordinary moving averages old histories, the least current events, are deleted from the computation as new events arrive. In exponential smoothing past events decline in importance but are never deleted entirely from the computations. They are discounted in geometric progression according to their position in the event sequence (Springer, 1965: 93).

Second, moving averages are more difficult to calculate. All events must be retained so the oldest one can be deleted as the newest one enters the calculations. In addition, all the remaining events must be moved to their new positions adjacent to their new weights. While this complicates calculations, it allows one to shape the memory retention characteristic of the equation. This may be a very desirable feature. Experiments to determine the effects of changing the number of events and values of the weights might be very useful.

On the other hand the influence of past events declines geometrically with exponential smoothing. It is accounted for in the last computed average. This simplifies calculations but saddles the researcher with a fixed decay curve. Some argue it may be a good approximation of our recollective process (Springer, 1965: 98).

Third, exponential smoothing uses a single constant, k to determine the relative influence of past and current events. Selecting a value for it is a compromise between stability (extensive historical influence, $k = .01$) and sensitivity to recent events ($k = .5$). The amount of variability of the ES equation as compared to a moving average can be determined by the formula $(2/k)-1$; thus $k = .4$ causes equation (b) to have a variability equivalent to a moving average composed of four events, while $k = .2$ would equate to nine events.

Equation (b) is single, first order, exponential smoothing. It works best if the data have no trend. Should a trend be present, as is true in many extended event sequences, single smoothing tends to understate the values. Recycling the single smoothed estimate corrects for trends. This leads to the equation for double, or second order, smoothing:

$$\text{(c)} \quad \overline{\overline{X}}_i = k\overline{X}_i + (1-k)\overline{\overline{X}}_{i-1}$$

Equation (c) is equation (b) with linear trend correction. The WEIS studies suggested it to be the preferred method. Resources and time prevented studies of third order, non-linear variants during Calhoun's tenure on the WEIS Project. Here again we identify further directions for event-sequence experimentation.

Before proceeding we should consider beginning points for exponential smoothing calculations. Since calculations iterate, the last term represents event history in the next cycle. To commence calculations, the equation must be jump-started with some reasonable estimate of the past. The mean of the first three events will suffice.

First and second order smoothed values are calculated for any pair of nations chosen by the user. We experimented with different smoothing constants from .4 to .2. For this research we employ the latter, thereby tending to moderate response. We can liken smoothing constants to "panic factors." Thus lower values might represent circumspection and prudence while higher ones uproar and tumult.

Being a time-series device, the model recalculates each time it encounters a day with events. In instances of days with multiple events, it calculates the algebraic sum of all event values for the day and then performs exponential smoothing. It does not take the mean of the event values for a day. This means that sudden redirection in the event stream will be acknowledged quickly should it persevere. For example, four force acts on the same day would sum to -16.00, enter the equation as 3.2 and should the historic flow be at neutral (0.0), redirect the event flow to -3.2. A second day of the same could move the plot past the conceptual limit of -4.0 down to -5.76.

This produces anomalies in some instances. The intense carnage of the Cambodian-Vietnam conflict of the 1970's drove the smoothed value through the conceptual floor. Beyond the pale, so to speak. In these instances, the graphing module merely plots to the conceptual limit (-4.00). The actual values are retained for computations. We believe this approach retains the flavor of the situation though we can't illustrate anything but a "smoking trench" along our plot.

We encounter very few days with multiple events like our example so our concerns may be exaggerated. Anyway we believe the perceptions of an event flood "piling on" in a single day would have a cumulative impact more properly represented by an algebraic sum than a mean. WEIS discerns events by days not hours, hence any discounting of values by recalculating events based on sequences encountered within days seems inappropriate.

Finally we should consider the graphics. Event/interaction studies focus on non-routine behavior (McClelland, 1968). They tell us what important things are happening and whether changes are afoot. In the absence of these we assume that the state of affairs and its tendencies remain much as we last saw them. On the other hand new events departing from expectation suggest otherwise and we rethink system state. In the absence of crises we don't know precisely how and when all the factors of changes occur, so for parsimony and simplicity we assume that they come in increments and so are usefully portrayed by a line connecting the event points that we do have. This model does just that, using a simple linear plotting routine to connect the smoothed values.

The following values are calculated and stored for each actor for each event-day using scaled values from the 1977 report: (1) first and second order smoothed values for composite indicators, (2) numbers of events for the day, (3) running averages for composite indicators, (4) daily potency values, (5) daily evaluative values, (6) smoothed values for evaluative and potency, and (7) a series of summary values for each year. In keeping with WEIS tradition, just about everything that looked reasonable is calculated. But we focus here on parts of items (1) and (6).

We chose three dyads: (1) Soviet Union and United States, (2) Soviet Union and Czechoslovakia, and, (3) the United States and United Kingdom. The first two cases have been popular WEIS foci, while the U.S. and Great Britain are reputed to have a "special relationship" that could set a perspective on what we call constructive behavior.

Happily, the splendid studies by Goldstein and Freeman (1988; 1990) offer us an opportunity to compare data and patterns. Further, the insights by Patchen (1990: 22) have particular relevance, notably the parallel tracking and gaps between the plots that we see in our event-by-event portrayals.

Our data and observations may differ from Goldstein and Freeman due to some scaling dissimilarities. YIELD is the major difference, where Goldstein and Freeman assigned a positive valence (estimated +3.5), while Calhoun's 1977 study assigned a negative value (-1.79), based on a survey of diplomatic practitioners. In contrast, Calhoun's 1972 findings showed a modest positive value (+0.72), based on a survey of students and faculty at USC. Apparently practitioners and observers differ on the nature of YIELD.

We find differences with THREATS, REDUCE RELATIONS, and WARNINGS. Calhoun found both populations assigning these less criticality than did Goldstein and Freeman. We must recall that we offer here a scale thought to be unlike the usual cooperative-conflict continua. But it may well be that the constructive-deconstructive scale will resemble other scales since it subsumes the conflict-cooperation continua. In fact we found relatively high correlations between the WEIS 1977 composite scales and Goldstein and Freeman's intuitive values. Table 4.8 summarizes our findings. The evaluative dimension emerges as the concept most closely associated with the composite scales, supporting WEIS Project suppositions that "evaluation" dominates event scaling schemes.

The graphics used here will appear in yearly segments for presentation convenience. The calculations continue across all years. When arranged end to end, they resemble a two-sensor electrocardiograph. To review, the top half of figure 4.1 shows a graph of the event flow as calculated by our model. Associated event descriptions can be selected and displayed on the bottom by placing cross-hairs over the date marks on the axis. Results of event-by-event calculations are stored chronologically for use by three dimensional plotters. Figures 4.2-4.4 show the two-dimensional plot on the top and three-dimensional variants beneath.

Superpower Competition—U.S. and USSR

Figures 4.2 through 4.4 show the U.S.-USSR event flow for 1985 and 1988-89. Goldstein and Freeman's splendid discussion and expanded plots for the period 1985-89 and their quarterly overview focus our discussion (Goldstein and

TABLE 4.8. Correlations between Events Scales

	G&F	Hi-Thr	Non-Thr	Hi-Thr-Ptn
Hi-Thr	.761			
Non-Thr	.813	.918		
Hi-Thr-Ptn	-.438	-.349	-.315	
Hi-Thr-Evl	.817	.954	.867	-.335

Freeman, 1990:145-157). We would like to see if our plots and addition of the evaluative and potency constructs might add to our insights.

First a word about the quarterly plot by Goldstein and Freeman (1990: 149, fig. 6.2). It displays the "total net cooperation" in the U.S.-USSR-China *triad*. A cyclical pattern emerges, but essentially driven, it appears, by the U.S.-USSR dyad. With about a five to one preponderance of events reported, the U.S.-USSR dyad could well be modulating the essentially flat pattern of the other two legs (p. 147,fig. 6.1). Thus Goldstein and Freeman's figure 6.2 can be considered a quarterly aggregation of figure 4.2 in this work (See also Goldstein and Freeman 1990: 42, fig. 2.2).

Quarterly aggregations seem to emphasize cyclical natures in the event stream more distinctly than monthly aggregations. From this, Goldstein and Freeman forecast a possible third cooperative period. Whatever the causes, the evidence does seem clear that U.S.-USSR relations rise and fall. The aggregate suggests that there are, "on average," good times and bad times.

Figures 4.2 through 4.4 illustrate in somewhat greater detail the changes in event flows noted by Goldstein and Freeman. Mid June 1985 seems to usher in a period where Soviet and U.S. behavior tracks more closely in both constructive or deconstructive situations. The distances between the U.S. and Soviet plot lines are metric units and thus display meaningful numeric distances between their respective behaviors. Thus the areas between the lines show amounts of discordant behavior in the event flow. By late June the gap narrows and in comparison with the previous twelve months. It has remained so ever since.

Studies of plots for the years 1966-87, not shown here, found the gaps to be widest and narrowest for intervals with popular labels like "East Politik," "Cold War I," "Cold War II," and "Detente." The narrowest gaps suggest progress and understanding-constructive behavior, and so are publicly noticeable. On the other hand, extended periods of wide gaps mean deconstructive behavior and similar popular notoriety. We believe this narrowing and widening of the behavior gap relates to Goldstein and Freeman's concept of stability. So deconstructive (unstable) conditions demand attention. The gap width indicates pressure levels for attention and actions. Hence, for example, President Ford's comment in 1976, after a lengthy period of deteriorating relations with the USSR, that he never wanted to hear the word 'detente' again.

Patchen (1990: 22) offers the insight:

> A nation's leaders may respond to a rival's actions not on the basis of the other's behavior in isolation but on the basis of the difference between the other's behavior and their own nation's recent behavior.

In Patchen's view, investigations into reciprocity could be a very promising direction for research.

This notion of tension levels (or response demand) using WEIS event values was being studied by Calhoun (1972) as he departed the project. But he focused

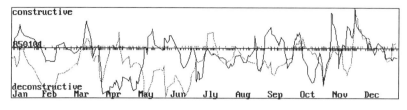

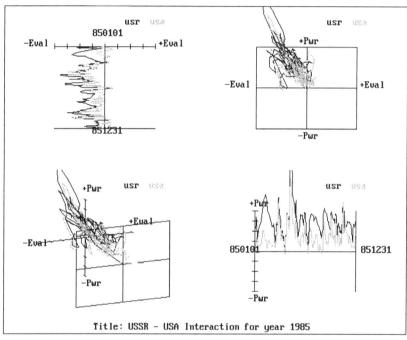

Fig. 4.2. World event/interaction survey scaled event flows

on the USSR-U.S.-China triad using a normalized formula based on net differences between positive (cooperative) and negative (conflictual) events for any nation pair for a given period. He calculated a metric quality (+1 to -1) for the dyad and called it 'tension' (Calhoun, 1972: 24a). Goldstein and Freeman's reciprocity propositions look like nominal level renditions of Calhoun's earlier explorations. Sheen Rajmaira and Michael Ward (1990) may, indeed, also be on the same trail.

Calhoun never linked exponential smoothing to his tension measure, but he again demonstrated that the WEIS metric means more than simple differences between quantities of negative and positive events (Calhoun, 1972: 32). Further explorations here must be considered as extensions of WEIS undertakings begun by McClelland.

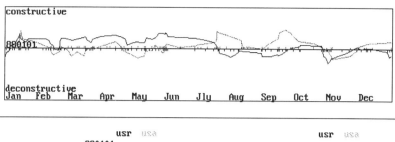

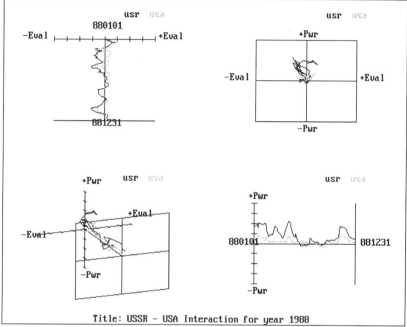

Fig. 4.3. World event/interaction survey scaled event flows

The three dimensional plots below each of the composite indicators show the evaluative and potency constructs for each actor's event stream. They look quite messy, having been compressed for printing. The event model permits user selection by month, quarter, half-year, and year for graphing. Figure 4.2 shows the full year. In addition each view can be expanded to full screen size and the '3-D' plot (lower left) rotated in space to display any perspective.

The evaluative and potency constructs occupy the horizontal and vertical axes that intersect the time (or "z" axis). They define a plane with a thickness of one day. All events for that date have their algebraic sum of item construct values plotted on the plane. The planes, or time slices, line up like slides in a projector. The time axis passes through the slices at the intersection of the x and y axes. The

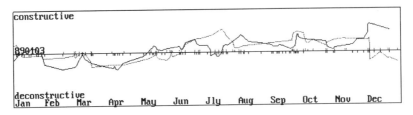

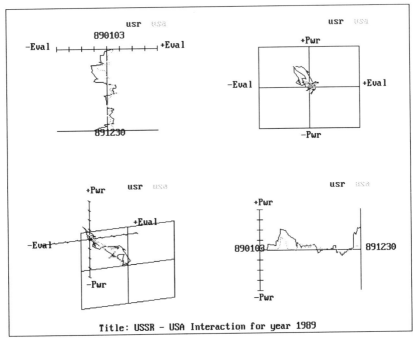

Fig. 4.4. World event/interaction survey scaled event flows

vertical axis "y" belongs to potency, and "x" to evaluative. Imagine countries to be worms munching through a loaf. Their trails' absolute (actual values) and relative (direction and distance between) positions interest us.

Since each slice corresponds to a day in real time, the worms may only appear intermittently through successive slices. We assume they travel directly between one observation to the next. We draw lines to show this. The spatial differences in worms' trails correspond to the gaps noted in our 2-D discussions.

We propose, as did Wright, that the relative and actual positions of the worms define one aspect of system state — its behavior dynamics. Anecdotal evidence from plots of twenty-five other dyads indicates that the upper left quadrant shows the tension-conflict dimension. The potency and evaluative constructs have a weak inverse correlation, so we expect high potency events to display negative valences on the evaluative side. Diplomats appear to perceive power (coercive) behavior as deconstructive activities.

We concur with Goldstein and Freeman that a qualitative change occurred sometime in late June of 1985. The alternating constructive-deconstructive behavior of the first half-year moderated somewhat and stabilized in early December. It continued with perturbations through the Libyan conflict, until 1987 when interactions tracked in "a very narrow range of net cooperation, at a level close to zero" (Goldstein and Freeman, 1990: 146). Figures 4.3 and 4.4 show modest levels on the potency construct and slight inclination towards a positive evaluative. Both remain near the origin, with some sorties into the second quadrant (positive power and evaluative), which we believe represents constructive approaches to problem solving short of war. The gap between the two behavior profiles has narrowed, suggesting that tensions have declined.

Perhaps Mikhail Gorbachev really deserved his peace prize. In reviewing our graphs, and asserting our metric to be valid, we find Soviet behavior throughout the run of WEIS data to have been more deconstructive than not. This finds support in Goldstein and Freeman's (1990: 165-167) table of monthly time series. Thus Gorbachev moved the Soviets into constructive dialogue and demonstrably reduced tensions (response-demand gap) between the superpowers.

Border Security and Ideological Purity—USSR and Czechoslovakia

The USSR-Czechoslovakian event sequence, illustrated in figure 4.5, could include ideological issues as important driving factors. The interaction sequence may, in this instance, illustrate a preordained conflict spiral that would find no resolution short of total victory by one side and complete capitulation by the other. A zero-sum game. This does not invalidate our event scales but suggests that in some instances our event monitor is only a seismograph measuring pressures along international fault lines. The ideological component could assure that the process ultimately will terminate in a cataclysmic event.

WEIS has little data on USSR-Czech. relations before 1968 and after 1969, largely, we suppose, because the Czechs conformed to the Soviet line. By 1967 it had become clear that the hard line regime of Antonin Novotny and elements of the dogmatic bureaucracy would have to go. In 1968 the progressive faction of the party succeeded in replacing Novotny with Alexander Dubcek, a Slovak. Dubcek began wide-ranging programs to liberalize and democratize the party and seek more independence from Moscow.

Despite repeated assurances and accommodations by the Czechs, the Soviets and their Warsaw Pact allies looked with increasing alarm on the reform program. As the exhilaration of freedom captured Czech hearts so too it reflected in their words and deeds. This writer, then in the area, learned that by February of 1968 the KGB was importing into Czechoslovakia caches of U.S. small arms captured in Vietnam and traceable to the U.S. This caused the U.S. Central Intelligence Agency to halt operations in Czechoslovakia by late March. The weapons eventually appeared July 19 amid Soviet allegations that counter-revolutionary forces were being armed.

The Czechs were not so accommodating to the Soviets as the data indicates, for much of the positive events came from meetings, visits, and consultations, which could be quite acrimonious. The Czech press accused the Soviets with complicity in the death of Jan Masaryk, the non-communist foreign minister, just before the communists took over in 1948. Furthermore, Joseph Smyrkovsky, a University Professor and close adviser to Dubcek, observed that reforms might include competitive elections and reinstitution of liberal democracy. Were this not enough, the Czechs extolled their reforms with broadcasts to the Ukraine in Ukrainian, then a banned language. This may have tipped the balance. No amount of accommodation, reciprocity, or anything else short of abject surrender would change the course of these events.

We know the Soviets had begun their contingency planning to thwart counterrevolutionary movements soon after Dubcek's election. The Czech reforms realized the Soviet's worst fears. The unfortunate culmination of this sequence appears in the Soviet-led Warsaw Pact intervention in the late summer of 1968. We consider now a relationship just the opposite.

Special Relationship—U.S. and United Kingdom

We selected two years for examination, 1982 with British involvement in the Falklands and 1985, an active year in U.S.-Soviet relations. Both indicate the resilience of the "special relationship" (figures 4.6 and 4.7).

The Falklands affair dominated the event stream from April through June of 1982 and residually during the United Nations General Assembly in November, when the U.S. cast an "incomprehensible and disappointing" vote contrary to British wishes. Concurrently some differences arose concerning President Reagan's decision to discontinue test ban negotiations with the USSR and his insistence that European manufacturers halt shipments of oil pipeline equipment to the Soviets. The 3-D plots illustrate the character of the relationship — co-occurring positive-valence interactions (PROMISE; GRANT) resulting in plots near the origin and in or nearly in the upper right quadrant.

With a backdrop of dynamic U.S.-Soviet activities, Britain and the United States *consulted, supported, assured,* and *promised* frequently throughout 1985. Contrary to our early expectations, we find constructive relationships staying close to the origin. We originally hypothesized greater distances. As expected, the plot occupies the upper right quadrant (positive evaluative and potency). Plots of other years reveal similar close alignments near the origin. We find U.S. and U.K. policy statements generally combine both negative and positive

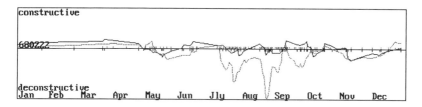

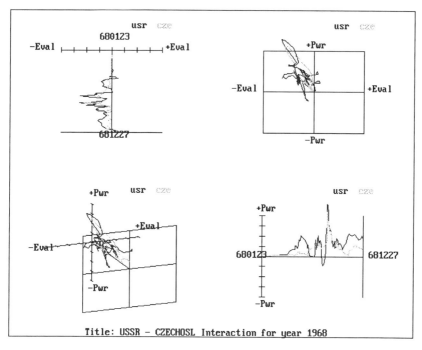

Fig. 4.5. World event/interaction survey scaled event flows

elements thus causing interaction plots to hover proximate to the neutral axis. For example, the U.S. promised a place for Britain in "Star Wars" development, but cannot give any assurances. This amounted to a promise (+1.11) and rejection (-1.18) for a near-origin final value of -0.07. We expect that event combinations could provide important clues to the general state of relations between international actors.

We suspect from our tentative evidence that healthy and stable relationships will be marked by openings toward compromising alternatives within each actor's event sequence. Thus rejections might include counter-proposals to keep communications open by providing the other party with more than just categorical

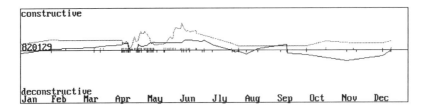

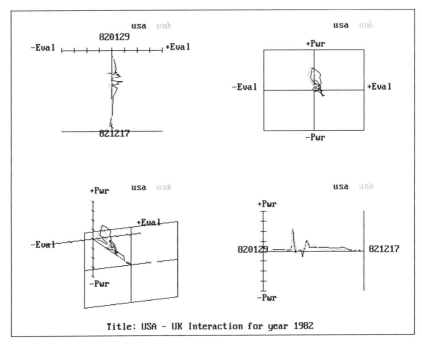

Fig. 4.6. World event/interaction survey scaled event flows

refusals. We label good news-bad news combinations as constructive behavior because the originator provides openings for continued dialogue pointing towards good faith resolution of differences. In contrast to the U.S.-U.K. dialogue, the Soviet-Czech sequence appears markedly short on constructive behavior.

Summary

1. The WEIS combined event scaling metric could be very useful for research today because it links meaning and distance.

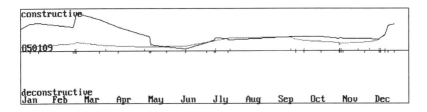

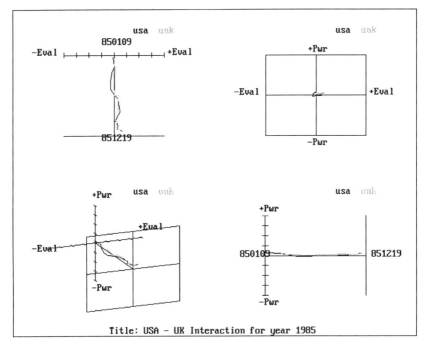

Title: USA – UK Interaction for year 1985

Fig. 4.7. World event/interaction survey scaled event flows

2. Exponential smoothing techniques should be considered in research related to event sequences. Links to microcomputer graphics capabilities could be very helpful.

3. The usual conflict-cooperative spectrum seems simplistic but useful in the absence of anything better. The perceptions of diplomatic practitioners about international events differ in some cases from those of academic observers.

4. The terms constructive-deconstructive are offered to differentiate WEIS multi-dimensional composite scaled events from other kinds in use.

5. The oscillations around the origin in constructive relationships should be further studied with the view to defining them in general terms.

6. The widening and narrowing of gaps between two actors' behavior in a dyadic time series should be studied further to identify conceptual links with the findings of Rajmaira and Ward (1990) and Goldstein and Freeman (1990).

7. The evaluative construct dominates most scaling formulations because its valences (+ & -) are adopted. That is to say, scales using cooperative-conflict appear to be primarily moral (evaluative) dimensions. The position of power, negatively related to evaluative, should be further studied.

8. There seems to be evidence of reciprocity in event sequences of less than one month aggregation.

9. The 3-D renditions of event flows should be further studied. This should include:
   a. Computation of "intermediate data" between observed data points to assure each daily (or other aggregations) time slice has a point.
   b. Facilities to extract single or successions of time slices for analysis of actual and relational differences between actor's behaviors.
   c. Presence and absence of different event types in flows to see if one kind or another or the mix and balance offers clues to the process direction. Combined events like GRANT, REWARD, PROPOSE, and AGREE appear more likely to appear in stable, constructive, event flows.

10. The effects of situations on perceptions should be studied further. It appears that high-threat situations degrade the constructive nature of many events, thus demanding more energies to achieve resolution. Calhoun remains convinced that the scales reported here possess objective reality and thus are insensitive to context. We are not so sure.

11. Event studies should move beyond the traditional, data-rich U.S.-USSR and others, for they might be biased.

REFERENCES

Azar, E. E. 1970a. "Analysis of International Events." *Peace Research Reviews* 4, 1: 1-113.

___. 1970b. "Methodological Developments in the Quantification of Event Data." Paper prepared for the Cooperation/Conflict Research Group of Event Data Conference. Michigan State University, East Lansing, MI, April 15-16.

Calhoun, H. L. 1971. "The Measurement and Scaling of Event Data Using the Semantic Differential." Paper presented at the 25th annual meeting of the Western Political Science Association. University of New Mexico, Albuquerque, NM, April 7-10.

___. 1972. "Exploratory Applications to Scaled Event Data." Paper presented at the 13th annual convention of the International Studies Association. Dallas, TX, March 15-17.

___. 1977. *The Measurement and Scaling of Event Data Using the Semantic Differential with Theoretical Applications*. Doctoral Dissertation, University of Southern California, Los Angeles, CA.

___. 1991. Visit with Tomlinson, March 1-3.

Corson, W. H. 1970. "Conflict and Cooperation in East-West Crisis: Measurement and Prediction." Paper prepared for Event Data Conference. Michigan State University, East Lansing, MI, April 15-16.

Goldstein, J. S. and J. R. Freeman. 1988. "Reciprocity in U.S.-Soviet-Chinese Relations." Paper presented at the 84th annual meeting of the American Political Science Association. Washington, DC, September 2.

___. 1990. *Three Way Street: Reciprocity in World Politics*. Chicago: University of Chicago Press.

McClelland, C. A. 1968. "International Interaction Analysis: Basic Research and Practical Applications." Technical Report #2, World Event/Interaction Survey, in support of ARPA/ONR contract #N00014-67-A-0269-0004. Los Angeles, CA: University of Southern California, School of International Relations. Mimeograph.

___. 1991. Interview with Tomlinson, Nipomo, CA, January.

McClelland, C. A., R. G. Tomlinson, R. G. Sherwin, G. A. Hill, H. A. Calhoun, P. H. Fenn and J. D. Martin. 1971. "The Management and Analysis of International Event Data: A Computerized System for Monitoring and Projecting Event Flows." Report in support of ARPA/ONR Contract #N00014-67-A-0269-0004 for Short-Term Conflict Prediction. Los Angeles, CA: University of Southern California, School of International Relations. Mimeograph.

Moses, L. E., R. A. Brody, O. R. Holsti, J. B. Kadane and J. S. Milstein. 1967. "Scaling Data on Inter-Nation Action: A Standard Scale is Developed for Comparing International Conflict in a Variety of Situations." *Science* 156, 3778 (26 May): 1054-1059.

Osgood, C. E., G. J. Suci and P. H. Tannenbaum. 1957. *The Measurement of Meaning*. Urbana: University of Illinois Press.

Patchen, M. 1990. "Conflict and Cooperation in American-Soviet Relations: What Have We Learned from Quantitative Research?" Paper presented at the 31st annual convention of the International Studies Association. Washington, DC, April 13.

Rajmaira, S. and M. D. Ward. 1990. "Reciprocity and Evolving Norms in the Reagan and Gorbachev Eras." Paper presented at the 86th annual meeting of the American Political Science Association. San Francisco, CA, August 29-September 2.

Springer, C. H., R. E. Herlihy and R. I. Beggs. 1965. *Advanced Methods and Models*. Homewood, IL: Richard D. Irwin.

Wright, Q. 1955. *The Study of International Relations*. New York: Appleton Century Crofts.

Young, R. A. and W. R. Martin. 1968. "Scaling Events Data." WEIS Project Research Memo. Los Angeles, CA: University of Southern California, School of International Relations. Mimeograph.

CHAPTER 5

Imagining the Possibilities: The Prospects of Isolating the Genome of International Conflict from the SHERFACS Dataset

Frank L. Sherman and Laura Neack

Abstract

Building upon the family of datasets that have sprung from the work of Ernest B. Haas, the SHERFACS dataset is designed to bridge the gap between structural attributes and behavioral explanations of conflict escalation and settlement. In this chapter, we demonstrated how SHERFACS enables analysts to compare phase "trajectories" or the sequencing of phases of escalation and de-escalation in cases with similar chronological structures. Specifically, we use SHERFACS to examine the structural factors that distinguish non-hostile from deadly international conflicts since World War II. We find that the structural factors of substantive issues, threats to values, and great power interests were the best indicators of phase trajectory groups, and power equality and ideology were the least important structural factors. Moreover, it appears that the presence of a bipolar rivalry and/or great power interest in disputes since 1945 have kept international disputes from escalating from mere disputes and mere crises to deadly conflicts.

A major challenge to research programs designed to measure international conflict has been to specify the ways in which conflicts develop — the pattern of actions and behaviors that lead to increased hostility, or alternatively, lead to resolution and settlement. Within quantitative approaches there have been at least two general approaches to structuring analysis about factors that exacerbate or ameliorate conflict. One approach focuses on the attributes and structural characteristics of the conflict situation, of the international system, or of the parties involved. In terms of their numbers and breadth, the cupboard storing quantitative case studies of episodic international conflict has been quite full. Another approach seeks understanding through the specification and analysis of the actual actions and behaviors undertaken by participants to the conflict. They seek to assess goals, values and intentions of decision-makers and their governments along the axis of the issue(s) under contention. Consequently, standard quantitative studies have been directed towards the analysis of events data, the perceptions of governmental leaders and diplomats, and textual analysis of speeches, memoirs, conference and treaty histories.

New research strategies and programs have been conceived to attempt a closer union of the two approaches. A number of them have been incorporated into the most recent round of DDIR coordinated NSF projects. One of the DDIR projects, SHERFACS, is well suited to analysis seeking to bridge the gap between structural attribute and behavioral explanations of conflict escalation and settlement. The preliminary analysis conducted for this paper will demonstrate both the depth of the SHERFACS study and the opportunities for further developments both in the area of expanded data acquisition and in the application of newer forms of computer-based analytical techniques.

As a start, this paper takes the SHERFACS international dispute data and asks the following questions:

What are the general patterns of conflict escalation and resolution extant in the international political system in the past 45 years?

What are the various measures that variously describe and perhaps account for these general patterns of escalation and resolution?

What judgments can be made from this preliminary analysis on the short-term developments in the international political system concerning the relative levels of conflict escalation and resolution among its many participants?

The Data

In order to illustrate these questions, we have used the SHERFACS conflict dataset which grew out of the empirical studies of conflict management begun in the late 1960s by Ernst B. Haas (1968) concerned with violent interstate conflict since 1945. Haas focused on the impact of collective security efforts of the United Nations on 55 interstate disputes (later more cases were added and the analysis published as Haas, 1983) referred to the United Nations for management. Joseph S. Nye (1971) added information on 24 interstate conflicts referred similarly to regional international organizations. A major expansion of the "Haas-line" of empirical studies was undertaken by Haas, Butterworth, and Nye (1972) and led to the inclusion of three categories of international disputes: (1) disputes in which an international organization sought involvement for purposes of conflict management, (2) civil strife in which at least one side of the dispute enjoyed the active and substantive political support of another government, and (3) "non-managed" interstate conflicts where fatalities occurred. Butterworth and Scranton (1976) and Butterworth (1980) improved the Haas, Butterworth, and Nye study by lengthening the historical period under analysis (with the last study through July of 1979) and added conflicts in which noninstitutional actors, individual nation states singly or in concert, and non-collective security international organizations provided management efforts. At this point the dataset comprised 307 cases of managed interstate conflicts.

Concurrently with the Haas, Butterworth, and Nye study and the later Butterworth efforts, Hayward Alker, James Bennett, Dwain Mefford, William Greenberg, and Cheryl Christensen used the Haas (Alker, Bennett, and Mefford, 1982; Alker and Christensen, 1972; and Alker and Greenberg, 1971) data to describe and develop various models of precedental logics used by the United Nations organization in the conduct of conflict management efforts. In 1980 Farris, Alker, Carley, and Sherman (1980) added to each of these cases three new kinds of information. First, their FACS dataset represented each conflict as a case which included a series of phases defined by the CASCON phase structure refined by Bloomfield and Leiss (1969). Simply put, when a conflict crosses a certain threshold (toward or away from violence) it passes from one phase to another. The six distinct phases identified in CASCON and FACS were dispute, crisis, hostilities, post-hostilities crisis, post-hostilities dispute, and settlement. The phase "trajectories" of conflicts need not include all these phases, and various conflicts have repeated a series or sequence of phases. Second, FACS expanded the management information available for each case by adding the preceding management referral process to the case as well as the specific subsequent actions taken by any management agent that achieve access to the case. Finally, FACS, using the 15 event summary categories developed by Edward Azar for COPDAB (Azar, 1982), added aggregate responses of the actions of all parties (both primary and secondary) involved in the conflict.

Sherman updated and expanded the FACS project by broadening the criteria for including conflicts and added an expanded list of conflict actors. The various actors could then include "internationally recognized" nonstate actors, domestic, or subnational actors (Karen tribesmen in Mynamar) as well as transnational actors (Arab League), and non-national actors (Pope Paul or ITT) that enjoyed some type of "verbal or physical support" from a national actor (Alker and Sherman, 1982; Sherman, 1987a, 1987b). Based upon the types of actors involved in the case, conflict was classified as "a situation where these exists mutually exclusive sets of competing claims or challenges to sovereignty between at least two actors, one of which must be an internationally recognized political actor" and divided into two sets: (1) international disputes (used in this analysis) in which parties on both sides of the issue are internationally-recognized actors, and (2) domestic quarrels where internationally-recognized actors are parties on only one side of the issue and when the issue in question is essentially domestic or internal.

Using these expanded criteria, Sherman produced a combined SHERFACS file of approximately 700 international disputes and 1000 domestic quarrels and included information on the conflict phases, means of referrals to management agents, and the nature of actions taken by the parties to the conflicts. A phase structure was created for domestic quarrels to mirror the CASCON structure for international disputes.

For the purposes of this analysis, the subset of international conflicts called disputes were selected.

The Dependent Variable: Phase Trajectory Group

For the most part typical contemporary analysis of conflict management activities has used a "static" view of conflict — describing and measuring conflict as a whole with gross characterizations of the varied attributes being studied. However, attempts at managing or resolving conflict should be assessed in terms of the pressure, structures, actions that fuel the conflict itself, either to or away from violence. Lincoln P. Bloomfield and Amelia C. Leiss have approached the study of local conflict in terms of this "internal dynamic" of conflict where conflict is seen "as a sequence of phases." Movement from phase to phase in a conflict occurs as "the factors interact in such a way as to push the conflict ultimately across a series of *thresholds* toward or away from violence" (Bloomfield and Leiss, 1969). Characteristics of disputes can be visualized as the timing and sequencing of movement between and among phases. Processes of the escalation of violence, resolution or amelioration of the seriousness (threat of violence-hostilities), and settlement are identifiable through the use of phase structures. Table 5.1 specifies each of the definitions used to describe the process of phase trajectories.

While we can compare like or dissimilar cases along gross characteristics such as parties, duration, number of dead, alignment of parties, inter alia, we can also model "phase trajectories" or the actual sequencing of phases within a particular case. In this sense, the phase information resembles a "genetic code" aiding in the comparison of cases with similar chronological structures. For example, phase sequence information, when coupled with collective conflict management referral/involvement/actions can measure hostility avoidance (cases ending in phase I, II, or VI), setbacks (cases having more than one hostilities phase), loose ends (cases where there are not phases V or VI), and either partial or complete settlements (phase VI).

There appears to be an innate tendency within either a dispute or a quarrel to move either to or away from hostilities. Incrementally, movement or transition *from* the current phase can either be to a phase type with lower expectations or threat of violence or to a phase type with a greater likelihood of hostilities. In the SHERFACS dataset there were over seventy unique phase trajectory patterns for the nearly 700 international disputes.

Disputes, with different phase trajectories, can have varying and hypo-thetically identifiable impacts, not only on the actors involved in the conflict, but also on the system-level structures and on the applicable or relevant security-seeking practices and conflict management. For the purposes of this paper, we have selected to merge phase trajectories into five distinct sub-categories.

Mere Disputes

These are cases in which the dispute did not escalate into a crisis phase (hostilities threatened or considered). Instead, the case either lapsed as a dispute phase or moved on to a settlement phase resulting in the resolution of the conflict. Conflicts remaining in the "dispute" phase without having a significant likelihood of escalation into a crisis situation, let alone escalation to hostilities, are likely to be of little systemic or global consequence. They may be of long duration, where the parties view the costs of escalation to outweigh the possible reward to be obtained from a "successful" but violent resolution of the case. Short-term

Table 5.1. Dispute Phase Structure Definitions

Phase Type	Description
Phase	One of six levels of disagreement and conflict; a given dispute may pass (repeatedly) through one or more of the phases.
Phase I	DISPUTE PHASE — a dispute claimed by at least one party to be an issue of substantive international political significance.
Phase II	CONFLICT PHASE — a dispute in which at least one of the parties has demonstrated a willingness to use military force to resolve the dispute but as yet has not actually done so.
Phase III	HOSTILITIES PHASE — a dispute involving systematic use of military force, over a specific military objective(s), causing casualties and/or destruction of property.
Phase IV	POST-HOSTILITIES CONFLICT PHASE — fighting no longer occurs as in Phase III, but at least one party continues to view the dispute in military terms. Sporadic violence may still occur, but evidence concerning the cessation of hostilities should suggest something more fundamental that just a temporary lull in intermittent hostilities.
Phase V	POST-HOSTILITIES DISPUTE PHASE — a dispute is no longer viewed in military terms. However, the issues of the dispute remain, although negotiations for resolution may be taking place.
Phase VI	SETTLEMENT PHASE — the final phase commencing with a settlement or agreement resolving the underlying issues or causes of the dispute.

Source: Farris et al., 1980

cases may be "off-shoots" (diplomatic, propaganda, international-political status cases) of chronic conflicts or long-term adversaries involved in other concurrent, albeit more serious, cases.

Mere Crises

These are cases in which the conflict did escalate beyond the initial dispute phase and the parties to the conflict (at least on one side) considered the necessity or actually threatened the use of military force to resolve the conflict. In this group, the escalation was halted at the crisis phase — the conflict did not proceed to actual hostilities. Subsequent phase transitions in this group could include a de-escalation to a dispute phase or movement to a settlement phase. In some rare instances, a case could oscillate between dispute and crisis phases.

Cooled-Down Hostilities

These are cases in which the conflict has proceeded into a hostilities phase. Following the transition to hostilities, these cases later moved beyond hostilities and ended either through dissipation or obsolescence in a post-hostilities dispute phase or through a settlement in a settlement phase.

Simmering Hostilities

These are cases that have also moved into a hostilities phase, but unlike the "cool-down" cases, these cases continued to "simmer" by remaining in a post-hostilities crisis phase. By remaining in a post-hostilities crisis phase, the participants are seen as still considering the use of military force and fighting to press their claims in the case. As such, hostilities could recur at any time.

Boiling Hostilities

Conflicts within this last category have also been called tenuously terminated hostilities (Sherman, 1987b). "Boiling" conflicts are those that have phase trajectories with repetitive hostility phases or are conflicts that are continuing and ongoing in a hostilities phase.

The Independent (Factor) Variables: Issue, Political Alignment, Ideology, Strongest Power, Power Disparity, System Dominance, Threats to Values, and Great Power Interests

Issue

The type of issue under contention in the dispute is another primary characteristic determining the response of management agents. Particularly for the United

Nations, the various types of substantive issues provide differing opportunities for management intervention. There have been varying operationalizations of the type of issue. The one used most frequently distinguished between general interstate conflict and internal conflict. Colonial issues and the impact of the cold war were also included. The present study describes the concept of issue in a different manner using eight categories of issue type. The issue categories are (1) colonial issues, (2) borders/territorial disputes, (3) international personality conflicts, (4) anti-regime and internal cases, (5) human rights violations and the status of repressive regimes, (6) resource oriented disputes, (7) navigation — both sea and air incidents — and military basing conflicts, and (8) terrorism. The first seven categories refer to the "objects" under dispute or those things sought by the parties to the dispute. The last category, terrorism, does not refer to a "thing" but to a method of political behavior. The underlying "cause" of the terrorist case (whether it be the rectification of a political or moral wrong or the "psycho-sexual" deviation of its practitioners) is not addressed in this analysis. Within the terrorism issue category we are only concerned with the dispute's substantive effects for the international actors "under the attack of terrorism."

Political Alignment

The indicator of alignment measures not only the cold-war political alignments but also the status of non-aligned and non-state actors. The actual values for the alignment measure are involved actors, including actors from opposing blocs, from the same bloc, bloc members against non-aligned states, both sides non-aligned states, and state actors versus non-state actors.

Ideology

SHERFACS continued the Haas-Butterworth-Nye tradition of viewing ideology in terms of the major contextual components of the cold war. The dichotomous values of this independent variable are (1) ideological factors not relevant to the case, and (2) ideological factors that are relevant and are contentious.

Strongest Power and Power Disparity

System power measures both the strongest power involved in a conflict and the relative power inequality between the opposing sides. Both the variables of strongest power and power disparity are based on an indicator of influence developed by Robert W. Cox and Harold K. Jacobson. They view power as having both a behavioral and a structural component. For them "power is conceived as a function of a number of component factors: the amount of resources, the extent to which these resources can be effectively mobilized to exert influence, skill in using resources, and willingness to use them" (Cox and Jacobson, 1974). As indicators of power, Cox and Jacobson use gross national product, per capita gross national product, population, nuclear capability, and prestige (table 5.2). From a composite of these scores, a ranking of nations is computed. For the purposes of this paper, these scores were collapsed into the following seven categories: (1) superpower, (2) great power, (3) large power, (4) middle power, (5) small power, (6) smallest power, (7) micro-power (non-national, sub-national actors). For purposes of this paper, large and middle powers were combined into a single category as were the categories of smallest power and micro-power. Table 5.3 lists the various rankings of actors in the international system based on their Cox-Jacobson scores used in this paper.

The largest power on each side of the dispute was identified. The difference between the ranking of the largest power (based on the seven point scale described above) on each side is the measure of power inequality. If the difference is one rank or less, the level of inequality is low. If the difference is four ranks or greater, the level of inequality is very great. A difference of two or three ranks is simply significant inequality.

System Dominance

Based on the level of inequality, power dominance is defined to be either significant or very great inequality. For great powers and the superpowers, their system scores could be either very great or significant inequality. For large or middle powers, it is only possible for them to achieve a significant unequal relationship and dominance. Table 5.4 illustrates the operationalization of "system dominance."

The first three levels of "power dominance" involve the United Nations veto powers as the strongest powers involved in a dispute. Cases of system power coded as "one" include disputes among the superpowers and the great powers. System power of "two" involve great powers and superpowers against middle-range powers (typically regional powers and leaders). Cases of system power coded "three" are instances of great and superpower "preying" on the smaller and weaker states of the international system. Fights among would-be powers (large and middle) and incidents of regional domination are isolated by the code levels of "four" and "five." The last category involves the disputes among the smallest and least powerful actors in the international system.

Threats to Values

This indicator was adapted for use from Michael Brecher and Jonathan Wilkenfeld's study on crises in world politics (Brecher and Wilkenfeld, 1982). A much more in-depth discussion of the concepts underlying their conception of this variable can be found in Brecher, Wilkenfeld, and Moser (1988). As used by SHERFACS the following categories were coded: (1) threat to existence, (2) threat of grave damage, (3) threat to influence in the international system, (4) threat of the loss of colonial territory, (5) threat to territorial integrity, (6) threat to the political system, (7) threat to diplomatic personnel and process, (8) threats to economic interests, and (9) threats limited to people and property. In the current analysis, several categories were combined: (1) extreme — either a threat of grave damage or a threat to the existence of the party, (2) great — threat of the loss of territory or of a colonial possession, (3) influence — threat of the loss of influence of the actor, either in the international political system or in its internal political system, and (4) instrumental — threats to diplomatic personnel, economic interests, and the property and lives of citizens.

TABLE 5.2. Cox-Jacobson Scale Scores

Cox and Jacobson calculate their measure of power from the five indicators of gross national product, per capita gross national product, population, nuclear capability, and prestige. Their ordinal measure is formed by the addition of each state's respective scores on the following operationalizations of these five concepts:

GNP at 1965 prices
(in billions of dollars):
1   under .9
2   1-3.9
3   4-6.9
4   7-9.9
5   10-19.9
6   20-29
7   30-39
8   40-59
9   60-99
10 100-199
11 200-499
12 500 and over

GNP per capita at 1965
(in dollars):
1   under 200
2   200-599
3   600-999
4   1,000 and over

Population (in millions):
0   under 2
1   2-19
2   20-59
3   60-99
4   100-249
5   over 250

Nuclear capability:
0   no foreseeable nuclear capability
1   ability to acquire nuclear weapons by 1980-1985
2   possession of nuclear weapons
3   developed "second strike" capability

Prestige:
0   nonindependent foreign policy
1   alliance-aligned
2   neutral or nonaligned, independent foreign policy
3   leader of alliance system or recognized leader-
    ship of a group of states or active independence
    in a hostile environment

Source: Cox and Jacobson, 1973: 438-439.

TABLE 5.3. Cox-Jacobson Scores of Significant International Actors

Actor	1945-55	1956-61	1962-71	1972-84
United States	super	super	super	super
USSR	super	super	super	super
China (Peking)	large	large	large	great
France	great	great	great	great
Germany (West)	middle	large	large	large
UK	great	great	great	great
Japan	middle	middle	large	large
India	middle	large	large	large
Italy	middle	middle	large	large
Canada	middle	middle	large	large
Sweden	middle	middle	middle	middle
Switzerland	middle	middle	middle	middle
Argentina	small	middle	middle	middle
Australia	middle	middle	middle	middle
Brazil	middle	middle	middle	middle
South Africa	small	middle	middle	middle
Belgium	middle	middle	middle	middle
Denmark	small	small	middle	middle
Indonesia	middle	middle	middle	middle
Netherlands	small	middle	middle	middle
Poland	small	small	middle	middle
Spain	middle	middle	middle	middle
Austria	small	small	middle	middle
Cuba	small	small	middle	middle
Germany (East)	small	small	middle	middle
Israel	small	small	middle	middle
Mexico	small	middle	middle	middle
Norway	small	middle	middle	middle
Pakistan	small	small	middle	middle
UAR	small	small	middle	middle
Yugoslavia	small	small	middle	middle
Czechoslovakia	small	small	small	small
Finland	small	small	small	small
New Zealand	small	small	small	small
Philippines	small	small	small	small
Turkey	small	small	small	small
Venezuela	small	small	small	small
Nigeria	small	small	small	small
Luxembourg	small	small	small	small
All Other State Actors	smallest	smallest	smallest	smallest
All Non-State Actors	micro	micro	micro	micro

Great Power (Superpower) Interests

This is another variable adapted from Brecher and Wilkenfeld (1982). Specifically, great power interests measure the level of threat to the bilateral global balance of power between the United States and the Soviet Union.

The interests lie along the following categorizations: (1) threat to an adverse change in the global balance, (2) threat to a decline of influence in the bloc, (3) threat to a decline of influence with the opposing bloc, (4) threat of a loss of influence with non-aligned states, (5) threat of a loss of influence within the adversary's bloc, and (6) no threat to superpower balance. To simplify the analysis the original values were recoded to only four categories: (1) global influence, (2) opposing bloc, (3) non-aligned, and (4) no interest.

The Analysis

Question One: What are the general patterns of conflict escalation and resolution extant in the international political system in the past 45 years?

Even though there were seventy-one separate unique phase trajectories for dispute cases in SHERFACS, the operationalization of "phase trajectory groups" described above has the virtue of simplicity while maintaining the substantive concept of escalation and its effects. Before proceeding with the description of the disputes, one alternative explanation needs to be addressed. Since cases in phase groups (1) mere disputes and (2) mere crises are so defined by their "failure" to escalate to hostilities, the inclusion of "ongoing" cases that are still in the dispute or crisis phases would be inappropriate. They have been dropped

TABLE 5.4. Computation of System Dominance (System Power)

System Power Value	Strongest Power in Disputes	Level of Power Inequality
1	1/2	0/1
2*	1/2	2/3
3*	1/2	4/5/6
4	3/4	0/1
5*	3/4	2/3
6	5/6/7	0/1

*Signifies instances of a dominance relationship.

from the 688 conflict cases. For those "ongoing" cases in phase escalation groups three through five, since they have already escalated to hostilities, their inclusion in the analysis remains appropriate. Table 5.5 displays the relative frequency of overall international conflicts in the phase escalation groups and the relative frequency when controlling for the "ongoing" nature of mere disputes and crises.

Question Two: What are the various factors that variously describe and perhaps account for these general patterns of escalation and resolution?

We have chosen to look among the following indicators to describe the structural components of the phase trajectory groups — Issue, Alignment, Ideology, Strongest Power, Power Equality, System Dominance, Threat to Values, and Great Power Interests. We undertook a series of simple bivariate analyses of variance — one for each indicator. In this form, we can assess the independent effects of each variable category on the dependent variable (phase escalation group). The statistics reported include the deviation from the grand mean (for phase trajectory groups the grand mean is 2.41), the amount of variance explained by the independent variable (Eta-squared), and the statistical significance. Tables 5.6 and 5.7 list the results. Of the eight indicators, only Power Equality did not indicate a significant relationship.

Overall it appears that Issue is the best indicator of the variation of phase trajectory groups, followed by Threat to Values and Great Power Interests. Of the least importance appear to be Power Equality and Ideology.

By viewing the deviations from the grand mean for each category of the indicator variables, we can ascertain the modal characteristics of "less than hostile" conflicts. It appears that mere disputes and mere crises are more likely

TABLE 5.5. Relative Frequency Distribution for Phase Trajectory Groups

Phase Trajectory Group Category	Number in SHERFACS	Percent	Controlling for Continuing Conflicts	
			Number	Percent
Mere Disputes	237	34.6	202	33.6
Mere Crises	190	27.8	143	23.8
"Cool-Down" Hostilities	111	16.2	111	18.4
"Simmering" Hostilities	93	13.6	93	15.4
"Boiling" Hostilities	53	7.7	53	8.8
	684	100.0	602	100.0

to be: (1) cases in which the issues under contention are international personality, human rights, resource or navigation cases, (2) conflicts occurring within the same bloc, (3) cases in which ideological factors are not relevant, (4) cases involving a superpower as the strongest power in the conflict, (5) cases in which there is an equality among great powers or the great power is only slightly dominant, (6) cases in which only instrumental values are threatened, and (7) cases in which global balance of power issues are not relevant.

The most vicious hostile cases appear to be those in which (1) the issues are colonial, terrorist, and anti-regime, (2) the alignment of parties is between states and non-state actors, (3) the strongest powers are small powers, large-middle powers, and smallest powers, (4) small power equality or middle power dominant status, (5) threats to existence and threats to actor influence, and (6) great power interests within opposing blocs or with non-aligned parties.

Simple Models of Explanation

Using the variables listed in tables 5.5 and 5.6, we posited three very simple multiple indicator models and tested each for interaction effects and to ascertain the amount of variation explained of the dependent variable of phase escalation group. Table 5.7 presents the results from each of these analyses. Interaction effects were not able to be computed due to the absence of cases in many of the group-indicator cells.

Cold War Model: By combining the measures of alignment of the parties and the presence of ideological components with the issue of the dispute we had a rough model that should illustrate the effects of "cold war" components on the escalation of conflict (table 5.8). As in all the models, the issue under contention is the greatest explanation for the variation in phase trajectory groups. Even

TABLE 5.6. Overall Main Effects Models of the Various Factors

Significance and Eta Values for Bivariate Analysis of Variance with Indicator Variables

Variable	Value of Eta	Significance of F
Issue	.47	.000
Alignment	.24	.000
Ideology	.12	.004
Strongest Power	.23	.000
Power Equality	.07	.244
System Dominance	.30	.000
Threat to Values	.38	.000
Great Power Interests	.36	.000

TABLE 5.7. Bivariate Analysis of Variance: Main Effects Model: Deviation from Grand Mean (2.41)

Variable and Category	N	Deviation
ISSUE		
Colonial	65	.42
Borders	166	.01
International Personality	38	-1.05
Anti-Regime	129	.90
Human Rights	5	-.62
Resource	54	-.85
Navigation	82	-.45
Terrorism	17	.58
ALIGNMENT		
Opposing Blocs	245	.02
Same Bloc	115	-.54
Bloc with Non-Aligned	126	.14
Both Non-Aligned	79	.20
State with Non-State	34	.73
IDEOLOGY		
Not Relevant	364	-.13
Yes-Contending	238	.19
STRONGEST POWER		
Superpower	196	-.40
Great Power	123	-.03
Large-Middle Power	116	.28
Small Power 1	25	.26
Smallest Power	42	.41
POWER EQUALITY		
Equal Powers 1	55	-.10
Minor Inequality	217	.12
Major Inequality	230	.04
SYSTEM DOMINANCE		
Great Power Equality	95	-.50
Great Power No-Equality	85	-.50
Great Power Dominance	148	.02
Middle Power Equality	61	-.11
Middle Power No-Equality	55	.72
Small Power Equality	158	.34
THREAT TO VALUES		
Threat to Existence	501	.28
Threat to Territory	233	.00
Threat to Influence	127	.32
Instrumental Threat	192	-.54
GREAT POWER INTERESTS		
Global with Opposing Bloc	90	-.12
Within Opposing Bloc	82	.46
With Nonaligned Parties	236	.40
No Great Power Interest	194	-.63

when adjusting for the other independent variables, the issue component's explanation only slightly decreases — that of the other variables decrease more drastically. Overall this model can be seen to account for over 25 percent of the variation in phase escalation group (with most of that accounted for by the issue of the dispute).

Power, Equality, and Dominance: Another consideration in the movement to a hostilities phase is the relative mix of "power" that each party to the dispute can call upon to promulgate their claims or contentions in the conflict. Initially, we looked at the effects of the strongest power in the case and the relative level of equality between the disputing parties. Again, issue is the most persuasive indicator; and in fact, both the strongest power and power equality main effects are not statistically significant when the effect of the conflict issue is taken into account. Intuitively we know that the power of the parties to a dispute are indicative of the types of actions to be taken — threatening policies of deterrence and compliance through the actual use of coercive force. Consequently, we used our computed indicator of system dominance (which combines the concepts of strongest power and the level of power equality in a case) with issue in another analysis. Here we found that, once again, issue is the greatest explanatory factor, but the computed system dominance indicator was significant. (The possible interaction between issue and system dominance was testable and found not to be significant.) The amount of overall variance accounted for by issue and system dominance was approximately 25 percent.

Level of Threat and the Interest of Great Powers: A final analysis was conducted to ascertain whether the level of threat and the interests of great powers were important joint explanations of conflict escalation. In a sense the level of threat and conflict escalation are somewhat tautological — if a party is involved in a general war in which the conduct of military operations is likely to led to its complete destruction, the level of threat would of consequence be quite high. Alternatively, states do not seem to be well motivated to spend considerable portions of their national treasure on disputes with others over issues and threats that are limited in nature. Our analysis did uncover some interesting results. First, the model tested did explain the highest level of phase group trajectory (approximately 33 percent of the variance). Second, the level of explanation for the issue of the dispute fell to its lowest level in any of the analyses. Third, both threats to values and great power interests seem to explain similar amounts of the variance of phase group trajectories; however, in a separate test of only those two variables, their interaction effects were found not to be statistically significant.

Question Three: What judgments can be made from this preliminary analysis on the short-term developments in the international political system concerning the relative levels of conflict escalation and resolution among its many participants?

TABLE 5.8. Results of Various Models of Relationships

Model One—Cold War:
Dependent Variable: Phase Trajectory Group
Grand Mean: 2.41
Number of Cases: 605
  6 Cases Missing

Source of Variation	Sum of Squares	DF	Mean Square	F	Sign of F
Main Effects	270.801	12	22.567	17.122	.000
ISSUE	203.743	7	29.106	22.084	.000
ALIGN	27.221	4	6.805	5.163	.000
IDEO	6.778	1	6.778	5.143	.024
Explained	270.801	12	22.567	17.122	.000
Residual	772.347	586	1.318		
Total	1043.149	598	1.744		

Multiple R^2 = .260
Multiple R = .510

Variable & Category	N	Unadjusted Dev'n	Eta	Adjusted for Independents Dev'n	Beta
ISSUE					
1 Colonial	64	.42		.37	
2 Borders	166	.02		.09	
3 Status	38	-1.04		-1.09	
4 Anti-Regime	128	.89		.81	
5 Human Rights	51	-.61		-.64	
6 Resource	54	-.84		-.77	
7 Navigation	82	-.44		-.44	
8 Terrorism	16	.53	.47	.47	.45
ALIGN					
3 Opposing Blocs	245	.02		.03	
4 Same Bloc	115	-.54		-.41	
5 Bloc with Other	126	.14		.16	
6 Both Unaligned	79	.20		.06	
7 State with Non-State	34	.73	.24	.43	.17
IDEO					
3 Not Relevant	364	-.12		-.10	
4 Yes Contending	235	.18	.11	.15	.09

TABLE 5.8. Continued

Model Two—Relative Power of the Participants
Dependent Variable: Phase Trajectory Group
Grand Mean: 2.42
Number of Cases: 605
  3 Cases Missing

Source of Variation	Sum of Squares	DF	Mean Square	F	Sign of F
Main Effects	250.495	13	19.269	14.086	.000
ISSUE	182.331	7	26.047	19.042	.000
STPW	9.570	4	2.392	1.749	.138
PWEQ	4.381	2	2.191	1.601	.202
Explained	250.495	13	19.269	14.086	.000
Residual	804.336	588	1.368		
Total	1054.831	601	1.755		

Multiple R^2 = .237
Multiple R = .487

Variable & Category	N	Unadjusted Dev'n	Eta	Adjusted for Independents Dev'n	Beta
ISSUE					
1 Colonial	65	.42		.36	
2 Borders	166	.01		-.01	
3 Status	38	-1.05		-.95	
4 Anti-Regime	129	.90		.83	
5 Human Rights	51	-.62		-.65	
6 Resource	54	-.85		-.84	
7 Navigation	82	-.45		-.29	
8 Terrorism	17	.58	.47	.56	.44
STPW					
1 Superpower	196	-.40		-.21	
2 Great Power	123	-.03		-.03	
3 Large-Middle	116	.28		.13	
4 Small Power	125	.26		.15	
5 Smallest Power	42	.41	.23	.25	.13
PWEQ					
1 None	155	-.10		-.16	
2 Minor	217	.12		.01	
3 Major	230	-.04	.07	.10	.08

(*Continued*)

TABLE 5.8. Continued

Model Two-A—Relative Power of the Participants (With System Dominance)
Dependent Variable: Phase Trajectory Group
Grand Mean: 2.42
Number of Cases: 605
  3 Cases Missing

Source of Variation	Sum of Squares	DF	Mean Square	F	Sign of F
Main Effects	263.015	12	21.918	16.032	.000
ISSUE	169.799	7	24.257	17.743	.000
SYSPOW	25.284	5	5.057	3.699	.003
2-Way Interactions	31.676	33	.960	.702	.894
ISSUE SYSPOW	31.676	33	.960	.702	.894
Explained	294.691	45	6.549	4.790	.000
Residual	760.140	556	1.367		
Total	1054.831	601	1.755		

Multiple R^2 = .249
Multiple R = .499

Variable & Category	N	Unadjusted Dev'n	Eta	Adjusted for Independents Dev'n	Beta
ISSUE					
1 Colonial	65	.42		.38	
2 Borders	166	.01		-.01	
3 Status	38	-1.05		-.99	
4 Anti-Regime	129	.90		.79	
5 Human Rights	51	-.62		-.59	
6 Resource	54	-.85		-.75	
7 Navigation	82	-.45		-.32	
8 Terrorism	17	.58	.47	.57	.42
SYSPOW					
1 GT EQ	95	-.50		-.26	
2 GT NE	85	-.50		-.29	
3 GT DOM	148	.02		.06	
4 MID NE	55	.72		.45	
5 MID EQ	61	-.11		-.09	
6 SM EQ	158	.34	.30	.14	.17

TABLE 5.8. Continued

Model Three—Threats to Values and Interests
Dependent Variable: Phase Trajectory Group
Grand Mean: 2.42
Number of Cases: 605
  6 Cases Missing

Source of Variation	Sum of Squares	DF	Mean Square	F	Sign of F
Main Effects	345.479	13	26.575	22.029	.000
ISSUE	88.262	7	12.609	10.452	.000
VALUE	48.294	3	16.098	13.344	.000
GTPWR	53.859	3	17.953	14.882	.024
Explained	345.479	13	26.575	22.029	.000
Residual	709.351	588	1.206		
Total	1054.831	601	1.755		

Multiple R^2 = .328
Multiple R = .572

Variable & Category	N	Unadjusted Dev'n	Eta	Adjusted for Independents Dev'n	Beta
ISSUE					
1 Colonial	65	.42		.20	
2 Borders	166	.01		-.01	
3 Status	38	-1.05		-.92	
4 Anti-Regime	129	.90		.62	
5 Human Rights	51	-.62		-.38	
6 Resource	54	-.85		-.46	
7 Navigation	82	-.45		-.26	
8 Terrorism	17	.53	.47	.58	.33
VALUE					
1 Extreme	50	1.28		.97	
2 Great	233	.00		-.03	
3 Influence	127	.32		.10	
4 Instrumental	192	-.54	.38	-.28	.24
GTPWR					
1 Global-Bloc	90	-.12		-.12	
2 Oppos-Bloc	82	.46		.38	
3 Non-Aligned	236	.40		.25	
4 No Interest	194	-.63	.36	-.41	.24

(*Continued*)

TABLE 5.8. Continued

Model Three—Possible Interaction Effects Between Threats to
        Values and Great Power Interests
Dependent Variable: Phase Trajectory Group
Grand Mean: 2.42
Number of Cases: 605
3 Cases Missing

Source of Variation	Sum of Squares	DF	Mean Square	F	Sign of F
Main Effects	257.217	6	42.870	32.092	.000
VALUE	123.697	3	41.232	30.866	.000
GTPWR	106.338	3	35.446	26.534	.000
2-Way Interactions	14.804	9	1.645	1.231	.273
VALUE GTPWR	14.804	9	1.645	1.231	.273
Explained	272.021	13	18.135	13.575	.000
Residual	782.809	586	1.336		
Total	1054.831	601	1.755		

Multiple R^2 = .244
Multiple R = .494

Variable & Category	N	Unadjusted Dev'n Eta		Adjusted for Independents Dev'n Beta	
VALUE					
1 Extreme	50	1.28		1.32	
2 Great	233	.00		-.04	
3 Influence	127	.32		.30	
4 Instrumental	192	-.54	.38	-.47	.35
GTPWR					
1 Global-Bloc	90	-.12		-.30	
2 Oppos-Bloc	82	.46		.43	
3 Non-Aligned	236	.40		.38	
4 No Interest	194	-.63	.36	-.51	.32

Our analysis in this paper allows us to make only very brief, cursory, and preliminary comments concerning the new "international political order" and possible short-range changes or effects on the conduct, number, hostility, and destructiveness of international conflicts and disputes. A few of the probable new futures are described below and for each, we have included a short discussion of some of the likely patterns of conflict escalation.

If the new world order consists of a multipolar world? We have found that conflicts in which the parties were members of the cold war political alignments were those in which escalation was least frequent. If the new world order consists of a political structure separate from the bilateral blocs of the cold war, disputes will consist primarily of those between former bloc members, non-aligned states, and with non-state actors — all of which have had significantly higher rates of escalation.

If the new world order consists of a unipolar (United States) world? It has been seen that conflict escalation is less likely or less severe in cases in which superpowers and great powers are involved as the strongest parties. It has also been the case that even when the superpowers or great powers are involved in cases in which there was significant inequality, the levels of escalation are far lower than when middle or large powers are in similar situations.

If the new world order consists of a unipolar (United States) world in which the United States does not take an active role in international affairs? While the role of the United States as the world's "policeman" has been derided in the scholarly and popular press as being chauvinistic and beyond the ability and resources of the United States as a world power, it is interesting to note that the conflicts in which the United States (or either superpower) becomes involved are less likely to escalate through to hostilities. In fact, if the new world order is one in which the superpowers "opt out" (the USSR for reasons of its inability to maintain itself as a cohesive international actor, and the United States because of a return to naive isolationism) leaving the leadership role for world order to large and middle powers, it is quite likely that the level of violent conflicts will increase. We have found that it is precisely those situations in which middle and large powers have a dominant power advantage over their opposition that are far more likely to proceed to violent confrontation and recurring hostility phases. Even among small power conflict, where the sides are relatively equal, the level of escalation is significantly higher than that for the great powers. If leadership in the new world order does not come from "above," the level of internecine and fratricidal conflict down "below" will only increase.

If the principles undergirding the new world order consist of the support for and active encouragement of "democratic" reforms in currently "non-democratic" states? And as a consequent question:

If the principles undergirding the new world order consist of "self-determination" of peoples and territories in contravention to the current principles that hold existing borders and national boundaries to be inviolate? One of the current popular themes of the prophesied new world order is the inculcation into the international political system of the principle of pluralistic free-market democracy as the model for internal political organization. Of all these probable "world models" listed here, this version is possibly the most dangerous and destabilizing one of all. Both anticipated and unanticipated effects abound. We have found that of all the various issue categories, challenges to the legitimacy and effectiveness of the domestic political regime (political independence) have been identified with the highest levels of phase escalation and hostility. Since the determination of "reforms" would lead to (or alternatively emanate from) destabilizing domestic situations, acts of pure terrorism could abound. Terrorism, as a basic issue component, was also found to be a positive indicator for significant escalation. By definition, these "liberalizing reforms" would necessitate the creation of and legitimation of non-state actors. We have also found that conflicts between state and non-state actors are much more likely to involve hostilities than any another combination of political alignments. Threats to the existence of the regime and to international influence will be higher and they also are positively related to the higher level of violent conflict.

Conclusion

We have found consistent statistical significance between the indicators of issue, alignment, ideology, strongest power, system dominance, threats to values and great power interests and the subsequent escalation of conflict to a hostilities phase.

For various likely "new world orders" we have also been able to hypothesize the effects on the presence or absence of violent hostile conflict based upon the relationship between phase escalation and our indicator variables. As others have stated, it appears that no matter what form the "new world order" takes, the challenges to international organizations and regimes, and the challenges to individual members of the political system will be fraught with danger, instability, and higher levels of violent conflict.

While it can be argued that many of the indicators used in this analysis measure similar phenomena, one cannot discount the considerable statistical significance of their individual explanatory power when compared to the assignment of conflicts to the various phase trajectory groups. At a minimum this analysis provides an insight to the structural components that distinguish between non-hostile and deadly international conflicts.

It also argues for the use of analytical techniques that are not dependent upon strict positivist statistical designs. Due to the qualitative nature of the described (by text and by numerical measures) history of the conflict episode, many of the elements of that description are co-related with each other. Some can be separated by time or sequencing of actions. Many cannot be so isolated. As a result, techniques that match on various criteria, either as a clustering technique or as a sequence of events in a "process-type" model, hold great promise for discovering further underlying patterns of relationship. Currently, work along these lines is being done at M. I. T. and elsewhere by John Mallery, Gavin Duffy, Sigrid Unseld, and Hayward Alker. This brief research paper finally concludes by pointing to the bright promise of their ongoing work.

APPENDIX

Some further information is warranted on the issue category "international political status disputes." Within this category, disputes include those over treaty interpretation, United Nations membership cases, the political status of various states, diplomatic disputes, as well as disputes germinating from the major power difficulties re-making the peace following World War II. The British-Iraqi 1936 Treaty Revisions (1947-56), the Baghdad Pact (1955-59), the Camp David Negotiations (1978-), U.S.-Japan Mutual Security Treaty (1958-60) are instances of disputes over treaty interpretation. A number of the most politicized United Nations membership cases are also included: People's Republic of China (1949-71), Mongolian People's Republic (1949-61). International status cases include disputes over the character of specific governments, the control over territorial areas, and the political "rectitude" of various governing ideologies. Examples of these disputes are Future Status of Berlin (1971-), Franco Government (1945-55), Gambia-Senegal Confederation (1961-82), Argentinian Political Intervention by the United States (1945-50), Status of Taiwan (1949-), among others. Diplomatic disputes have also occurred since 1945. Among these types of disputes are: Soviet Romanian Rift (1964-68), Sino-Albanian Rift (1972-), Taiwan-Netherlands Submarine Dispute (1980-81), U.S.-Canada CIA Brainwashing Experiments (1983-), French Withdrawal from NATO (1958-64), Skybolt Crisis (1962-63), the Indonesian United Nations Withdrawal (1965-67), Israel-Norway Murder Dispute (1973-74), Saudi Arabia-United Kingdom "Death of a Princess" (1980), and PRC Diplomatic Disputes (1967-71).

The navigation component of disputes in the SHERFACS study includes cases involving sea, air, and land incidents among international actors where the rights of navigation have been abused. These incidents can occur either through the intentional and conscious design of a particular actor or by virtue of an accidental cause. Also collapsed into this category are disputes over the rights of both the host country and the outside state concerning the establishment and operation of military bases. Representative disputes in this category include: U.S.-Libya Air Bases (1947-50), PRC-Bandung Plane Crash (1955), Japan-Soviet Union Submarine Incident (1980), American Bases in Greece (1983-), the ANZUS Nuclear Weapons Basing Dispute (1984-), U.S.-Spain H-Bombs Air Incident (1966), U.S. Seventh Fleet (1950), Czech Overflights of U.S.-German Zone (1950-53), C-47 Shootdown (1951-54), Polish Airspace (1956), and the KAL-007 Shootdown (1983-84) among many others.

Disputes arising from claims of human rights violations in a cold war context include the following: Russian Wives (1948-50), East European Human Rights (1949-56), Yugoslavian Anti-Church Activities (1951-66), Hungary Church-State Conflict (1946-74), PRC Anti-Church Activities (1951-), Soviet Dissidents and Human Rights (1967-), and Czech "Charter 77" Human Rights (1976-). Non-cold war claims of human rights comprise the basis of the following disputes: South Africa-Basutoland Ganyile Kidnapping Case (1961-62), Expulsion of Greeks from Egypt (1961-62), South African Bantustan Policy (1973-), Latin American Human Rights (1977-81), Haitian Human Rights (1964-71), Zairean Human Rights (1980-), Chinese Expulsion from Mongolia (1983-), South African Race Policies (1946-60), Mass Deportation of Europeans from Egypt (1956-57), Persecution of Greeks (1964-65), Chilean Repressions (1973-81), Iraqi Political Prisoners (1975-79), Repressions in South Africa (1946-76), Dominican Tyranny (1959-65),

Northern Ireland (1968-), and South African Persecutions (1976-). Instances of refugee problems include the following: Vietnamese "Boat people" (1975-), Uganda-Rwanda Refugees (1981-), Djiboutian-Ethiopian Refugees (1977-83), Indian Exodus from Burma (1964-65), Ghanaian Refugees (1966-67), Burmese Refugees (1974-79), US-Haitian Refugees (1980-), U.S.-Cuba Mariel Boatlift (1980-84), and Zimbabwe Refugees in Botswana (1983).

Trade patterns, economic dependency, and resource dependency have all been identified as providing "demographic sources" of conflict by international scholars. Nazli Choucri, Robert North, and Johan Galtung, among others, have dealt with these "lateral pressures" for structural violence on the international political behavior of states. Edward Azar has coined the term "structural victimization" as being the basis for protracted social and economic conflict. While the sources of domestic political-security disputes often lie in the economic deprivation and dependency of the central governments involved, in the realm of disputes and for the purposes of this paper, resource and economic disputes are considered to be general interstate conflict over resources, fishing rights, ownership of foreign capital, and the legal guardianship of various types of assets (mainly gold reserves of foreign currency). Representative resource disputes contained within the present dataset include the following: U.S.-Yugoslavian Gold (1947-49), Swiss-Romanian Assets (1948-49), Icelandic Fisheries #1 (1952-59), the Pearl Fishing Dispute (1953-54), Norwegian Loans (1957), "Lidice" Incident (1959), U.S.-Mexico Colorado Waters Dispute (1962-65), United Kingdom-Libya Oil Nationalization (1971-73), OPEC Oil Embargo (1973-74), Angolan Fisheries Dispute (1975-78), U.S.-Canada Georges Bank/Gulf of Maine (1977-), Sweden-Denmark Offshore Oil Rights (1978-), Anglo-Norwegian Fisheries (1960-61), New Zealand-Japan Fisheries (1966-67), Bolivia-Gulf Oil Company (1969-70), Canada-USSR Fisheries (1976-78), Indus Canal Waters Disputes (1948-60), Icelandic Fisheries (1958-71), among others.

Border and territorial disputes, as well as disputes concerning the political independence of state members of the international system, have been operationalized as stemming from Article 2(4) of the United Nations Charter. Situations of international disputes considered under Article 2(4) include both the classical territorial integrity issues as well as the inviolability of the political independence of member states. For purposes of this paper, issues comprising organization concern under Article 2(4) have been divided into two categories. The first category contains the typical border/territorial disputes between adjacent international actors. These disputes include invasions, border skirmishes, irredentist territorial claims, and legal claim to specific territories. For example, the following disputes are considered part of the border/territorial issue category: Saseno Island Dispute (1943-50), Malacca Straits Dispute (1957-), Venezuela-Guyana Essequibo Dispute (1981-), Italy-Yugoslavia Continental Shelf (1968), Soviet Claims on Turkey (1945-48), Kashmir Accession (1947-65), Korean Invasion (1950-53), Somali Borders (1960-75), Ogaden War (1974-), and Kampuchean Invasion (1975-), among many others. Finally, the last category includes those cases concerning the political independence of states in the international system. This category, termed Anti-Regime issues, contains cases of civil wars (both cold war and non-cold war), secessionist movements, insurgencies, guerrilla wars, and ethnic/minority/religious tensions. Disputes concerning exiles seeking to re-establish themselves in their former countries are also included. Within these cases of domestic or internal political-security disputes, aspects of what Azar terms protracted social conflict can be isolated and analyzed.

REFERENCE

Alker, H. R., Jr., J. P. Bennet and D. Mefford. 1982. "Generalized Precedent Logics for Resolving Insecurity Dilemmas." *International Interactions* 7, 2: 165-206.

Alker, H. R., Jr. and C. Christensen. 1972. "From Causal Modelling to Artificial Intelligence: The Evolution of a UN Peace-Making Simulation." In *Experimentation and Simulation in Political Science*. Eds. Laponce, J. and P. Smoker. 177-224. Toronto: University of Toronto Press.

Alker, H. R., Jr. and W. J. Greenberg. 1971. "The UN Charter: Alternate Pasts and Alternate Futures." In *The United Nations: Problems and Prospects*. Ed. Fedder, E. H. 113-142. St. Louis: University of Missouri, Center for International Studies.

Alker, H. R., Jr. and F. L. Sherman. 1982. "Collective Security-Seeking Practices Since 1945." In *Managing International Crises*. Ed. Frei, D. 113-145. Beverly Hills, CA and London: Sage Publications.

Azar, E. E. 1982. *The Codebook of the Conflict and Peace Data Bank (COPDAB)*. College Park, MD: University of Maryland, Center for International Development and Conflict Management.

Bloomfield, L. P. and A. C. Leiss. 1969. *Controlling Small Wars: A Strategy for the 1970's*. New York: Alfred A. Knopf.

Brecher, M. and J. Wilkenfeld. 1982. "Crises in World Politics." *World Politics* 34, 3 (April): 380-417.

Brecher, M., J. Wilkenfeld and S. Moser. 1988. *Crises in the Twentieth Century: Volume I Handbook of International Crises*. New York: Pergammon Press.

Butterworth, R. L. 1980. *Managing Interstate Conflict, 1945-1979: Data with Synopses*, Final Report, February.

Butterworth, R. L. and M. E. Scranton. 1976. *Managing Interstate Conflict, 1945-1974: Data with Synopses*. Pittsburgh, PA: University of Pittsburgh, University Center for International Studies.

Cox, R. W., H. K. Jacobson, et al. 1973. "The Stratification of Power." In *The Anatomy of Influence: Decision Making in International Organizations* by R. W. Cox and H. K. Jacobson. 437-443. New Haven, CT and London: Yale University Press.

Farris, L., H. R. Alker, Jr., K. Carley and F. L. Sherman. 1980. "Phase/Actor Disaggregated Butterworth-Scranton Codebook." Cambridge, MA: The Massachusetts Institute of Technology, Center for International Studies. Working paper.

Haas, E. B. 1968. "Collective Security and the Future International System." Monograph No. 1. Monograph Series in World Affairs, Vol. 5, No. 1. Denver, CO: University of Denver.

___. 1983. "Regime Decay: Conflict Management and International Organizations, 1945-1981." *International Organization* 37, 2 (Spring): 189-256.

Haas, E. B., R. L. Butterworth and J. S. Nye. 1972. *Conflict Management by International Organizations*. Morristown, NJ: General Learning Press.

Nye, J. S. 1971. *Peace in Parts: Integration and Conflict in Regional Organization*. Boston, MA: Little, Brown and Company.

Sherman, F. L. 1987a. "Four Major Traditions of Historical Events Research: A Brief Comparison." Paper presented at the Second DDIR Event Data Conference. Boston, MA, The Massachusetts Institute of Technology, November 13-15.

___. 1987b. "Partway to Peace: The United Nations and the Road to Nowhere." Ph.D. dissertation. State College, PA: The Pennsylvania State University.

CHAPTER 6

Automated and Machine-Assisted Coding of Event Data: The BCOW Approach

Russell J. Leng

Abstract

The gains and limits of automated and machine-assisted coding of event data are examined, with illustrations from the Behavioral Correlates of War (BCOW) project. The focus of the chapter is on the tension between gains in reliability and efficiency and potential trade-offs in validity as the data generation process becomes increasingly automated. The gains in reliability and efficiency are dramatic, but the author warns of the need to keep validity considerations at the forefront of the data generation effort.

The Problem

The event-data approach to the analysis of international behavior has had more than its share of difficulties with the three most basic problems associated with data-based research: efficiency, reliability, and validity. The development of procedures that enable us to move more and more of the data generation and analysis efforts from human coders to machines promises dramatic gains in reliability and efficiency. The challenge is to achieve those gains without sacrificing validity. This paper presents a practical illustration of the gains and limits of machine coding of event data, through a description of some recent developments in the Behavioral Correlates of War (BCOW) data generation effort.

Efficiency

Some perspective on what can be gained by automated or machine-assisted coding can be gained by considering the process when it is done entirely by hand, and it has been on the BCOW project until very recently. Once we have identified the militarized interstate crisis (MIC) and its participants, there are four steps to the data generation process:

Step 1: Coders search the data sources to identify events meeting the BCOW criteria.[1] Descriptions of these events are then transcribed as formatted verbal chronologies.

Step 2:   The chronologies are checked for errors, duplicate events, and missing data. A single, master chronology is prepared.

Step 3:   The verbal descriptions are coded into categories and descriptions meeting the criteria of the BCOW typology (Leng and Singer, 1988).

Step 4:   The coded data are entered on-line, with some additional formatting to facilitate analysis.

Step 1 has required human coders to plow through newspapers and diplomatic histories in order to identify international actions, and then write a description of each action on a 4x6 card. The preparation of the master chronology in step 2 has meant sifting through decks of cards, comparing duplicates, and, when the funding has been available, entering the verbal chronology on-line. The coding in step 3 has required the coder to work his or her way through the 4x6 cards containing the chronology of events, and enter the coded version on standardized forms. The proper codes for each event have been found by checking the instructions and action categories in the 80 page *Coder's Manual* (Leng, 1986). Finally, in step 4, the coded data have been typed on-line for data analysis. It has been slow and painstaking work. The careers of our BCOW coders have been solitary, tedious and, too often, short.

Given the current state of computer science, coupled with the availability of on-line news services, all this seems a little archaic. In theory, *each* of the steps described above can be performed by machine. In practice, at a minimum, the data entry in steps 2 and 4 can be eliminated, and the tasks in steps 1 and 3 greatly facilitated by machine-assisted coding. How far one can go in fully automating steps 1 and 3 depends on the answers to validity questions, which will be discussed below. There is no doubt, however, that the gains in efficiency that one achieves by moving to machine generated data, or even machine-assisted data generation, are dramatic.

Reliability

The reliability, or internal consistency, obtained in generating descriptions of events is a potential problem whenever human coders are required to interpret coding rules. Inconsistencies occur when different coders interpret the rules differently, or when the same coder interprets the rules one way on one occasion, and another way on another occasion. Inconsistency is not a problem that afflicts automated coding. Consequently, the more coding decisions that can be automated, the higher the reliability. In sum, there is little doubt that machine coding of event data will produce dramatic gains in efficiency and reliability. Validity is another matter.

Validity

The validity issue can be stated quite simply: Do the data provide an accurate representation of the variables that the researcher is attempting to describe and analyze? In event-data research, the answer must be stated in relative terms. To begin with, we cannot observe directly the phenomena we wish to describe. We are second-hand, or more often, third or fourth-hand, recipients of information that has been described by others, and, no less important, *for* others. We are choosing our suits off the rack, and they have been tailored to fit the needs and tastes of someone else. This problem, needless to say, has validity implications, and, while I do not want to rehash the long-standing discussion of validity issues in event-data research, a brief summary of the nature of the problem will help place the relationship between machine coding and validity in perspective.

We need to begin by recognizing several things about the information provided by the sources of event data. First, the person who is observing[2] and reporting the events of interest is doing so for purposes that are different from those of the researcher. What the source decides to observe and report, and how the source decides to describe what he or she has observed, are dependent on considerations that are only coincidentally consistent with the objectives of the event-data researcher. This is not quite as serious as it appears at first glance, because both parties are likely to be interested in an accurate account of what is happening; nevertheless, both observation and reporting are likely to be affected by considerations that are distinct from those of the event-data researcher. To put it another way, the observer takes the first step in the coding process. Each event is categorized according the observer's understanding of reality and described according to his or her understanding of language and grammar. Whatever regularities we may find in the "deep structure" of human grammar, what we see on the surface is likely to vary with the observer's verbal competence, style, culture, and concern with precision. A statement that one observer does not consider worth mentioning, another observer may interpret as a serious warning of potential coercive action, and yet another, as an outright threat. Moreover, how the statement is characterized, that is, which particular word is chosen by a source to describe the statement, may be dependent on nothing more than stylistic considerations. The variation in attention, interpretation, and in the wording used to report events can vary not only from one observer to another, but on the part of the same observer. Thus, what we call the "raw" data is, in fact, a coded interpretation of those events to which the source directed his or her attention. Moreover, it may represent an interpretation that not only is at variance with that of the researcher, but that lacks consistency in its own right. Variation of this sort creates problems of reliability, as well as of validity. In sum, the information that forms the raw material of event-data research is, in fact, not "raw" at all, but coded by the source in a manner that is likely to present distortions and ambiguities for the event-data researcher.

In the BCOW project we have attempted to deal with the problem of uneven reporting of events by relying on multiple sources. We also have had the advantage of dealing with events in situations — militarized interstate crises — that attract a good deal of international attention, so that the under-reporting of events is not as serious as it can be when one attempts day-to-day global or regional coverage of international events. But what of the descriptions accompanying the events that are reported? The transformation of the noise-laden, or ambiguous, information that the researcher receives from the source into event descriptions that are valid representations of the researcher's own conceptions of international actions, requires another stage in the coding process. Understanding the nature of this step, and the problems that it presents, is critical to the event-data collection effort. On the one hand, simply to accept the descriptions of events as they are provided by the source is to accept whatever coding rules the source was applying, for whatever reasons, and to accept the inconsistencies in interpretation that are bound to occur both across sources and, to some extent, within the same source. It is for these reasons that event typologies that are constructed according to key words used by the source to describe actions present serious validity problems, particularly when they describe verbal actions. On the other hand, a coding scheme like that employed by the BCOW project attempts to reinterpret and code the source descriptions into event descriptions that are consistent with the conception of types of international actions held by the researcher. This improves the degree of construct validity, but the added burden of interpretation increases the likelihood of reliability problems.

It is at this point that the nature of the tension between reliability and validity in event-data collection becomes most apparent. Resolution of the ambiguities and inconsistencies in the information provided by the source requires reinterpreting the meaning of the information; yet as soon as the researcher begins to attempt more than a simple categorization of the events based on the wording employed by the source, reliability becomes a problem. In the BCOW project we have placed considerations of validity first, and treated reliability as a practical problem to be solved through consistent and exhaustive coding instructions (Leng, 1986), and carefully trained coders. To the extent that we have been successful, however, we have paid a price in efficiency. Standing alongside the mountains of event data produced by the WEIS and COPDAB schemes, the BCOW project is a cottage industry. We think that the finished product is of high quality, with subtleties of detail not found in other event datasets, but the level of productivity is low. For us, the challenge is take advantage of the gains in efficiency and reliability offered by machine coding without sacrificing what we have achieved in validity. How we are attempting to do this in the BCOW project can be illustrated through a discussion of the application of these techniques to each of the four steps in the data generation effort.

Humans, Machines, and the BCOW Data

Data Generation Steps 1 and 2: With NSF support of the recent DDIR proposal, the first two steps in the data generation process — constructing and merging verbal chronologies of events — will be undertaken by the Global Event-Data System (GEDS) project at the University Maryland. The agreement across event-data projects to centralize what had been a great deal of duplication at this stage of the data generation effort is one of the most significant achievements of the DDIR project.[3] Thanks to the availability of on-line news sources, such as Reuters and NEXIS, along with the development of new software, much of that effort is being automated. Certainly, the days of human coders pouring over microfiche and entering descriptions on 4x6 cards is fading into the past. We may find it necessary to add some additional sources for particular crises of interest to the BCOW project, but the lion's share of the most time-consuming component of the data generation effort will be undertaken by GEDS.

Data Generation Step 3: The verbal chronologies prepared at Maryland will be available on-line and in a format that will enable us to automate some of the simpler coding tasks in step 3 — the transformation of verbal chronologies into data coded in accordance with the BCOW typology. Those decisions that still must be made by a human coder are now made in response to on-line prompts as the coder works on a micro-computer (Macintosh), with detailed coding instructions from the *BCOW Coder's Manual* accessible, whenever necessary, through a "help" command. This can be contrasted with the procedure up to now, which has been for coders to work their way through a stack of 4x6 chronology cards, with an 80 page *Coder's Manual* to flip through for added information, as they inscribed the numerical codes on standardized forms. Working from the terminal, with on-line information, the coder has no need to remember any numerical codes, or to fill out forms. He or she simply hits a single key in response to prompts from the computer.[4] The gain in reliability is obvious to anyone who has attempted to remember multiple sets of numbers, such as the combinations to several different lockers.

The questions that must be answered by a BCOW coder to code physical and verbal actions are listed below, with the decisions that now are automated (performed entirely by the computer) identified by asterisks.

Coding a Physical Action

1. *When is the action occurring (date)?
2. *What international actor(s) are taking the action?[5]
3. *Who are the target(s) of the action?
4. *Where does the action take place?
5. *Is the actor acting alone, or with others?
6. What is the action tempo (starting, increasing, decreasing, stopping)?

7. Is the medium of action military, diplomatic, economic, or unofficial?
8. What type of military, diplomatic, economic, or unofficial action is it?

Coding a Verbal Action

1. *When is the verbal action occurring (date)?
2. *What international actor(s) is making the statement?
3. *Who is the target(s) of the statement?
4. *Where does the verbal action take place?
5. Is this a two- or three-line verbal act? (Is the action that the actor is commenting upon, intending, or requesting, physical, *or* verbal?)[6]
6. *Is the actor issuing the statement alone, or with other actors?
7. What is the tempo of the action?
8. Is the actor commenting upon another action, intending to undertake an action, or requesting an action by the target?

If the verbal action is a *comment on another action*, the following questions must be answered:

9. Is the actor commenting on a past or future action?
10. Is the source of the comment an official, or unofficial, spokesperson?
11. Does the comment indicate approval, disapproval, denial, or is it neutral?

If the verbal action indicates that the actor *intends to take some future action* the following questions must be answered:

9. Does the actor indicate that it intends to *take* action? or that it intends to *refrain from* taking action?
10. Under what conditions will the actor take the action? (Unconditionally? Action by the target? Inaction by the target? Action or inaction by some third party, or because of certain circumstances?)
11. Has the actor specified the time when the action would be taken?
12. Has the actor specified the action that would be taken?

If the actor *requests the target to take action,* the following questions must be answered:

9. Does the actor request that the target *take* action? or that the target *refrain from* taking action?
10. What conditions are attached to the request? (None? Action in return by the requesting actor? Inaction by the requesting actor? Other conditions?)

11. Does the requestor specify a deadline for when the requested action should be taken?

12. Does the requestor specify the action to be taken?

Then the coder proceeds to code the verbal or physical action commented upon, intended, or requested. The questions posed by the computer vary according to the type of verbal action and whether the action commented upon, intended, or requested, is verbal or physical. To simplify the illustration, we will assume that the actor indicates that it *intends* to take some *physical* action.

13. When would the physical action be taken? (Automated if the answer to question 10 is "no.")

14. What actor(s) would take the physical action?

15. Who would be the target(s) of the physical action?

16. Where would the action take place?

17. Would the actor be acting alone or with others?

18. What would the tempo of the physical action be? (Start, increase, decrease, stop, refrain from acting, or continue existing action.)

19. Would the action be military, diplomatic, economic, or unofficial?

20. What type of military, diplomatic, economic, or unofficial action would be taken?

As the reader can see, whereas the coder must answer only 3 questions to complete the coding of a physical action, the coding of verbal actions still requires that the coder answer 15 questions for most verbal actions, and, in those few cases where the verbal action refers to another verbal action, the coder must answer 22 questions. Thus, at first glance, the gain in efficiency is mostly mechanical: hitting certain keys in response to questions from the computer, and having a well-directed "help" command, as opposed to flipping through a coder's manual. That gain, of course, is by no means trivial. For example, many actions involve multiple actors and targets. Our coding rules identify a separate action from each action directed by each party on one side to each party on the other side. For example, if negotiations begin among five states, there will be 20 separate events to record. With computer assisted coding, once the first act has been coded, the coder needs only to identify the other parties as additional actors and targets, and all subsequent combinations are coded by the computer.

On the other hand, it is difficult, at this point, to speculate on how much further we can go in the foreseeable future in automating the coding decisions listed above. In *theory,* all categories could be machine-coded provided that we were able to foresee all possible syntactical combinations and to provide a large enough dictionary, but the application is another matter. The syntactical understanding that comes so easily, almost unconsciously, to humans outstrips our ability to develop software capable of making comparable interpretations. Consequently, our approach will be to proceed incrementally, beginning with those categories of coding decisions that provide reliability problems that might be alleviated, perhaps even eliminated, by imaginative programming.

To gain some perspective on what can be accomplished with machine-assisted coding, and where we might take the extra step of moving to fully automated coding, let me describe a reliability problem surrounding one of our most complicated coding decisions, that is, coding the "tempo" of certain types of actions. The "tempo" category is very important to describing the dynamics of physical actions, that is, when they begin, increase or decrease in intensity, or stop. It also is a category that presents reliability problems for coders, particularly with certain categories of verbal actions. Consider the following verbal action as an example: "The President stated that he intended to begin the blockade on the following day." The reader will remember that the first step in coding verbal actions is to describe the attributes of the verbal statement per se, and that the second step is to describe the physical action to which it refers. In the description of the verbal component of this two part (verbal and physical) coding, the tempo code is "discrete," indicating a verbal action (stated). Then, when the intended physical action (begin the blockade) is coded, the tempo is "start," indicating the beginning of a physical action extending beyond one day. This alerts our counting and search program to count this action as occurring on each day until the action ends. Now consider this example: "The President stated that he would not stop the blockade." If the tempo is coded as "discrete" in the description of the verbal action (stated), and as "stop" in the description of the intended physical action (blockade), the action appears as if the President intends to stop the blockade, whereas his actual intention is to *refrain from* doing so. Thus, the coder is instructed to code "refrain from" as the tempo of the verbal action, and "decrease" as the tempo of the physical action. There is a logic to this method, but it complicates the coding procedure, and it can be a source of reliability problems.

The reliability problem introduced by this case is largely a function of the coder's confusion over encountering what appears to be a third tempo descriptor, that is, the "refrain from action." The instruction to substitute it for the coding of "discrete" — the standard tempo descriptor for verbal actions — introduces an exception to the rule, and exceptions cause reliability problems. This component of the reliability problem can be reduced significantly by machine-assisted coding. With the computer programmed to make the decision as to what tempo descriptors should be used and where they should be placed, an potential cause of confusion and error is eliminated. The coder is simply prompted in the following manner:

> Does the verbal statement indicate that the actor intends to refrain from taking the action?

If the answer is "yes," then the computer simply asks the coder to describe the tempo of the physical action (blockade), which, in this case is "decrease." The decision of where and what to enter in the tempo columns of the coded description is left to the computer software.

Determining whether the verbal action is stated in the negative is not a difficult decision for the coder, but it also is a decision that appears to be a good candidate to automate. There is a limited vocabulary of terms that can be used to indicate that the actor intends *not* to take action, or requests that the target *not* take action. These could be identified by the computer so that the decision is removed entirely from the hands of the coder. In fact, the vocabulary associated with the tempo category more generally may be sufficiently limited to automate the entire coding of what is — for the human coder — the most difficult BCOW coding decision.

Another way in which the efficiency and reliability of automated coding may be attained at this stage of the data generation process is by working with a *limited vocabulary* at the verbal chronology stage, that is, at step 1 in the data generation process. For example, coders preparing verbal chronologies could limit their description of the tempo of actions to the seven descriptors used in the final coding (discrete, start, increase, decrease, stop, refrain from action, continue action). This approach would make it easier to make the transition to machine coding in step 3. On the other hand, the overall effect is simply to move the problem from one stage of the data generation process to another. The same human interpretations and decisions must be made; it is just that they now would be made at step 1, rather than at step 3, in the data generation process. Our experience to date has suggested that greater reliability is achieved by breaking the coding process into discrete steps, with the identification of an action and its basic components (date, actor, target, location, and action description) in step 1 and the categorization and description of its attributes in step 3.

In sum, at the current stage of our efforts, we have been able to improve significantly both the efficiency and reliability of the data generation effort, with no loss in validity, by moving to machine-assisted coding. We also have been able to automate some of decisions in the coding process. Our intention is to continue to move incrementally to increase the degree of automated coding to the extent that it is possible to do so without sacrificing validity.

Conclusion

The immediate returns on automated and machine-assisted coding will produce dramatic gains in efficiency and reliability in the generation of BCOW data. Moreover, the centralization of most of the first stage of the data generation process through GEDS will yield significant gains for the entire event-data community. These gains have grown out of the DDIR effort, and there is reason to believe that we will achieve even greater gains in the near future. Nevertheless, we need to remember that validity concerns remain at the heart of the event-data generation enterprise.

In the BCOW project our concern with validity has led us to take a conservative, incremental, approach to automated coding by mixing it with machine-assisted coding. We have begun with machine-assisted coding and are moving step-by-step to automate more and more of the coding process, rather than attempting a complete overhaul of the BCOW typology to obtain fully automated coding. I believe that we have developed an unusually rich and fine-screened data base, and I do not want to take any actions that would compromise its quality to achieve greater efficiency. Over the long run, it may well be that the data generation process can be automated fully with no loss in validity, but we need to take care to avoid compromising what we already have achieved.

NOTES

1. Operational definitions of crisis, international actions, and other key variables are defined in Leng and Singer (1988).
2. To simplify the discussion, I will assume that the source is working from a direct observation of the event. This, of course, frequently is not the case, and, in those instances in which it is not, the event has cycled through the steps that I am about to describe as many times as the source is removed from the original observation.
3. I have argued for many years (see Leng, 1978) that the first step in any cooperative effort to generate event data should occur at this phase of the process to eliminate unnecessary duplication. It is a tribute to the mediating efforts of Dina Zinnes and Richard Merritt that this cooperative venture finally has been launched.
4. The programming for the automated and computer-assisted coding routines described in the following sections were performed by Ding Chun. The programs are written in Modula 2 for use on a Macintosh or Mac II microcomputer.
5. If there is more than one actor or target, the computer creates an additional action for each possible action-target combination.
6. An example of a two line verbal action would be: "The U.S. requests a cease-fire." An example of a three line verbal act would be: "The U.S. states that it intends to request a cease-fire." In the first example, the verbal action (requesting) is described on the first line, and the requested physical action (cease-fire) is described on the second line. The second example requires three lines of description: the initial verbal act (the U.S. statement that it intends to request...), the intended verbal act (requesting), and the physical action requested (cease-fire).

REFERENCES

Leng, R. J. 1978. "Event Data Validity: Comparing Coding Schemes." In *Measuring International Behavior: Public Sources, Events, and Validity*. Ed. Munton, D. Halifax, NS: Dalhousie University.

___. 1986. *Coder's Manual for Describing and Coding International Actions*, 6th ed. Middlebury, VT: Middlebury College. Mimeograph.

Leng, R. J. and J. David Singer. 1988. "Militarized Interstate Crisis: The BCOW Typology and Its Applications." *International Studies Quarterly* 32, 2 (June): 155-173.

CHAPTER 7

Machine Coding of Event Data

Philip A. Schrodt

Abstract

This paper reports on the development of machine coding systems for generating event data. Machine coding provides event data at a dramatically lower cost than human coding; the accuracy of machine coding is somewhat less than that of human coding but in many statistical applications the increased quantity of data compensates for the decreased quality. NEXIS and other machine-readable databases are discussed as a source of event data. NEXIS provides a convenient source of real-time events from a number of international sources. Two systems using machine-learning and statistical techniques for natural language processing are described and tested. WINR generates a statistical classification scheme using a set of pre-coded training cases; it is tested using the text summaries from various WEIS datasets. Kansas Event-Data System (KEDS) uses pattern recognition and simple linguistic parsing; English and German dictionaries for coding WEIS data using this system are currently being developed at the University of Kansas under DDIR funding. The accuracy of the KEDS system is also evaluated using a set of WEIS summaries originally coded from the *New York Times*. Both systems run on Macintosh computers rather than on specialized hardware.

Introduction

Within political science the prospect of machine coding of event data has often been regarded as impossible; in fact it is a relatively straightforward computational problem for which a very substantial literature exists. The perception of difficulty is due in large part to two factors. First, the initial efforts on the related problem of automated content analysis, using the General Inquirer program (Stone et al., 1966), were largely a failure, at least in political science.[1] General Inquirer was an effort of thirty years ago which originally ran on hardware possessing a fraction of the computational power of a Nintendo game and therefore is not representative of the current state of the art. Second, machine coding is often confused with the much more difficult problem of general natural language comprehension and machine translation. These are more complicated problems because they require mapping a domain with a complex structure — natural language text — into a range with a complex structure — another natural language or a knowledge base. Machine coding of events, in contrast, maps language into a very simple range — nominal codes.

This article contends that machine coding of machine-readable news sources provides a practical and low-cost alternative for generating event data. While such data will generally be of somewhat lower quality than human-coded events, the *quantity* of information provided will outweigh that decreased quality in many applications. Machine-coded data are actually superior to human-coded data on some dimensions, for example in reproducibility and the explicit speci-fication of the coding rules. Machine coding also simplifies the implementation of new coding schemes, since a natural language event source can be recoded in a few hours with appropriate software and coding dictionaries.

Two systems using machine-learning and statistical techniques for natural language processing will be described. The WINR system is "trained" using examples of coded natural language text, it generates a statistical scheme for classifying unknown cases and is tested using the text summaries of various WEIS datasets. KEDS uses pattern recognition and simple linguistic parsing; English and German dictionaries for coding WEIS data using this system are currently being developed at the University of Kansas under DDIR funding. KEDS is evaluated using a set of WEIS summaries originally coded from the *New York Times (NYT)*. Our systems generate WEIS codes but should in principle be able to code COPDAB, and possibly BCOW.[2]

Natural Language Processing for Machine Coding

Natural Language Processing

The machine coding problem is related to that of automated information retrieval and text analysis. Salton (1989) provides an excellent discussion of this field with an extensive bibliography; Joshi (1991) provides a variety of more recent bibliographic references; Forsyth and Rada (1986) deal with the issue from a machine learning perspective. While this field is relatively new — it experienced considerable development in the 1980s as machine-readable text became widely available — it has been the focus of extensive work in computer science and library science. A variety of proven techniques are available; the work proposed here merely adapts existing methodologies rather than inventing new ones.

Fundamentally, machine coding is a *classification problem*: A natural language description of each event must be associated with a specific category. Most approaches use variations on clustering and "nearest neighbor" algorithms: Each individual event is described by a vector based on the words in the sentence describing the event; each category is associated with a point in that vector space,[3] and classification is made by assigning the event to the category which it is closest to according to some metric. Salton (1989: ch. 10) describes a variety of methods for doing this; most are taken from the automated document retrieval literature.

Adapting these methods to the coding of events is fairly straightforward. One starts with a very large and representative set of cases — natural language events along with their associated event codes — and constructs a vector space and a metric which maximizes the clustering of the events using either statistical or machine learning techniques; each category is then assigned to the centroid of its cluster. Once the vector space, metric and centroids have been obtained, new cases are classified using the nearest neighbor method. The method is conceptually identical to the technique by which discriminant analysis is used to predict unknown cases on the basis of a sample of known cases.

As Salton (1989: chapter 11) points out, statistical and pattern recognition approaches are used in lieu of formal linguistic analysis in almost all existing document retrieval systems; Fan (1988) has also been using statistical methods for doing content analysis of wire service stories in studying public opinion. The statistical approach is insensitive to linguistic nuance and presupposes a great deal of regularity in the original text, though journalistic texts such as those provided by Reuters or UPI have a relatively limited vocabulary and are fairly regular. WINR is an example of a statistical system.

Rule-based systems, which are based theoretically in the expert systems literature of Artificial Intelligence (AI), use classification rules provided by the coder, rather than deriving the classification scheme through statistical induction. The disadvantage of this approach is that the coder must first solve the classification problem, which requires expertise and may be quite time-consuming in complex problems; the computer merely implements that solution. The advantage is that the coder usually has a good idea of the true classification rules, particularly in the case of classification schemes such as WEIS or COPDAB designed for rule-based implementation; it is also relatively straightforward to incorporate some linguistic processing into such a system. KEDS is an example of such a rule-based system.

The Quantity-Quality Tradeoff

Event-data collections have been developed largely independent of the statistical techniques by which the data are analyzed. While substantial effort has been devoted to the problem of *measurement* — for example in the construction of the COPDAB scales — very little effort was spent in any formal analysis of what might be done with those measures. This problem is anything but trivial: There is no point in collecting data which is more accurate than the statistical technique can use. To use a familiar analogy, if a drawing is created accurate to 1/300 inch but printed on a dot-matrix printer at a resolution of 1/72 inch, the additional precision was wasted effort.

Most existing general events datasets have internal intercoder reliability in the range of 80 percent to 90 percent. Inter-project reliability is less clear, though Burgess and Lawton (1972) report a 42 percent agreement at the discrete event level between the original WEIS and student coders at Macalester College; and Vincent (1983) notes that the correlation (r) between WEIS and COPDAB conflict scores (by year across countries) ranges from 0.92 in 1969 to 0.14 in 1972, with an average of 0.66. Event data generation is not a precise business; even human coding contains a lot of uncertainty.

The most likely measurement tradeoff is quantity versus quality: Given finite resources, the greater the effort devoted to reliability, the fewer events will be coded. In the case of the most common statistical manipulation in events data — aggregation — the quantity-quality trade-off can be analyzed explicitly.

Assume, as is typical, that the events data are used to estimate a value, ω, (e.g., an hostility score) by taking the mean of a sample of observations:

$$\omega = \overline{X} = \frac{1}{n} \sum_{i=1}^{n} x_i$$

Assume that each x_i can be decomposed into three parts

$$x_i = \mu + e_i + m_i$$

where μ = true value, e_i = true error (in other words, deviation due to the intrinsic variability of the underlying random variable) and m_i = measurement error. Assuming e_i and m_i have mean zero,[4] from the Central Limit Theorem, ω will be distributed

$$\text{Normal}\left(\mu; \frac{\text{Var}(e) + \text{Var}(m)}{n}\right)$$

whatever the underlying distributions of e_i and m_i.

Suppose there are two measurement instruments A and B which have sample sizes N_a and N_b and measurement error variances v_a and v_b, respectively. Assume that $N_a > N_b$ and $v_a > v_b$, in other words, A has a larger number of observations but also has a higher measurement error. Let s_a and s_b be the error variances of the ω measured using A and B. Under what circumstances will $s_a < s_b$?

Assuming without loss of generality that $\text{Var}(e) = 1$, a bit of algebra will show that this is true provided

$$v_a < v_b \left(\frac{N_a}{N_b} \right) + \left(\frac{N_a}{N_b} - 1 \right)$$

Since the second term is greater than zero, this means that $s_a < s_b$ so long as the variance of the less accurate measure increases proportionately to the increase in the sample size. For example, if method A provides twice the number of data points as method B, it can have at least twice the measurement error ($\text{Var}(m)$) and still produce more accurate ($\text{Var}(\omega)$) measures of ω.

In addition to its reduced costs and immediacy, an advantage to machine coding is that coding systems are *cumulative, transferable,* and *explicit.* Within a given system, any additional development can pick up where the old left off — subsequent effort adds to the knowledge already incorporated. Development undoubtedly follows a classical learning curve — it shows diminishing returns — but it need not start over from the beginning. The knowledge of student coders, in contrast, is lost when they graduate.

The knowledge is transferable — a machine coding system can be transferred to another institution by mailing a disk. At Kansas, we are currently developing a dictionary of phrases for the assignment of WEIS codes; this same dictionary could provide the basis of dictionaries for coding other schemes, or the same dictionaries could be used for coding a different dataset.

Finally, the coding rules are explicit, which cannot be said of human coding no matter how elaborate the coding manuals and coder training. Some of our coding is questionable due to ambiguities in the WEIS scheme itself; inter-coder ambiguities are also embedded in the phrase set. But these decisions are explicit, so one could code data in 1999 using precisely the same coding rules and interpretation of those rules as we used in 1991. This allows a greater degree of reliability in the coding, and in applications studying change over long periods of time, this may be more important than validity.

The existence of a *consistent* pattern of incorrect classification provides another possibility for statistically correcting aggregated event data. Assume that the misclassification matrix $\mathbb{M}$, where

m_{ij} = probability an event of type j will be classified as type i

can be estimated and let $\underline{t}$ be the true event frequency vector in a set of data. In the absence of censoring, the observed frequency vector $\underline{x}$ is simply

$$\underline{x} = \mathbb{M} \, \underline{t}$$

An improved estimate of $\underline{t}$, adjusting for misclassification, would be

$$\underline{x}^* = \mathbb{M}^{-1}\underline{x}$$

With machine coding, $\mathbb{M}$ is straightforward to compute: One human-codes a suitably large and representative set of data,[5] recodes the same data by machine and estimates $\mathbb{M}$ by

$$m_{ij} = \frac{\#\ \text{events coded } i \text{ by machine and } j \text{ by human}}{\text{total } \#\ \text{events coded } j \text{ by human}}$$

Reducing the variance of a sample mean and determining aggregate event frequencies are not the only items of interest in event-data analysis,[6] though they probably are of interest in most *existing* applications. My point is simply that the issue is open. In a world of finite resources — the world with which most of us are best acquainted — the quantity-quality tradeoff is real. For certain analyses the reliability of human coded data will provide an advantage over the superior quantity of machine coded data. However, this cannot be taken for granted, particularly given the cost and consistency advantages of machine coding. On a per-event basis, machine-coded data generated from machine-readable sources, with human error checking, costs perhaps 1/10th as much as human coded data generated from hard-copy source. That data certainly does not have 10-times the error variance. When the alternative to machine-generated data is *no* data, the quantity-quality tradeoff must be carefully considered.

Hardware Requirements

Natural language processing has acquired a quite inappropriate mystique of being suitable only for specialized workstations such as $30,000 LISP machines and Kurzweil document processors. In fact, it is well within the capabilities of personal computers such as the Macintosh II or IBM AT series provided suitable programs are used. Most of the work reported here was done on a circa-1988 Mac II; the programs are in Pascal.

In both WINR and KEDS, the bulk of the computational time — aside from input and output — is spent searching for individual words. With appropriate programming, the average number of words which must be checked to see whether a word is in the system is proportional to $\log_2(N)$ where N is number of words in the system's dictionaries.[7] Thus a search among 16,000 words would require on average only about 14 or fewer comparisons.

While the English language contains several hundred thousand words, the vocabulary used in the international news media is substantially more restricted, and the vocabulary required for classification even more so. WINR's analysis of 8,000 International Public Policy Research Center (IPPRC) WEIS descriptions required a vocabulary of fewer than 5,000 words, well within the constraints of a modest personal computer. In developing a very successful computer program to solve the somewhat similar problem of interpreting news articles about terrorist incidents in Latin America, Lehnert et al., (1992; also see Lehnert and Sundheim, 1991) use a dictionary of about 6,000 terms, so the possibility of coding with a vocabulary in the thousands, rather than tens of thousands, of words seems realistic.

WINR is quite fast: On a Macintosh II it processed about 3,000 cases per minute when coding IPPRC WEIS textual summaries. KEDS — which does considerably more linguistic analysis than WINR — is slower, coding about 200 Reuters leads per minute, though the program has yet to be optimized for speed. Either of these speeds is quite sufficient for coding large datasets: For example at the speed of KEDS, one could code 144,000 Reuters leads in a 12-hour overnight run; this is roughly the size of the entire COPDAB dataset,[8] and by current standards, a Macintosh II is not a particularly fast machine. In short, any machine capable of doing serious statistical analysis or desktop publishing is sufficient for the task of machine coding.

Machine-Readable Data Sources

NEXIS

NEXIS is the on-line news data base of Mead Data Central.[9] It contains over 100 distinct data files, though most of these are specific to narrow economic topics. The file we have been working with is the "WIRES" file, which contains wire service reports from Reuters, Xinhua ("New China") General News Agency, United Press International (UPI), the *London Daily Telegraph* and an assortment of other European and Japanese press agencies. Because of the "pyramid style" of journalistic writing — the most important aspects of a story are given first, followed by the details — wire service stories are particularly useful input for machine coding systems.

While NEXIS provides the full text of articles, the NEXIS "citation" form provides a date and a one-sentence "lead" which provides the gist of the article. A typical Reuters lead is

> 4. Copyright (c) 1989 Reuters The Reuter Library Report, March 31, 1989, Friday, AM cycle, 224 words, ISRAEL SUMMONS CANADIAN AMBASSADOR TO DISCUSS PLO. JERUSALEM, March 31, ISRAEL-CANADA, LEAD: Israel has summoned the Canadian ambassador to protest Canada's decision to upgrade talks with the Palestine Liberation Organization (PLO), a Foreign Ministry spokesman said on Friday.

NEXIS is searched using keywords, which can be arranged into Boolean statements of considerable complexity. For our project, which focuses on the Middle East, the search command is:[10]

> HEADLINE(ISRAEL OR JORDAN OR EGYPT OR LEBANON OR SYRIA OR PLO OR PALEST!)

NEXIS is downloaded using a modem and an 800-number; a 1000-record file is about 500K, and takes about an hour and a half to download, but this process is easily automated with the appropriate software. Mead Data Central, unlike some data services, explicitly permits downloading and states that data can be held for 30 days and used for research purposes. While NEXIS data initially contains quite a bit of garbage — page headers, serial numbers, copyright notices, control characters and so forth — these can be filtered using a simple utility program. The WIRES file is updated at least once a day, so the data are current to within about 24-hours. While a variety of sources are available on NEXIS, we've used Reuters almost exclusively since it seems to be the most thorough English-language source covering the Middle East.

Duplicate stories are very common on NEXIS, particularly for Reuters. Duplicates occur when Reuters issues an update to an earlier story, and can be identified by leads which are similar, but not identical to the original lead. On some days up to 40 percent of the stories will be duplicates. We are detecting these by computing a signature on each lead consisting of the count of the frequency of each letter of the alphabet in the text. If the signatures of two leads on the same day differ by less than a fixed threshold — currently set at 20 — they are considered to be duplicates and only the most recent version of the story is coded. This method captures the most obvious duplicates, for example those leads which are identical, differ only by a misspelling or word order, or which have added a couple of words. It results in virtually no incorrect rejections; in fact the threshold may be too low. The method does not detect duplicates where substantial new information has been added to the lead, such as a new phrase, and does not deal with the same event reported in two sources.

Density

One complaint about the Inter-University Consortium for Political and Social Research (ICPSR) event datasets is their low density — the small number of events reported per day. While the Middle East may not be completely typical for NEXIS, it consistently reports about 700 reports per month during the 1988-1989 period. In contrast, the ICPSR WEIS dataset generated from the *NYT* has about 700 events per month for the *entire world* during 1968-1978 (McClelland, 1983:172); this is also roughly consistent with COPDAB's 400 events per month density for 1948-1978. The NEXIS density is even higher when one considers that many NEXIS reports would generate two or more individual WEIS or COPDAB events due to event pairs, so a 1000 events per month density is probably in the ballpark.

The approximate density of interactions within the Middle East is given in table 7.1. These are the result of machine coding NEXIS for actors and are probably not entirely accurate, though the system had a fairly complete list of Middle Eastern actors. Since this period includes both the Palestinian *intifada* and the Lebanese civil war, this density is not necessarily typical for the entire world, but it is promising. Note in particular that the coverage does not dramatically drop during 1989; in contrast the *NYT* international coverage focused almost exclusively on Eastern Europe and Panama during the autumn of 1989.

For purposes of comparison, figure 7.1 shows the distribution of event counts for the Egypt-Israel dyad in COPDAB. The frequency of events varies substantially over time, rising to about 150 events per year during periods of military crisis (1955-1957; 1967-1973) and dropping off to fewer than 25 in other periods prior to 1974. After 1974 the level is about 75 events per year. If the 150 percent ratio of stories to events is accurate and 1988-89 has Israel-Egypt interaction levels comparable to 1974-1978 (which is plausible), then NEXIS is recording about twice as many events as COPDAB in the Middle East.

A wide variety of additional sources — for example the *NYT*, *Wall Street Journal*, *Washington Post*, *The Times* (London), TASS, and some Japanese news services — are available on NEXIS and if, as has been suggested, these newspapers provide complementary coverage of the world rather than overlapping coverage, these would potentially provide substantially enhanced coverage. However, this comes with three costs. First, the downloading time increases. Second, many

TABLE 7.1. Dyadic Interactions Reported in the NEXIS "WIRES" File

1988	ISR	PAL	LEB	JOR	UAR	SYR
ISR	--	1002	179	12	45	13
PAL	934	--	66	103	48	59
LEB	34	28	--	10	1	58
JOR	78	163	2	--	28	24
UAR	109	66	4	34	--	7
SYR	21	68	86	10	9	--
Total	3301					

1989	ISR	PAL	LEB	JOR	UAR	SYR
ISR	--	737	206	20	102	36
PAL	686	--	43	34	62	25
LEB	30	7	--	3	6	108
JOR	46	44	10	--	15	12
UAR	137	50	14	15	--	30
SYR	23	24	175	4	17	--
Total	2721					

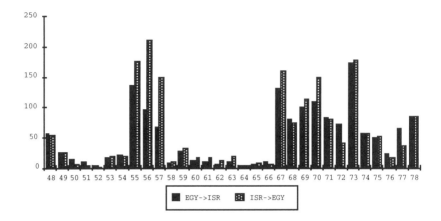

**Fig. 7.1. Frequency of COPDAB interactions by year
for the Egypt-Israel dyad**

of these "new" sources primarily use Reuters or UPI material; the apparently complementary coverage simply reflects different editorial selections.[11] Finally, searching the *NYT* and *Los Angeles Times* (*LAT*) for Middle Eastern targets results in a very large number of false positives — as much as half the data — since *Jordan* is a very common surname in the United States. These can be weeded out, but increase the downloading time, particularly during basketball season.

CD-ROM and Other Machine Readable Sources

While NEXIS is free to researchers at institutions with a subscription to LEXIS, it is quite expensive otherwise. A number of additional sources are available on CD-ROM which might be suitable for machine coding.

FBIS Daily Reports. The Foreign Broadcast Information Service is a daily compendium of foreign radio, television and newspaper reports monitored by the Central Intelligence Agency. It is unclassified and currently available by subscription (about $400 per year) in hard copy and microfiche; it is supposed to be available in CD-ROM format in the near future. FBIS has problems of coverage bias — it disproportionately monitors geographical areas of concern to the United States — but has far greater density than the *NYT*.

Facts on File. This source, long a favorite of event-data coders, is available on CD-ROM covering 1979-1989. While *Facts on File* has some coverage biases and would require a somewhat different approach to event generation than used with NEXIS,[12] it might provide a useful and relatively inexpensive source.

UMI Newspaper Abstracts. The Newspaper Abstract CD-ROM produced by University Microforms Inc. indexes eight United States newspapers — including the *NYT, Wall Street Journal, Washington Post,* and *Christian Science Monitor* — and is available in many libraries. This provides coverage of major international events, though it suffers the usual coverage bias problems of U.S. newspapers, and there is considerable redundancy in the eight papers. The abstracts also provide somewhat less detail than Reuters leads.

Optical scanning. When a concentrated event source is available only in hard copy, optical character recognition (OCR) is a possibility. OCR software has improved substantially in recent years — particularly with respect to speed and its ability to deal with proportionately spaced fonts — and when combined with a spelling checker, it is relatively easy to generate machine-readable text from hard copy.[13]

The most concentrated sources of international events we have found are the chronologies produced by specialized publications: for example the journal *Middle East International* produces such a chronology for the Middle East on a monthly basis. Under the DDIR funding, we are currently experimenting with this option using English-language chronologies for the Middle East and German-language chronologies for Central Europe; we also intend to experiment with scanning copies of microfilmed newspapers such as the *Times* (London) to test the possibility of generating event data from historical sources.

The WINR Machine Coding System

WINR[14] is an almost purely statistical system and was the initial attempt at Kansas in developing a machine coding system; the results of experiments with WINR are given in detail in Schrodt and Donald (1990). It is a useful illustration of how a machine learning system might work, and might still be useful in some specialized circumstances, such as coding-by-example from non-English source material.

The Algorithm

The classification metric used in WINR is similar to that used in fuzzy sets; this extends work done earlier in Schrodt and Leibsohn (1985). Each word w is associated with a vector v^w indexed on the event codes (c) where

$$v_c^w = \frac{\text{\# of occurrences of } w \text{ in events of type } c}{\text{total \# of occurrences of } w}$$

In short, v_c^w is the conditional probability that w is found in an event of type c given that w occurs in a sentence. For example, when using a set of 22 codes (e.g., the 2-digit WEIS), the maximum value of v_c^w would be 1.0, which would occur if a word were only found in events having a single code. The minimum value would be 0.045 (1/22), which occurs if the occurrences of the word are spread equally across all of the categories. These vectors are determined empirically from the frequency of tokenized words in the English text in the training set.

The initial classification criterion is the code c which maximizes

$$\underset{c \in C}{\text{Max}} \sum_{w \in S} v_c^w$$

where C is the set of event codes and S is the set of tokenized words found in the text describing the event. In other words, the system simply sums the conditional probabilities and takes the maximum value. WINR implements this basic algorithm with a few minor modifications (see figure 7.2).

1. Elimination of stopwords on an entropy criterion. The information theoretic concept of entropy (see Pierce, 1980) is ideally suited to a classification problem such as this. This measure — identical to the H_{rel} used in some of McClelland's early studies — is effectively a measure of the ability of a feature (in this case, a word) to discriminate between categories. A word with zero entropy is associated with only a single category (in other words, it classifies perfectly); one with high entropy is scattered more or less equally across the various categories. Entropy is defined as

$$E = -\sum_i p_i \log_2(p_i)$$

where p_i = proportion of times the word is observed in category i. In the IPPRC WEIS, "low" entropy tends to be anything below 0.5; "high" entropy above 1.5.

High entropy words were eliminated in a two-stage process. First, the data were tokenized using a "universal" stoplist of about forty common words (e.g., numbers, days of the week) and proper nouns (actors). The entropy of the remaining words was then computed and all those words above a threshold (set somewhat arbitrarily at 1.5) were added to the stoplist. The final stoplist contained about 700 words for the IPPRC WEIS set. The elimination of high entropy words decidedly speeds up the computation; it has only a small, though positive, effect on the classification accuracy.

2. Keywords. A few of the WEIS categories are strongly associated with single words. These were detected, using machine learning methods, by looking for high-frequency words with exceptionally low entropy. Table 7.2 shows the set of words from the IPPRC WEIS with entropy less than 0.5 and a frequency greater than 10; the two-digit numbers are the WEIS categories they are most

Source text:		"Mubarak Receives Message From Mitterand"								
Tokenized words:		RECEIV MESSAG								

WEIS Codes			01	02	03	04	05	06	07	...	22
Vectors: RECEIV			.00	.25	.30	.00	.02	.10	.33	...	00
MESSAG			.00	.30	.30	.20	.10	.10	.00	...	.00
Total		.00	.55	.60	.20	.12	.20	.33	...	00	

Classification: WEIS code 03

In this example, there are two keywords in the source sentence, "receives" and "message." Each word is found in sentences in various WEIS codes-code 02 is "comment," 03 is "consult," 04 is "approve," 05 is "promise" and 06 is "reward." These probabilities were determined empirically from the actual data. When the probabilities are summed, the maximum category is 03, "consult."

Fig. 7.2. WINR example

strongly associated with. This set corresponds quite closely to the keywords in the various WEIS categories; these were the only words with high frequency and low entropy.

3. *Tokenizing*. Most natural language processing systems have a means of reducing verbs to their roots, a process known as "stemming."[15] WINR uses a very simple stemming technique: Words were truncated to tokens of six characters. This works relatively well for English: For example REJECTS, REJECTED, REJECTING all go to REJECT. In cases where it does not work — for example SHOT, SHOOTS, SHOOTING — separate counts are maintained. This approach is simpler and computationally more efficient than a system with greater information on rules of English verb formation (e.g., Lovins, 1968) but results in relatively few incorrect roots because of the limited vocabulary used in describing international events. A formal stemming algorithm would probably improve the performance of the system by a couple percentage points, but not dramatically.

4. *Low frequency words*. Words which are very infrequent in the training set are problematic when these occur only once and therefore are strongly associated with a single category. These enhance the internal consistency of the test but result in overtraining since such words result in misclassification when they occur in a different context. The solution to this problem was to eliminate

TABLE 7.2. Keywords with High Frequency and Low Entropy

03	'MEETS'	05	'ASSURE'	08	'AGREE'	09	'CALLS '
10	'URGES'	11	'REJECT'	13	'PROTES'	14	'DENIES'
15	'DEMAND'	16	'WARNS'	20	'EXPELS'		

the use of any low-frequency word occurring in only a single category. In the tests reported here, "low frequency" was < 2. This reduces the internal consistency of the system from 95 percent to 90 percent in the IPPRC WEIS, but has little effect in the FBIS or ICPSR WEIS sets; it raises the external accuracy by about 3 percent. This may be too low a threshold, and one might eliminate any low-frequency cases where there is an equal distribution among categories.[16]

Coding WEIS Summaries Using WINR

Schrodt and Donald (1990) report the results of split-sample testing of WINR on the textual summaries in three datasets of increasing linguistic complexity. Since the objective of this work is developmental and the ultimate objective is coding NEXIS, not WEIS, these datasets are a convenience sample rather than a random sample; table 7.3 gives examples of the text in the three sets.

TABLE 7.3. Sample WEIS Text Summaries

FBIS INDEX

025:Abd al-Majid, Algerian Ambassador On Cooperation
033:Arab League Official Arrives In Cairo 2 April
065: Membership In Arab Mining Company Restored
081:Electricity- Grid To Link With Asian Countries
032:Egyptian Assistant Foreign Minister Arrives 5 April
033:PRC Vice Minister Concludes Visit, Departs
033:Ghall Meets Ethiopian Envoy 10 April
031:Mubarak Receives Call From Mitteran On Lebanon

ICPSR WEIS

121:syr in note to uno accused isr of preparing a raid into syr
223:syr and isr exchange fire
223:isr and syr tanks clash on border in two hour battle
121:isr prm calls use of syr tanks in dmz a serious violation of the armistice agreements
160:isr warns if harassment continued isr would determine her response
121:syr said isr opened fire first

IPPRC WEIS

94:Pope John Paul II calls for the survival of Solidarity, saying the union has become an integral part of the heritage of the workers of Poland and of other nations.
101:Saudi FM Saud al Faisal says that in return for Israeli recognition of Palestinian rights and the return of occupied lands, the Saudi gvt is prepared to accept Israel.
121:Saudi FM Saud al Faisal charges that Israeli policy is to try to precipitate war.
121:Saudi FM Saud al Faisal charges that if USA policy in the Middle East is not changed, conflict in the region will occur.
94:Polish PM Jaruzelski calls for a meeting with ten European Community ambassadors.

FBIS Index: About 450 entries from the Newsbank *Index to the FBIS Daily Reports* from the Middle East in April 1989; these were assigned WEIS codes.

ICPSR WEIS: 1200 cases taken from the standard ICPSR WEIS data from an assortment of years. The ICPSR WEIS descriptions are quite short and generally are in an abbreviated English.

IPPRC WEIS: This is the "fugitive" WEIS that was collected by the International Public Policy Research Center for Richard Beal's National Security Council event-data project during the early years of the Reagan administration. The source is the *NYT*, and the project was directed by former McClelland students, so it is probably fairly close to "true" WEIS. The descriptions are substantially longer than the IPPRC WEIS and appear to be similar to *NYT* leads. The sample is about 8,000 events.

The overall accuracy of the WINR system is summarized in table 7.4; the misclassification matrices are presented in Schrodt and Donald (1990). The internal accuracy of WINR across the three datasets is comparable; the external accuracy differs considerably on the simple external test, and then converges again when learning is incorporated.

The "Internal Consistency Test" is the result of recoding the training set after the classification matrix had been determined: It is basically a measure of the extent to which that matrix has incorporated the information in the training set. The "External Validation Test" is the test against cases that were not in the training set. The FBIS index entries have the highest accuracy since these are both very abbreviated and deal almost entirely with comments and consultations. The low external accuracy of the ICPSR data may be due to the fact that the training set depleted the validation set for many of the categories, and almost half of the validation set was a single category, "Accuse." In the IPPRC set the "Comment" category caused problems — less than 10 percent of these are categorized correctly, and comments were about 25 percent of that dataset.

In the "Learning" results, whenever a case is misclassified, the information on that case was added to the distribution matrix. Unsurprisingly, this helps the overall accuracy considerably, bringing it to around 63 percent for all of the cases. The 63 percent includes the initial misclassification as an "error"; when the validation sets are retested after the iterative learning phase, the accuracy goes to about 80 percent, roughly the inter-coder reliability for human coders. Iterative learning dramatically improves the accuracy in the "Comment" category

TABLE 7.4. Accuracy of WINR Coding (2-digit codes)

Source	Internal	External	Learning
FBIS Index	96%	51%	64%
ICPSR WEIS	94%	33%	64%
IPPRC WEIS	90%	43%	62 %

on the IPPRC set, which would suggest that comments were being misclassified in part because of different word combinations.

Discussion

WINR is in many ways an extreme test. It is almost a pure statistical, example-based scheme — the program had no linguistic information except for an initial stoplist. It is also a relatively simple classification system: There was no attempt to estimate *optimal* weighting vectors for the various words using regression analysis or some comparable linear technique, nor was there a sophisticated attempt to generate an optimal training set. For all of these reasons, this should be interpreted as a lower bound on the accuracy of machine coding using statistical techniques, not as either an upper limit or typical performance. The basic representational scheme is clearly sufficient, since the internal consistency is greater than 90 percent. The performance drops to around 40 percent on a simple external validation test; this can be increased to about 62 percent with iterative learning and 80 percent accuracy on reevaluation of the entire set. The external validations are considerably below the within-project coder reliabilities in the existing projects, though they may be approaching the between-project reliabilities using human coders.

KEDS : A Pattern-Based Approach

The pure machine learning approach of WINR is a useful exercise if a large amount of coded data is available, but it makes almost no use of the linguistic regularities of natural language. The alternative is to incorporate some linguistic knowledge and use human-designated patterns rather than statistical inference. The disadvantages of this approach is that a human must interact with the data and the patterns will be language-specific. However, a human coder can bring to bear linguistic knowledge and will probably reach a convergence on the common categories much more quickly than will a system relying solely on statistical inference.

KEDS is a pattern-based coder that uses dictionaries of actors and verb phrases to do three-digit WEIS coding. The program runs on Macintosh SE and II computers, has a regular Macintosh interface, and is designed to be used by individuals with only minimal computer experience; it can be used for either machine-assisted coding or fully automatic coding. The program is reasonably bug-free and copies are available from the author. We have been developing the system by coding Reuters leads from the Middle East; the system presently has about 300 phrases identifying actors and about 800 verbs and patterns.

KEDS uses three types of information:

Actors: Proper nouns used to identify the political actors recognized by the system.
Verbs: Since WEIS codes are primarily characterized by the actions that one actor takes toward another, the verb in a sentence is usually the most important aspect of an event.
Patterns: Patterns are usually fragments of verb phrases and are used to distinguish different uses of a verb — for example PROMISED TO SEND versus PROMISED TO CONSIDER.

Patterns can also provide syntactic information on the location of the source and target within the sentence; for example reversing the source and target when a sentence is in passive voice. Consistent with similar work in text analysis (Lehnert and Sundheim, 1991), KEDS relies on simple parsing of sentences — primarily identifying proper nouns (which may be compound), verb phrases and direct objects (using patterns), and dereferencing pronouns — rather than using full syntactical analysis. As a consequence KEDS will make errors on oddly constructed sentences but accurately deals with the sentence structures most commonly encountered in news articles.

By foregoing the use of a full parser and relying on universal linguistic traits such as nouns, verbs and objects, KEDS can also be easily modified to handle languages other than English. At Kansas, Ronald Francisco is using KEDS to code events dealing with Central Europe from the German-language foreign policy chronology *Informationen*, a fortnightly publication of the German Ministry for Inter-German Relations in Bonn. German language coding involves entirely new actor, verb and pattern dictionaries, but otherwise has required very few modifications in the basic program. For obvious reasons, English parsing is not applied to the German text, but the system recognizes passive voice in German. Because the "bureaucratic German" of *Informationen* is far more regular than the "journalistic English" in Reuters, and because Central European international events are more straightforward than those in the Middle East, the accuracy of German-language coding has been very high, often exceeding 90 percent. If a machine-readable source text is located, we are also planning to test the system in Arabic.

Results

Because KEDS is still in the development stage and because we do not have available a large set of WEIS-coded Reuters data, we have yet to subject KEDS/ Reuters to as much systematic testing as WINR. However, we have done an initial test against a subset of the IPPRC summaries:[17] The results of this test are reported in Table 7.5. The over all accuracy in assigning event codes is about 60 percent for two-digit codes and 32 percent for three-digit codes; this is almost a 50 percent improvement over WINR on the two-digit codes. Since we have been coding Reuters only for Middle East articles, KEDS does not have a complete actor list and some incorrect classifications were due to errors in the actor identification; on the subsample where KEDS could find a source and target, the two-digit accuracy rises to about 67 percent.[18] Finally, we have not completed the incorporation of three-digit codes into our dictionaries; if one looks only at those cases where KEDS assigned a three-digit code and found two actors, the accuracy of three-digit coding is about 60 percent.

The test of KEDS against the IPPRC summaries is a strong one in the sense that the KEDS dictionaries were developed using Reuters, not IPPRC: Any commonality between the two rests on their English language content rather than the statistical characteristics of the source material. The coding accuracy of KEDS is certainly in the ballpark for the inter-project coding reliabilities discussed above, and since the KEDS dictionaries are still relatively small, there is ample room for improvement. It is also reassuring to note that the three-digit accuracy is not substantially less than the two-digit accuracy, so the transition from two-digit to three-digit coding seems to be causing little problem.

Schrodt and Donald (1990) reported the results of an experiment on an earlier version of KEDS testing the accuracy of two-digit codes. While this test produced an overall accuracy of only 38 percent, certain categories had unusually low levels of false positives — for example 'Accuse' (6 percent error ; $N=300$), 'Reject' (11 percent error; $N=83$), 'Demand' (21 percent error, $N=47$) and 'Consult' (26 percent error, $N=700$). Based on those results, Gerner (1990) used machine-coded Reuters leads for December 1987 to February 1990 in a study of Israel's reaction to adverse international opinion as reflected in the change in the number of deaths of Palestinians inflicted by Israeli forces in dealing with the *intifada*. The question is a nontrivial one, since Israel has been accused both of being *insensitive* to international opinion on this issue (mostly by critics on the left) and of being *too* sensitive (mostly by critics on the right). The only WEIS categories in the study are the negative interactions 'Accuse,' 'Protest,' 'Demand' and 'Warn,' which had low false positive classification rates. Gerner's test showed not only a statistically significant correlation between deaths and international protest, but also found that non-Arab accusations and demands had a significant negative effect on the change in deaths but that accusations and demands from Arab states had no significant effect. The ability of machine

TABLE 7.5. Accuracy of KEDS Coding of IPPRC Summaries

Cases	N	2-digit	3-digit
All	2740	59.3%	31.8%
Two actors found	2431	66.9%	35.9%
Two actors, 3-digit code	1461	—	59.7%

coded data to reflect such relatively subtle political distinctions provides at least some indication of its validity.

The KEDS dictionaries are still relatively primitive: We currently have a vocabulary of about 1,100 words and phrases; the final coding system will probably incorporate three or four times that many. We suspect that once we have developed the dictionaries to handle WEIS coding, that dictionary can be used as a basis for other coding systems, since it will contain a substantial percentage of the phrases likely to be encountered when coding international events from a news source, and the actors dictionary will need only minimum modification. Based on the success of KEDS in coding the *NYT*-based IPPRC summaries, the dictionary does not seem to be excessively source-dependent.

The IPPRC data dealt only with international events and explicitly identified the actors involved. Reuters leads are not always as clear, and the source material causes some problems. Some of the most common problems, with examples of actual leads, are the following.

Implicit actor identification: The identification of one or more actors is sometimes dependent on context:

> An Israeli army commander shot dead a 14-year-old Palestinian boy and an Arab informer armed with an army-supplied gun killed another teenager in the occupied West Bank on Thursday, Israeli military sources said.

The "Arab informer" is presumably working for Israel, the dead teenager is presumably Palestinian; but there is no explicit indication of this in the lead.

Internal events: Keyword searching retrieves stories where there is internal debate about international affairs:

> U.S. Democratic Party Chairman Ron Brown demanded on Thursday that President George Bush suspend talks with the Palestine Liberation Organization until it condemns a seaborne raid by a PLO faction on Israel.

Coding is also difficult when complex events of a quasi-international character are encountered, such as stories on the Lebanese civil war or the Palestinian *intifada*,[19] the activity by autonomous "internal" actors, and activity of international organizations such as the United Nations, European Community, and the Arab League. Some of these cases, of course, would pose problems for human coders as well; interactions in this region are much more complicated than those of the Westphalian nation-states presupposed by the WEIS coding scheme.

Complex sentence structures: Reuters occasionally contains sentences that cannot be handled by the parser and which have not been anticipated in the verb phrase patterns:

> Talks between Israel and Palestinians about elections in the Israeli-occupied territories would be impossible unless the PLO was represented at those discussions.

> Resumption of ties between Egypt and Syria may spur reconciliation between Iraq and Syria, and Syria and the PLO, the Qatari newspaper al-Raya said on Friday.

In Reuters, complex sentence structure is definitely the exception rather than the rule; most leads are quite regular in structure. This regularity allows operations such as the assignment of pronoun references and implicit subjects in compound sentences to be done with simple rules.

Feature stories: Some leads introduce feature stories rather than events:

> The U.N. armored car careered down a steep street in pursuit of Israeli-backed militiamen, whipping past the slow lines of mules loaded with smuggled fuel from Syria.

> The Israeli army, accustomed to glory on the battlefields of the Middle East, is uncomfortable in its role as policeman in the narrow streets of Palestinian villages.

Many feature story leads do not contain references to multiple actors and are rejected automatically, but problem cases remain.

After the KEDS dictionaries are more fully developed, we will attempt to develop filters to eliminate many of these problem cases. KEDS currently tries to code everything; a more practical version would code only those sentences that fit known patterns and leave the complicated cases to a human coder.

Conclusion

On the basis of our experiments, several generalizations can be made about machine coding within the WEIS framework. The most basic result is that the task is not only possible but relatively straightforward using ordinary personal computers. Specialized hardware is not necessary, and techniques developed in the literature on automated text retrieval and text analysis can be applied effectively to the machine coding problem. While the methods used with Reuters and foreign policy chronologies would probably not work on less structured text such as political rhetoric, merely being able to code Reuters is sufficient for most existing applications of event data. Our experience to date in coding a language other than English has also been encouraging, which opens the possibility of reducing the existing dependence of event data on English-language sources.

Fully-automated machine coding systems can be used in machine-assisted coding to gain substantial savings in costs. While a fully-automated system may have only 70 percent overall accuracy, it usually gets the source and target assignments correct even if the event is wrong, or gets the event correct with an incorrect target, so the accuracy as a percentage of the number of items assigned is 90 percent.[20] This reduces by a factor of ten the labor required for coding. Machine coding also substantially reduces the effort involved in assigning codes when a large number of actors are involved: With an appropriately complete dictionary actor codes are almost never assigned incorrectly, and software can be written so that changing the role of an actor (i.e., from source to target) can be done with a single keystroke or mouse click.

Machine coding is useful for generating specialized datasets from regionally-specific or historical sources, which might not otherwise be coded due to the labor involved. The preparation of the input text can be done by individuals without special training, such as work-study students or university wordprocessing centers; specialists can focus on the coding itself. This same task differentiation applies to material in languages other than English: The expertise of a multi-lingual coder can be concentrated on the difficult cases.

I suspect that a major use of machine coding will be for re-coding existing datasets to fit new paradigms and test new hypotheses. Because of the tremendous effort involved in generating human-coded data, the WEIS, COPDAB, CREON and BCOW coding systems were designed to be as general as possible, rather than being designed with specific research hypotheses in mind. However, once a set of natural language texts are available — whether a journalistic source such as Reuters or the *Facts on File* CD-ROM, or a set designed for event coding such as Maryland's GEDS project — it will be practical to develop customized event-data coding schemes for testing specific hypotheses. The coding system appropriate for a study of international trade negotiations would presumably be quite different than that used to study the effects of arms transfers on conflict. With machine coding, recoding a large existing event set is within the capabilities of a single researcher with modest computer resources — for example a graduate student doing dissertation research. Most of the effort in the project can go into developing the appropriate coding scheme rather than the rather tiresome process of coding or supervising coders. Where copyright is not a problem — for example with historical news texts — machine-readable natural language texts themselves become a reusable resource for international relations research that could be archived with the ICPSR.

Automated actor assignment is particularly useful if one is dealing with internal actors, since these are substantially greater in number than international actors, they change over time, and the degree of specificity of actor identification may vary with the research question. In the Middle East, for example, some research designs would require coding all PLO-affiliated Palestinian groups as PLO, others would distinguish between parties within the PLO (e.g., Fatah, PFLP, DFLP), still others might distinguish between individuals within those parties. Such changes can be made very quickly using machine coding.

Finally, machine-coding systems provide a backup for the existing system of human coding. During the 1980s event-data research was severely hampered by the fact that the existing datasets ended about 1978, and the most widely available event dataset, the ICPSR WEIS, covered only about a decade. With funding from DDIR and the University of Maryland, a systematic event-data collection is again underway. As long as this effort continues, the Maryland datasets will likely be of higher quality than machine-coded data. However, should those funding sources terminate, a machine-coding system could take over. With an institutional subscription to NEXIS and some fraction of a graduate research assistant, an up-to-date machine-coded event dataset based on

Reuters could be maintained for a few thousand dollars a year, perhaps under the sponsorship of the ICPSR or some public-spirited university-sponsored center for international studies. The knowledge that event data will be a continuing resource should encourage further utilization of and research with such data.

NOTES

This research was supported by National Science Foundation Grant SES89-10738 and DDIR. My thanks to Christopher Donald and Cory McGinnis for coding on WINR, to Fritz Snyder of the University of Kansas Law School Library for assistance with NEXIS, and to Llewelyn Howell for assistance in obtaining the IPPRC WEIS data. Tony Nownes, Deborah Gerner, Ronald Francisco, Julia Pitner, and Judy Weddle have served the difficult role of alpha-testers for KEDS; Nownes and Weddle are responsible for most of the English vocabulary development.

1. General Inquirer is still in use and has its share of advocates, but has never played a central role in international relations research.
2. BCOW is more difficult because it codes the continuation and cessation of events as well as their initiation. This characteristic, rather than the greater number of BCOW categories, might cause problems.
3. The dimensions of the vector spaces in question are usually associated with specific words or terms, and hence the dimensionality is extremely large: The use of one or two thousand dimensions is not uncommon. While the similarity metric is usually non-Euclidean, these systems are conceptually similar to Euclidean nearest neighbor systems such as discriminant analysis.
4. A weak restriction since any known bias can be adjusted by subtracting a constant.
5. Human coding also presumably involves some errors, but for the purposes of event coding, it is as close as one gets to the "true" codes. In this article, the term "accuracy" refers to the ability of a machine coding system to assign the same code as that assigned by a human coder.
6. For example, in some pattern recognition studies, the superior ability of a human to code discrete secondary events buried in a story might be a more important consideration.
7. KEDS uses a binary search of a list of words indexed on their first two letters; if trying to locate the word AGREE, it searches only words with the first two letters greater than or equal to AG and less than AH. As with most text analysis systems, KEDS uses verb "stemming" so that the single entry AGREE matches AGREES, AGREED and AGREEING as well as AGREE.
8. Many Reuters texts generate multiple events due to compound verb phrases, compound actors and paired events so 144,000 Reuters leads would probably generate about 250,000 WEIS events.
9. At the University of Kansas, NEXIS is available during off-peak hours through the Law School subscription to the LEXIS legal service. The university pays a fixed subscription price for the service, rather than paying by citation; for faculty research purposes, it is effectively free.
10. This retrieves only a small number of totally irrelevant stories, primarily UPI stories on basketball player Michael Jordan and Reuters reports on international soccer,

tennis and cricket competitions. The "PALEST!" construct uses a wildcard character to match "Palestinian," "Palestinians" and "Palestine."

11. This is true even for papers with reporters in the area: the herd mentality of the international press is well documented and the Reuters teletype is prominently available in the major international hotels in Middle Eastern capitals. Since most international events are either unpredictable acts of violence only occasionally witnessed firsthand by Western reporters, or are official statements released at press conferences, the presence of reporters will contribute little in the way of new events, however useful their presence may be for analysis.

12. *Facts on File* aggregates events by topic rather than strictly chronologically. However most sentences containing a date (e.g., "25 April") refer to an event, so by filtering for such sentences one might be able to produce a useable events dataset.

13. At the University of Kansas, OCR is available as a word processing service, so we were able to experiment with the technology without investing in additional equipment.

14. A recursive acronym for "WINR Is Not Relatus."

15. Tokenizing is primarily done for the purposes of computational efficiency; the classification algorithm works just as well with complete words if a suitably large training set is used. Lovins (1968) provides a much more complete system for the derivation of English stems which we may eventually incorporate into KEDS; van Rijsberger (1979) also discusses stop word and stemming systems in detail.

16. For example a word occurring twice, once in 02 and once in 12. These are not captured by the high entropy measure since, strictly speaking, they have dramatically reduced the uncertainty, from 22 categories to only 2. Still, this configuration provides less confidence than a word which occurs 10 times in 02 and ten in 12, even though the entropy is the same.

17. The IPPRC set was edited so that if the same event text appeared multiple times (e.g., meetings), the event text was coded only once. The accuracy comparison applies only to the event code assignment, not the source/target assignment.

18. This is a lower bound: The incomplete actor list meant that sometimes an incorrect actor was identified, which can lead to incorrect identification of the relevant verb. Correcting that problem might raise the accuracy an additional percentage point or two.

19. For purposes of KEDS' development, we are treating as many political groups as possible as actors; depending on the research question, these may or may not be considered international events.

20. 70 percent are totally correct; in the remaining 30 percent two out of three items (source, target, or event) are assigned correctly.

REFERENCES

Burgess, P. M. and R. W. Lawton. 1972. *Indicators of International Behavior: An Assessment of Events Data Research.* Sage Professional Paper in International Studies, Vol. 1, Series No. 02-010. Beverly Hills, CA and London: Sage Publications.

Fan, D. P. 1988. *Predictions of Public Opinion from the Mass Media.* Westport, CT: Greenwood Press.

Forsyth, R. and R. Rada. 1986. *Machine Learning: Applications in Expert Systems and Information Retrieval.* New York: Wiley/Halstead.

Gerner, D. J. 1990. "Evolution of a Revolution: The Palestinian Uprising, 1987-1989." Paper presented at the 31st annual convention of the International Studies Association. Washington, DC, April 10-14.

Joshi, A. K. 1991. "Natural Language Processing." *Science* 253, (September 13): 1242-1249.

Lehnert, W., C. Cardie, D. Fisher, J. McCarthy, E. Riloff and S. Soderland. 1992. "University of Massachusetts: MUC-4 Test Results and Analysis." in *Proceedings of the Third Message Understanding Conference.* 151-158. San Mateo, CA: Morgan Kaufmann.

Lehnert, W. and B. Sundheim. 1991. "A Performance Evaluation of Text Analysis Technologies." *AI Magazine* 12, 3: 81-94.

Lovins, J. B. 1968. "Development of a Stemming Algorithm." *Mechanical Translation and Computational Linguistics* 11, 1-2: 11-31.

McClelland, C. A. 1983. "Let the User Beware." *International Studies Quarterly* 27, 2 (June): 169-177.

Pierce, J. R. 1980. *An Introduction to Information Theory.* New York: Dover.

Salton, G. 1989. *Automatic Text Processing.* Reading, MA: Addison-Wesley.

Schrodt, P. A. and C. Donald. 1990. "Machine Coding of Event Data." Paper presented at the 31st annual convention of the International Studies Association. Washington, DC, April 10-14.

Schrodt, P. A. and D. Leibsohn. 1985. "An Algorithm for the Classification of WEIS Event Code from WEIS Textual Descriptions." Paper presented at the 26th annual convention of the International Studies Association. Washington, DC, March 5-9.

Stone, P. J., D. C. Dunphy, M. S. Smith and D. M. Ogilvie. 1966. *The General Inquirer: A Computer Approach to Content Analysis.* Cambridge: MIT Press.

van Rijsberger, C. J. 1979. *Information Retrieval,* 2d ed. London: Butterworths.

Vincent, J. E. 1983. "WEIS vs. COPDAB: Correspondence Problems." *International Studies Quarterly* 27, 2 (June): 160-168.

CHAPTER 8

Making Peaceful Sense of the News: Institutionalizing International Conflict-Management Event Reporting Using Frame-Based Interpretive Routines

Hayward R. Alker, Jr.

Abstract

As a contribution toward the development of a news monitoring component of a United Nations oriented conflict warning and analysis system, this article explores several frame-based ways of automating preliminary interpretive codings of conflict management relevant information generated by the GEDS system. These include conflict characterization frames, conflict sequence scripts, case-based reasoning about conflict precedents or analogies, and explanation-based learning from new disputes; relevant software has been developed by Schank and Riesbeck, Pazzani, Haase, and Lehnert. The integration of such procedures into SHERFACS coding practices will be a principal concern. All software to be explored will be COMMON LISP based, affordable, and usable on either UNIX-based work stations, MAC II's or MSDOS 386 operating systems; the use of such routines by other GEDS users will also be explored.

Institutionalizing a globally oriented system for monitoring threats to, and breaches of, the peace will not end war — after all, timely crime statistics certainly have not ended crime. But good data on crime and anti-crime efforts can help society learn better how to define and achieve its goals. Analogously, such an information monitoring system could facilitate the early warning efforts of the Office for the Research and Collection of Information in the United Nations Secretariat; and a regularly updated, computationally accessible historical record of conflicts and conflict management activities could help scholars, diplomats and conflict managers remember and reassess the successes and failures of the United Nations Collective Security system. By facilitating research on "avoidable wars,"[1] such an information system, if organizationally implemented, would be a modest scholarly contribution to world order, a small step towards the "domestication" of *The Anarchical Society*.[2]

Working in conjunction with Frank Sherman and other participants in the Data Development for International Research project (DDIR), I propose to develop several semi-automated components of such a conflict management system. It will be a software development and revision effort focused on, and presupposing, the Reuters-based, humanly-coded events stream generated by the Global Event-Data System (GEDS).[3] Specifically, this interpretive software should help speed SHERFACS codings of conflict management cases and their subsequent comparative, precedential analysis.

At the end of the two year project, I want to make publicly available, at minimal cost, a series of interpretive computer routines for making peaceful sense of DDIR/GEDS event-data[4] from an early warning, conflict management perspective. These routines — oriented toward the Haas-Butterworth-Alker-Sherman series of conflict management studies — can also be applied, with varying degrees of reworking, by others with different empirical, theoretical or practical interests in using the DDIR/GEDS data stream.[5]

Although event-data research (and GEDS in particular) can rightly be proud of the evolution of international, domestic and transnational "layers" of data making, I shall focus here on a different, linguistic, hierarchy of research orientations. In increasing order of semantic and pragmatic complexity, the three components of a DDIR/GEDS event-data record are:

1.   the organizationally contextualized GEDS action/events codes,
2.   the humanly constructed, source-specific narrative summaries of each event, and
3.   the quotations attributed to principal actors/interactors as integral parts of the event being described.

At a minimum, I am assuming that these three-tier event descriptions will all be in the same data record; hopefully, original source story(-ies) in their entirety with codings attached to, but not obliterative of, relevant text fragments, will also be conveniently accessible.[6] That way events, acts and quotations (interpretable as public speech acts)[7] could be linked at modest cost to richer historical, institutional, precedential and journalistic characterizations of their significance available in, or outside of, the original source text.

The Linguistic, Interpretive Philosophy of the Present Proposal

In either case, this proposal assumes that increased attention to, *and multi-perspective understanding of*, public international conflict and conflict management events is a worthy research focus.[8] Moreover, it is assumed that the *practically relevant meanings* of such internationally relevant conflict events require *multi-perspective descriptions* which the apparently consensual judgments of student coders only partially approximate, but which GEDS's multi-source coding strategy greatly facilitates.

Whether an *act* should be described as a threatening, promising, or mocking *action* is determined by the perceptions, interpretations, judgments, commitments and shared meaning conventions of the parties involved.[9] The correct *description* of a social action is thus more than a reliable *convergence* of coder and/or diplomatic judgments; its *meaning and identity* is *constituted* by the *multiple* interpretive perspectives of the principal actors in such events. Such interpretive complexities, I believe, are an appropriate emphasis for an institutionally-aware and internationally constituted political science.[10]

An illustrative multi-perspective event description. Let me illustrate several of these points with an example taken from my 1975 application of "Reason Analysis" accounting schemes. Table 8.1 suggests historical and practical idealizations of positions in the UN debate on its Congo operation. It is the custom of event-data coding practices to summarize a news report as containing at most one or two "events;" let us assume that the news report's "event" in question would be summarily coded as "UN Security Council takes conflict management/peacekeeping action directed at the Congo." Table 8.1 suggests just how distinctive interests, preambular conflict situation descriptions, and diplomatic expectations partially converged in this particular historic event.

Among diplomatic conflict managers (and sympathetic scholars) seeking to probe, to reach and to extend institutional "limits of the possible" peace-bringing roles that the UN might play during the Cold War, some of the specific situational features in table 8.1 were widely recognized as especially significant. Let me recall several of them.

First, the limited convergence of First, Second and Third World "general interests" in conflict limitation in this case suggests "anti-imperial"/ "self-determination"/ "decolonialization" conflicts as a potential future domain for UN actions; more precisely, the remarkable convergence of resistance to encouraged secession by the resource-rich province of Katanga suggests important support for the "territorial integrity" norm of "the anarchical society of states," even in Africa.

Subtler judgments about the infeasibility of alternative "direct intervention attempts" are also brought to our attention by the "justifiability" considerations at the end of table 8.1. The "limits" set by continued referral to "host state" agreement plagued subsequent efforts by UN peacekeeping forces to prevent renewed outbreaks of Arab-Israeli hostilities, for example.

A third set of considerations relate to the institution-specific convergence suggested by the "Veto weighted acceptability," crudely summarized in the table 8.1. Of course, the Veto provision of the Charter is being referred to; Security Council actions are required for the authorization of UN peace forces. Besides the weakening of Charter barriers against dealing with matters of "domestic jurisdiction" like breakdowns in "public order," this decision strengthened the precedents for decisive action even when certain Great Powers (but neither the Superpowers, nor the Third World bloc numerically predominant in the General Assembly and quite strongly present in the Security Council as well) are highly ambivalent about UN actions. Coming after the successful UN Suez crisis role, ONUC actions helped broaden this expansive rewriting of Charter language for a time.

Subtler precedential issues ride just below the surface, and contribute

TABLE 8.1. An Accounting Scheme for UNOC Security Council Votes

Veto Weighted Acceptability	Hypothetical Positions	I. *Interests of the Actors*
		A. General interests
-	(+,-,?,-)	1. Interest in solidarity with Free World bloc leader
-	(-,+,-,?)	2. Interest in solidarity with anti-imperialist cause
?	(+,?,+,?)	3. Interest in saving (white) lives, preventing bloodshed
?	(?,+,-,+)	4. Interest in Third World independence, self-determination
-	(+,?,-,+)	5. Interest in enhanced UN capabilities
		B. Specific objectives
-	(+,-,+,+)	1. Interest in preventing Soviet foothold in the Congo
-	(+,-,+,-)	2. Interest in supporting colonial governments and settlers in Africa
-	(+,-,+,-)	3. Interest in transnational economic investments in Katanga
?	(?,?,-,+)	4. Concern for enlarging UN role in other decolonization/postcolonial disputes
+	(+,+,?,+)	5. Concern that Soviet-American conflict might devastate the Congo and spread elsewhere
+	(?,+,+,+)	6. Concern that a precedent for new boundaries not be created by successful Katangese succession

		II. *Nature of the Conflict Situation*
		A. Inside the Congo
-	(-,+,+,+)	1. The conflict is seen as basically anti-imperial.
?	(+,?,+,-)	2. The dispute is between Belgium and the Congo.
-	(+,-,+,-)	3. The primary conflicts are due to a breakdown in public order, as evidenced by mutinies.
+	(?,+,+,+)	4. The government of the Congo wants UN help vis-à-vis the Belgian troops (and their support of the Katangese).
?	(+,?,+,?)	5. The Congolese request really involves an admission of civil incapacity to govern.

TABLE 8.1. Continued

Veto Weighted Acceptability	Hypothetical Positions	II. *Nature of the Conflict Situation* (cont.)
		B. Outside of the Congo
		1. The conflict is pivotal in the emergence and maintenance of
?	(?,+,+,?)	a) anti-imperialist coalitions.
?	(?,+,+,?)	b) neutral states friendly to the West.
?	(?,?,+,+)	c) independent Africa.
		2. The conflict is pivotally important for the definition of the UN's role in
?	(?,?,?,+)	a) containing the Cold War.
+	(?,+,+,+)	b) speeding decolonization.
+	(+,+,+,?)	c) peacekeeping questions where veto powers may not all completely agree.
		III. *Expectations about UN Actions and Alternatives*
		A. Historical-legal justifiability of UN peacekeeping role
?	(+,?,-,+)	1. Willingness to see UN involvement as binding Security Council action
-	(+,+,-,+)	2. Validity of Suez peacekeeping precedent
?	(?,?,+,+)	3. Domestic interventions only valid when host state agrees.
		B. The UN can mobilize sufficient
+	(+,+,?,+)	1. troops
+	(+,?,+,+)	2. logistics
?	(+,?,-,+)	3. administrative personnel
?	(+,?,-,?)	4. financing to be quickly effective.
		C. Considerations regarding alternate influence actions.
+	(+,+,+,?)	1. Awareness of vulnerabilities of their own large-scale direct intervention attempt
		2. Awareness of some options for continued
+	(+,+,+,?)	a) United States influence
+	(+,+,?,?)	b) Soviet influence
+	(+,+,?,?)	c) European influence
+	(?,+,+,+)	d) Afro-Asian influence within the confines of a UN operation.

Note: Hypothetical positions of the United States, the USSR, France, and black Africancountries are on the left. Reprinted from Alker, 1975: 172-183, with the permission of F. I. Greenstein and N. W. Polsby, *Handbook of Political Science*, Vol. 7: Strategies of Inquiry. (Reading, Mass: Addison-Wesley).

significantly to the *now limited precedential meaningfulness* of the Congo operation. If Security Council decisions are required for force deployments, are they still binding when subsequent French and British (and then Soviet) objections stall the Security Council's further actions? Is the "Uniting for Peace" *procedural* ploy of moving the conflict to the General Assembly applicable in this case, with its attendant financial obligations? Will Soviet votes support such a move despite, for them, its distasteful Korean antecedent?

In this partial discussion of the legitimating rationale for (and the UN resolution authorizing) the Congo operation, I have referred repeatedly to the language of its multi-actor authorization, approximately summarized in the reasoned account of table 8.1. *None of these crucial features of the UN's action are explicitly referred to in the conventional "event data" description above! How then can such behaviorally oversimplified descriptions adequately inform subsequent practical or theoretical deliberations about the UN's peace bringing limits and possibilities?*

Improving on DDIR/GEDS Events Codings Using a Mature Lasswellian Action/Interaction Coding Framework

As Edward Azar and Richard Merritt have already argued[11], the original framework/paradigm/mapping sentence/coding schema of WEISS and COPDAB events measurement — with events seen as actors taking typed actions vis-à-vis targets — was consistent with, and partially inspired by, Harold Lasswell's (1936) famous instrumentalist and positivistic definition of *Politics: Who Gets What, When and How?* In his postwar work, consistent with the "contextual" orientation elaborated in his other pre-war writings, Lasswell himself adopted a more hermeneutically oriented perspective.[12]

After emendations to take into account more reflectively oriented, but still Weberian[13] perspectives, this approach forms the analytical basis for the present proposal.

In his later work, Lasswell sees interactive events, or interactions, as:

Interactions

Actor A acts   ⇔   Actor B acts

To this, interactively and contextually, I would add: (as facilitated/hindered by Actor C, within context/situation D).

The simplest, i.e., top level, form of his mature "schema" (or "frame," or "mapping sentence"[14] for actors, actions and targets) now reads:

Participants, with Perspectives, use Base Values (Resources) according to Strategies, in Situations/thru Institutions, wherein certain Outcomes are evaluated as (un-)desirable, with related institution-sustaining or modifying Effects.

Surely this interpretively-oriented, rather Weberian list is cumbersome. But it is also relatively comprehensive, distant from the logical atomism of much early positivism, resonant with many of the newer features of GEDS coding practice, and sensitive to the special features of the situational/institutional contexts within which most international conflict and conflict management takes place.[15] In this latter regard, rethink the Charter-sensitive descriptions of the ONUC operation suggested above; and recall any of the case-based event-data generating efforts linked to Ernest Haas, Lincoln Bloomfield, Jonathan Wilkenfeld, and Michael Brecher. From a BCOW perspective, think similarly of how vastly different the politically motivated killing of a single American, Russian, Panamanian, El Salvadorean, Palestinian, Kuwaiti, Saudi, or Ethiopian *would be/should be* considered in various different disputes.

One may find elements of the contemporary concern with the social aspects of language in general, as well as speech and conversation in particular settings, in Lasswell's work on legal interpretation and in his occasional citations to George Herbert Mead's prescient but behaviorist appreciation of the self- and other-constitutive functions of language.[16] Limiting oneself additionally to a mention of several giants of recent analytically-oriented Anglo-American language philosophy and social theory — Austin, Chomsky, Grice, Goffman, Labov, Lakoff, and Searle — motivates the post-positivist view that the social, political and scientific uses and functions of language far exceed those proposed by the logical positivists. Their views, in turn, heavily influenced the early event-data researchers and quantitative content analysts, including Lasswell.[17]

Going through and beyond theories of the illocutionary linguistic "force" of direct and indirect speech acts mentioned at the beginning of this paper (such as promising, threatening, declaring, performing, interrogating, ordering, arguing, justifying or questioning), work in the last two decades on the ethnography of speaking, for example, has focused on "the notion of a *speech event*, or culturally recognized social activity in which language plays a specific, and often rather specialized role."[18]

From a developmental research perspective, I believe that future event-data research should be guided by continuing developments in operationally oriented language philosophy, including more recent contributions to empirically oriented social and political science from hermeneutically oriented social and political theory, text linguistics and discourse analysis, cognitive and social psychology, and natural language processing research within artificial intelligence. Such a cumulation-oriented perspective seeks to benefit from both accomplishments as well as recognized limitations of earlier styles of work, described above as unequally co-present layerings in current scientific practice.[19]

Although I do not propose in this project to develop a mature speech act/event-oriented "interface" system for all of DDIR event data — limiting the effort, for the sake of intellectual and financial feasibility, to *SHERFACS facilitating, intentionally-oriented, context-sensitive, multi-perspective interpretive software adaptation and development* — it is my intention to continue to review and learn from other computationally-oriented investigations of how this might be achieved.[20] System development considerations need at the earliest stages of projects like the present one to take into account many such exciting evolutionary possibilities.[21] Giving prominent attention to newsworthy "speech events" in DDIR data-making practices must be left to a later effort. The convergence of interest between traditional, historically-oriented, social and political scientists, speech/conversation social theorists, and artificial intelligence specialists interested in newsworthy speeches or official texts, speaks forcefully to the value of recognizing the worthwhile character of such a subsequent focus.

Redefining the Schank-Abelson-Riesbeck Repertoire of Interpretive Routines in a Lasswellian Events Framework

To illustrate more concretely the first stages of how I propose interpretively to enrich institutionally linked, multi-perspective DDIR/GEDS event codings, and move towards the more difficult but challenging interpretive analysis of event narrative summaries, I refer to the SHERFACS reconstruction of table 8.2.

In table 8.2 I present a reorganization of certain variables from Frank Sherman's Haas-tradition SHERFACS Codebook in terms of a mature Lasswellian "event description framework." Obviously some, but not all of these features will be available in the full DDIR event report (and backup sources). But enough of these elements are likely to occur in either connected series of DDIR/GEDS event codings or their associated summary accounts for us to want to construct interpretive search routines capable of looking through — interfacing with — large data and text files reorganized within such context- and perspective-sensitive interpretive frameworks. I want both to assist SHERFACS coding practices and the subsequent analyses of SHERFACS datasets.

Some time ago I proposed[22] a Lasswell-inspired, intentionalist respecific-ation of political measurement practices modeled on recent developments of human interpretation, reasoning and/or action-understanding processes. The reasons-based, multi-perspective account of arguments shaping the original UN intervention decision in the Congo Crisis was summarized in table 8.1, taken from that article.

Figure 8.1, also taken from Alker (1975), contains an Abelson-Schank Conceptual Dependency formal representation of another example text, a Sheik Yamani speech fragment:

> The advanced industrial nations have long been able to dominate and monopolize, directly or indirectly, the four elements of development [raw materials, including energy, capital, technology, markets]. Being the owners of capital and technology, those nations were enabled through their international companies to dominate the sources of raw materials and energy and to place these elements at the disposal of

their own industries, which in turn controlled their markets throughout the world, allowing no outsider to approach them.

On the other hand, the countries of the third world, or the developing countries, devoid of capital and technology, had no real power over the raw materials or sources of energy of which, in many cases, they were the rightful owners. Their role in the international economic game was merely that of exporter of raw materials and energy at unrealistically low prices, the supplier of cheap labour, and as an open market for the manufactured goods that inundated them, making it impossible for them to establish industries in their own territories except within the narrow limits permitted by the advanced industrial countries. (Yamani, 1974)

TABLE 8.2. SHERFACS Variables as Lasswellian Interaction Event Categories

PARTICIPANTS
such as Bolivian_Dissidents, FSLN_Nicaragua, the Big Four, U.S., grouped into Primary and Secondary Parties on two sides, with

PERSPECTIVES
including relevant preceding, coincident, subsequent cases, context-specific expectations of continuity, spread, intensity, Soviet-American war outbreak

employing *RESOURCES*
costing < 1%, 1-9%, or 10%+ of their total resources

using/initiating/stopping *STRATEGIES*
such as threatening, expressing displeasure, engaging in unconventional war, undergoing dissension, repressing, ignoring protocol, assisting, asymmetrically willing to talk, publicly supporting

[towards unspecified primary or secondary parties on side A or B]

in *SITUATIONS/INSTITUTIONS*
identified as to conflict phase, system period, mode of consensus mobilization, issue type (e.g. colonial or internal Cold War, with/without ethnic aspects, various patterns of party alignment, management agent involvements (managers C, from a list of dozens) wherein parties D (up to 7) were identified as promoting or opposing particular manager actions (sending aid, investigating, calling for sanctions, employing peacekeeping forces or a mediator, etc.), judged in terms of their biases, separately coded within conflict phase

with *OUTCOMES*
described in terms of parties prevailing, hostilities being stopped or disputes settled, or phase changes resulting from such actions, the judged-outcome-difference-were-manager-absent vis-à-vis spread, intensity, U.S.-USSR war variables mentioned above, conflict casualties (totals, on a logged scale), etc.

and *EFFECTS*
including (calculated) average within period or by organization success rates. Managerial institution's success or failures mentioned above might also be included here. Calculations of individual actor successes and failures, as they influence subsequent agenda dispositions should also be mentioned.

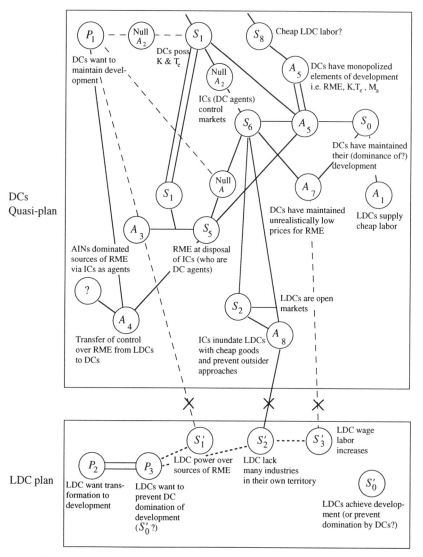

Fig. 8.1. Elements of a functional-dominance theme implied by Yamani speech fragment

This fragment developed an OPEC-oriented "common history" of the economic conflicts between primary-product-producing developing countries and the industrialized countries.

Without reviewing its "chemical" construction out of subatomic, atomic and molecular meaning units, one can say that figure 8.1 provides a scripted, multi-plan respecification in Schank-Abelson Conceptual Dependency analysis terms of the Sheik Yamani speech fragment. Indeed, reading some of the instrumentally manipulative stories generated and semantically /pragmatically "computationally analyzed" or "scientifically understood" in Schank and Abelson's classic 1970s text,[23] one sees many examples of instrumentally purposive Lasswellian agents seeking or getting "what, when, and how" in a context of their goals, institutional expectations, and previous interaction histories. Coercion, deception, bargaining and rational persuasion processes are dynamically represented in context-sensitive, multi-perspective, practical ways.

As interpretive software oriented towards operationally reconstructing perspective-linked, situation-specific *understanding*, software modules in the Schank-Abelson tradition *sew together interpretively redescribed event and state*[24] *sequences into intentionally linked plans, action strategies, thematic relationship characterizations, or context-linked case descriptions.* This is possible because words are treated not merely as bit strings but as symbols in an operational semantic lexicon (roughly, explicit-enough-to-be-computable dictionary definitions), in which the intentional implications of particular types of actions or interactions are explicitly elaborated.

More complex interpretive understanding from various perspectives is computationally simulated when elementary meaning structures are discovered to fit into more complex ones, such as the "No Win implication molecule" simulating an interventionist rationale of American Cold Warriors, Abelson's famous "Cold War" script which has been argued as relevant for both U.S., Soviet and Chinese understanding, Yamani's statist version of economic dependency relationships, or the Rhodesia, Congo, or Suez-like precedential case redescription or "policy lessons" one might discover in trying to make historical sense of the recent United Nations reversal of the Iraqi invasion of Kuwait. (This latest case would also be extremely interesting to study, were it in the DDIR event-database, because of the *partial* convergence of Soviet, Egyptian, American, West European, and Japanese interpretations, and the "anti-Arab" "pro-imperialist" interpretations that the Iraqis have tried to persuade others of. Careful searching through large, internationally oriented news reporting, like Reuters reports or FBIS documents, would tell many of us new things about international crisis politics.)

There are two ways to proceed in trying to make peaceful interpretive sense of GEDS data reports, one much simpler than the other; both will be explored in the present effort. *First, one can take the humanly supplied event codes and try to fit them into larger interpretive structures. Secondly, one can use machine-based natural language parsing routines, applied to GEDS narrative summaries, and try to fit (partially) parsed, or "mechanically understood" text accounts into such larger interpretive structures.*

Because modular LISP versions of much of the computational text analysis routines of the Schank-Abelson tradition are publicly available[25] — clearly relevant to the textual bases of DDIR coding practices and the products of this data-making approach, and closely analogous to the Lasswellian conception of social events, acts and interactions — I propose to use the relevant segments of this work[26] as the computational basis for the proposed interpretive software development. To the extent that a shoestring effort relies on packaged software prepared by, and owned by, others, an effort will be made to use software that is well documented, able to work on UNIX or MSDOS/386 or Macintosh IIci platforms, and not very expensive.

Beyond the obvious and desirable feasibility of this exercise — which derives from the cumulation-oriented efforts of several generations of computer science graduate students — to further justify this usage for a project of national significance, I add that work in the Schank-Abelson tradition has slowly been gaining recognition in political scientific studies of cognition and reasoning.

Subsequent offshoots in the areas of dynamic memory research, case-based reasoning modeling and media argumentation analysis are now already recognized, outside of political science, as important areas of text linguistics, news analysis and artificial intelligence research on natural language processing. If the extension of such widely used tools to different cases or contexts is not effortless, the present effort, within a sharply defined research context, should increase our understanding of humankind's politically relevant interpretive abilities.

From a conversational analysis and modeling perspective, the limited vocabulary of DDIR event data and its impoverished events frames or story narratives are clearly regrettable limitations, with only a few operationally beneficial consequences. But this simplicity — which facilitates trend updatings and replications of earlier work — greatly facilitates the redeployment of the rather positivistic Schank-Abelson-Riesbeck interpretive routines in such standardized meaning contexts. Coders trained to search for the "narrative sense" of a lengthy news report are also likely to look for, and compose, intentionally meaningful narrative summaries that will be a useful illustration of, as well as a relevant challenge for, this approach.

With MIT student help, I plan to adapt, reprogram and selectively synthesize the software products of this approach in a DDIR-connected COMMON LISP programming environment.[27] Validity and reliability oriented comparisons of original sources, DDIR event codings, human narrative summary descriptions, speech fragments and computational interpretations will constructively focus subsequent analyses of media texts by political scientists. Indeed, to the extent that DDIR funding allows, such comparisons should help define new directions for appropriate further work.

As a regulative ideal for such work, where political research is seen as one link in a continuing, critically reflective social communication process, I propose a concluding quotation from Teun van Dijk, which explains why the proposed interpretation-modeling software routines would benefit the DDIR event-data user:

> To be able to participate in a communicative event, we again build a model of the context, featuring a communicative setting, location, circumstances, speech participants, and the kinds of speech acts or other communicative acts involved. The representation of the text or dialogue itself may be thought of as the kernel of the model of that communicative event. (van Dijk, 1988: 23)

A Summary of Expected Products

An advanced, working subset of the proposed interpretive routines, pointed towards SHERFACS case coding needs, written in COMMON LISP and working on one or several intermediate level computational platforms would be made available, at the lowest possible cost, to DDIR event-database users at the end of the project.

Basically, I shall focus on facilitating SHERFACS quantitative and narrative data-making within the DDIR/GEDS system. I shall further limit my Schank-Abelson-Riesbeck style analyses to the disputes/cases that Sherman has already created, those since 1984 he is encoding with DDIR help, and those, post-1990, that SHERFACS users would want to see encoded as they enter, and are processed by, the augmented UN conflict management system. Since SHERFACS is a complex dataset, with both "quantitative" event data and narrative summary information incorporated within it now, it turns out to be no small task to translate such datasets into the representations that parse-based interpretive routines can work upon directly.

An effort would be made to stay compatible with, as well as complimentary to, software development at Maryland associated with the present project. For example, record access and retrieval software developed at Maryland (or Kansas, Middlebury, Illinois, or at M. I. T., e.g., Mallery's COMMON LISP data record handling system), may be used as foundational bases for the interpretively and historically oriented software that will be the principal product of this effort.

Supplementary to, and illustrative of the uses of this software, will be a series of papers and user manuals oriented towards SHERFACS/GEDS materials.

Finally, further suggestions about next steps toward a more fully communicative, conversational mode of computer-assisted event-data analysis, conceived of scholarly historical reenactments and counterfactual interpretive explorations of both past and future, can be reliably anticipated.

NOTES

This paper presents a slightly revised and updated version of a portion of the Data Development for International Research (DDIR) event data proposal submitted in 1990 to the National Science Foundation of the United States. Contributions to this project from other participants in the DDIR project are readily acknowledged.

1. See Alker (1988a).
2. Of course I have in mind Hedley Bull's (1977) book of that name.
3. See John L. Davies and Chad K. McDaniel, "The Global Event-Data System," chapter 2 in this volume. GEDS synthesizes certain categories from: (a) the Conflict and Peace Data Bank (COBDAB, initiated by Azar), (b) the World Event Interaction Survey (WEIS, initiated by McClelland), (c) the Behavioral Correlates Of War dataset (BCOW, initiated by Leng and Singer), (d) the World Handbook of Political and Social Indicators (WHPSI, 3d edition by Taylor and Jodice, 1983), and (e) SHERFACS (a Haas-inspired, Sherman-Alker continued conflict management dataset). It will include the actions vis-à-vis each other of (a) nation-states, (b) major non-state communities, and (c) international organizations; when appropriate, the organizational contexts within which actions occur will also be recorded, information that will be especially helpful for determining the operational conflict handling routines of such organizations.
4. The "Global Event-Data System (GEDS)" proposed by John L. Davies, Ted Robert Gurr, and Chad K. McDaniel of the University of Maryland at College Park is summarily described in DDIR's 1990 proposal to NSF. See also the present volume.
5. In particular, I have in mind Steven Seitz's and Russell Leng's interest in "interpretive frameworks," and Russell Leng's semi-automated judgmental coding of BCOW crisis actions.
6. Archaeologically, the three-tiered data record form represents differently timed but overlapping methodological artifacts, layered deposits from three traditions of language-based and text-oriented social science research: positivistically (and statistically) oriented event or content analysis, interpretively and generatively oriented semantic/pragmatic theorizing about narrative structure, function and content, and the emerging paradigms of conversationally oriented social theorizing.
7. In the DDIR project, Chad McDaniel has described direct quotations as the locutionary or utterance aspect of speech acts; this close-to-the event characterization obviously calls for further investigation of the action-constituting "illocutionary" and situation-affecting "perlocutionary" aspects of such events.

In Anglo-American language philosophy, "speech acts" have been recognized by Wittgenstein, Austin, and Searle as performative linguistic activities beyond, and different from, the referencing functions emphasized by logical positivists and early event-data researchers. Christening a ship, legitimating a marriage, and creating binding contractual obligations through public promises are examples of such activity. A clear, recent recognition by an international theorist of the constitutive, "illocutionary" force of promises, as distinguished from the "perlocutionary outcome" or consequence of promises is (Kratochwil, 1989):

The binding character of contracts, as mutual promises, depends for its validity not on the "reliance" which one of the contracting parties might have placed on the promise of the other, but on the institution of contract itself. Not the perlocutionary effect but the illocutionary force of the mutual promises establishes the binding character of contracts.

8. A good but partial indicator of the generalized North American recognition of the methodological importance of the interpretive "moment" of empirically oriented political science is the extent to which Moon (1975) has been understood, accepted, and used in graduate training programs. Moon cites von Wright, Habermas, Kuhn, and Weber as relevant, influential advocates of the independent significance for social science of an interpretive (or hermeneutic) knowledge interest. Alker (1975) followed this lead.

9. In the speech act terminology of footnote 7, we distinguished locutionary acts from illocutionary actions, the intentional action socially constituted by a verbal locution. Although all actions are certainly not speech actions, the meaningfulness of nonverbal actions partakes of similar, symbolic, convention-shaped, intentional, or accidental linguistic complexities.

10. Having written my own 1975 chapter on "Polimetrics: Its Descriptive Foundations" to bring out the implications of interpretive concerns for polimetric practice, I have pursued this orientation ever since. A partially coded description of UN intervention in the Congo Crisis, taken from this chapter, is given in table 8.1.

   In Alker (1984) I further introduced Rescherian formalisms for analyzing political argumentation, reviewed von Wright and Abelson's modes of representing practical cum interpretive reasoning, illustrated Abelson and Reich's early Artificial Intelligence modeling of ideological interpretations of international news events, and suggested how both Weberian action theory and "the temporal self-understanding of a continuing human society," Olafson's definition of "historicity," could be empirically reconstructed using Abelsonian simulations.

11. I refer to Azar's verbal remarks at earlier DDIR meetings. See also Merritt (1990). Many of Merritt's points are incorporated in the DDIR Event-Data research proposal.

12. The event/action mapping sentence to be discussed below is clearly presented in Lasswell and Kaplan (1950), the basis for his teaching at Yale in the Law School and the Political Science Department in the 1950s and 1960s; I draw from the late version described in (Lasswell, 1971: 18-29). In my experience, his most analytically advanced, hermeneutically informed treatment of interpretive processes is McDougal, Lasswell, and Miller (1967), a book of 400 pages focused on the interpretive roles of politicians, lawyers, judges and citizens. Also of note is his late work with Zvi Namenwirth in analyzing American party platforms with a specially constructed "Lasswell Value Dictionary" and the General Inquirer computer content analysis system.

13. Despite their different vocabularies, the similarities in research orientation should be readily apparent to others who have taught both Weber and Lasswell in a philosophy of social science course. Compare for example, Weberian action theory and Lasswell's action/interaction schema presented below, or contrast the disciplined self-limitation of Lasswell's "policy science" and Weber's "Science as a Vocation."

   Although I do not know of a textually detailed study arguing this interpretation, I have stressed the deep similarities of Lasswell's "garrison state" developmental construct, Weber's "iron cage" prophecy, and Orwell's 1984 (Alker, 1989).

14. I use "action" (in the Weberian or Parsonian mold), "frame" (as technically developed by Goffman and Minsky), "schema" (in the Piagetian sense), "mapping sentence" (as used by Guttman), or "paradigm" (in the Mertonian sense), not because they are exactly equivalent, but in order to enlist the reader's prior understanding of the largely overlapping roles played by these scientific concepts in a rich variety of interpretively oriented social research programs. Jurgen Habermas (1984 and 1989) has written perhaps the most impressive published synthesis of these perspectives, fully cognizant of the communicative functions of speech acts and social conversation.

15. McDougal, Lasswell, and Miller (1967: 99 and fn. 71) argue that "the United Nations Charter and the practice in which it is applied in fact constitute a continuing, contemporary communication," suggesting its history-rich interpretation to be like that of the U.S. Constitution: "The goal for interpreting the Constitution which appears to be accepted in practice is that of the closest possible approximation to the contemporary expectations created in the general community by the entire flow of past communication from all constitution makers."

16. Mead's most enduring work is *Mind, Self and Society* (Mead, 1962). I use "communicative action," or the "conversational paradigm," growing out of and going beyond speech act theory, as ways of signaling a more complex conception of communicative social action than that of intentional, purposive action. Especially helpful in this regard is Habermas' discussion (1984: ch. 5).

17. For those with a strong behavioral or mathematical orientation but little knowledge of linguistics or computer science, as introductions to the revolutionary changes in formal language theory in the 1950s and 1960s, I have found especially helpful: Noam Chomsky and George Miller (1963), John R. Searle (1969), and David D. Clark (1983).

18. This quotation is from an especially well regarded textbook by Stephen C. Levinson (1983: 279). For social and political scientists interested in the content and role of news reports, such as those serving as bases for the DDIR effort, Teun van Dijk (1988) has an excellent introductory chapter on recent, socially and politically oriented text and discourse analysis. See also recently started journals like *Discourse and Society* (published by Sage in London and edited by Van Dijk) and *Argumentation* (with Frans H. van Eemeren a central editor, and active participation by a number of American "speech and communication" specialists).

19. For present purposes, four published articles most fully explicative of the archaeological sense of linguistic computation are Alker (1988b), Mallery, Hurwitz, and Duffy (1987), Winograd's (1985) amazingly prescient event-data focus, and Alker, Duffy, Hurwitz, and Mallery (1991: 97-126).

20. I should mention the comparative, software competition aspect of the "Third Message Understanding Conference," being held this year (1991) with DARPA support, under the auspices of Beth Sundheim at the Naval Ocean Systems Center, San Diego; for more details, contact sundheim@nosc.mil. Two very relevant reports of results are Lehnert and Sundheim (1991) and Lehnert et al. (1992).

21. John McCarthy, the principal inventor of LISP, and a founding father of Artificial Intelligence, has recently lectured at Harvard about an Elephant 2000 computer

language capable of speech actions ordering, promising, debiting, inquiring, justifying, etc., from one of its users to another, or to authoritative record data bases. He distributes a relevant bibliography and not yet citable draft paper on this subject. Because of its political subject matter, a very recent example of a related form of computational analysis of newspaper editorializing something not totally absent from the news pages of even our most authoritative sources is Sergio J. Alvarado (1990). Philip R. Cohen, Jerry Morgan, and Martha E. Pollack (1990) is an impressive summary of Stanford-Berkeley approaches to representing communicative actions. Despite its tremendous formal and linguistic acuity, the book downplays, like John McCarthy, certain pragmatic normative conditions, such as "sincerity conditions" affecting the reception of intentional communications.

22. Alker (1975). This citation is perhaps the earliest extended reference to the Abelson-Schank mode of computational text analysis in a mainline political science source. Among political scientists, Robert Axelrod, Mathew Bonham, and Michael Shapiro in the United States, and Victor Sergeev in the Soviet Union were working along somewhat similar lines at approximately the same time. Related work by Herbert Simon, J. Patrick Crecine, and others might also be mentioned.

23. Shank and Abelson (1977). As a thesis student of Michael Dyer's, whose thesis work was supervised by Wendy Lehnert, a student and collaborator of Schank and Abelson, Alvarado qualifies as a "great grandstudent" of Abelson and Schank.

24. It is worth noting that most of the simple Abelson and Schank structures, such as implication molecules, plans, themes and scripts, are constructed out of alternating action and state sequences. Hence DDIR/GEDS codings may require revised representations indicating plausibly appropriate enabling and consequential state descriptions. How difficult this problem is, is not now clear.

25. Schank and Riesbeck (1981). Particularly relevant to BCOW or SHERFACS "case style" event datasets are the program miniatures in Riesbeck and Schank (1989). Alternatively, Michael J. Pazzani (1990) has provided a Schank-influenced, publicly available OCCAM explanation-based learning software. A good reader, with many suggestive applications in what I have called the "precedential reasoning domain," is Kolodner and Riesbeck (1986).

26. An alternative approach, consistent with this intent, but not using Conceptual Dependency formalisms, is the rewriting of Abelson-Schank interpretive routines within the facilities of Ken Haase's Arlotje and Huh representational, parsing, and script-fitting capacities. Haase is developing educationally oriented interpretive software for use on MacIIci and Unix software systems; he teaches a course on "The Art of AI Programming" at the Media Lab at MIT. His approach has the additional advantage of having been extended to "case-based" and "explanation-based" domains. Dwain Mefford (1991) has made a convincing argument for the relevance of these representational and reasoning modeling approaches in international institutional domains.

27. An effort to redeploy software developed or adapted for present purposes to the UNIX/AIX environment of MIT's ATHENA project will be undertaken as well. But MSDOS/386 and Macintosh IIci environments may win out because of the greater frequency of their use by the relevant programmers.

REFERENCES

Alker, H. R., Jr. 1975. "Polimetrics: Its Descriptive Foundations." In Vol. 7 of *Handbook of Political Science*. Eds. Greenstein, F. and N. Polsby. 139-210. Reading, MA: Addison-Wesley.

___. 1984. "Historical Argumentation and Statistical Inference: Towards More Appropriate Logics for Historical Research." *Historical Methods* 17, 3 (Summer): 164-173 (plus Erratum on p. 270 of the next issue).

___. 1988a. "Bit Flows, Rewrites, Social Talk: Towards More Adequate Information Ontologies." Reprinted in *Between Rationality and Cognition*. Ed. Campanella, M. 237-256. Torino: Albert Meynier.

___. 1988b. "Toward Globalized Event-Data Research on Avoidable War." *DDIR Update* 3, 2 (October): 2-5.

___. 1989. "An Orwellian Lasswell for Today." In *The Orwellian Moment: Hindsight and Foresight in the Post-1984 World*. Eds. Savage, R. L., J. Combs and D. Nimmo. 131-155. Fayetteville: University of Arkansas Press.

Alker, H. R., Jr., G. Duffy, R. Hurwitz and J. C. Mallery. 1991. "Text Modeling for International Politics: A Tourist's Guide to RELATUS." In *Artificial Intelligence and International Politics*. Ed. Hudson, V. M. 97-126. Boulder: Westview Press.

Alvarado, S. J. 1990. *Understanding Editorial Text: A Computer Model of Argument Comprehension*. Boston: Kluwer Academic Publishers.

Bull, H. 1977. *The Anarchical Society*. New York: Columbia University Press.

Chomsky, N. and G. Miller. 1963. "Finite State Languages." In *Readings in Mathematical Psychology*. Eds. Luce, R. D., Bush, R. R., and E. Galanter. 156-171. Vol II. New York: John Wiley

Clarke, D. D. 1983. *Language and Action: A Structural Model of Behavior*. International Series in Experimental Social Psychology, 7. Oxford: Pergamon Press.

Cohen, P. R., J. Morgan and M. E. Pollack. 1990. *Intentions in Communication*. Cambridge, MA: MIT Press.

Habermas, J. 1984. *Theory of Communicative Action*. Vol. 1. Boston: Beacon Press.

___. 1989. *Theory of Communicative Action*. Vol. 2. Boston: Beacon Press.

Kolodner, J. L. and C. K. Riesbeck, Eds. 1986. *Experience, Memory & Reasoning*. Hillsdale, NJ: Erlbaum.

Kratochwil, F. 1989. *Rules, Norms, and Decisions: On the Conditions of Practical and Legal Reasoning in International Relations and Domestic Affairs*. New York: Cambridge University Press.

Lasswell, H. D. 1936. Politics: Who gets What, When, How. New York: McGraw-Hill.

___. 1971. *A Pre-View of Policy Sciences*. New York: Elsevier.

Lasswell, H. D. and M. A. Kaplan. 1950. *Power and Society*. New Haven: Yale University Press.

Lehnert, W., C. Cardie, D. Fisher, J. McCarthy, E. Riloff and S. Soderland. 1992. "University of Massachusetts: MUC-4 Test Results and Analysis." in *Proceedings of the Third Message Understanding Conference*. 151-158. San Mateo, CA: Morgan Kaufmann.

Lehnert, W. and B. Sundheim. 1991. "A Performance Evaluation of Text Analysis Technologies." *AI Magazine* 12, 3: 81-94.

Levinson, S. C. 1983. *Pragmatics*. Cambridge Textbooks in Linguistics. Cambridge, Eng.: Cambridge University Press.

Mallery, J., R. Hurwitzs and G. Duffy. 1987. "Hermeneutics." In Vol. 1 of *Encyclopedia of Artificial Intelligence*. Eds. Shapiro, S. C., Eckroth, D. and G. A. Vallasi. 362-376. New York: John Wiley.

McDougal, M. S., H. D. Lasswell and J. C. Miller. 1967. *The Interpretation of Agreements and World Public Order*. New Haven: Yale University Press.

Mead, G. H. 1962. *Mind, Self and Society*. Ed. Morris, C. Chicago: University of Chicago Press.

Mefford, D. 1991. "Steps Toward Artificial Intelligence: Rule-Based, Case-Based, and Explanation-Based Models of Politics." In *Artificial Intelligence and International Politics*. Ed. Hudson, V. M. 56-96. Boulder: Westview Press.

Merritt, R. L. 1990. "Data in International Research: Confluence of Interest and Possibility." *DDIR Update* 4, 3 (April): 1-11.

Moon, D. 1975. "The Logic of Political Inquiry: A Synthesis of Opposed Perspectives." In Vol. 1 of *Handbook of Political Science*. Eds. Greenstein, F. I. and N. W. Polsby. 131-228. Reading, MA: Addison-Wesley.

Pazzani, M. J. 1990. *Creating a Memory of Causal Relationships*. Hillsdale, NJ: Erlbaum.

Riesbeck, C. K. and R. C. Schank. 1989. *Inside Case-Based Reasoning*. Hillsdale, NJ: Erlbaum.

Schank, R. C. and R. P. Abelson. 1977. *Scripts, Plans, Goals and Understanding*. Hillsdale, NJ: Erlbaum.

Schank, R. C. and C. K. Riesbeck. 1981. *Inside Computer Understanding: Five Programs Plus Miniatures*. Hillsdale, NJ: Erlbaum.

Searle, J. R. 1969. *Speech Acts: An Essay in the Philosophy of Langauge*. New York: Cambridge University Press.

Taylor, C. F. and D. A. 1983. *World Handbook of Political and Social Indicators,* 3d ed. New Haven: Yale University Press.

van Dijk, T. 1988. *News Analysis: Case Studies of International and National News in the Press*. Hillsdale, NJ: Erlbaum.

Winograd, T. 1985. "Moving the Semantic Fulcrum." *Linguistics and Philosophy* 8, 1 (February): 91-104.

Yamani, S. A. 1974. Speech before Sixth Special Session of United Nations General Assembly.

CHAPTER 9

Through Rose-Colored Glasses: Computational Interpretations of Events

Steven Thomas Seitz

Abstract

This chapter outlines a strategy for the systematic analysis of textual material that differs from semantic parsing and hermeneutic contextualism. The strategy proposed here begins with libraries of interpretive frameworks (metaphors & parables) and works backward to the structuring of text streams. Although the volume of textual information is great indeed, a relatively small number of interpretive frameworks can cover much of the textual material of general interest to political scientists. An interpretive framework that meets the user's goodness-of-fit standards can, in turn, serve as the basis for generating projections that utilize dynamic components of each interpretive framework.

Textual materials have long occupied a pivotal position in the conduct of political research. Generations of political scientists before and scores of individuals following the behavioral revolution have argued that documents, speeches, statutes and other textual sources contain the raw materials of politics. Older generations have further argued that the only available tools for exploiting these resources were subjective textual exegesis, explication, and commentary. Behavioralists of the post-World War II era recognized the importance of textual documents while also recognizing the scientific limitations of subjective textual exegesis. Several alternate tools were proposed and employed as means for increasing the systematic and inter-subjectively verifiable use of such textual materials. Content analysis, especially the counting of key words in important texts, was one such tool. Another was the use of coding schemes to reduce textual materials to machine-readable data files. A more promising but as yet unrealized potential lay in machine-based semantic parsing and/or link list systems for analyzing ordinary language texts.

Much can be said about the difficulties associated with automated language parsing and meaning analysis. Some early problems could be attributed to technological limitations, but these are rapidly being addressed. The current generation of LISP-based machines, for example, provides considerable capacity to link words and lists of words to one another. Parallel processing, coupled with newer storage and retrieval systems, will exponentially expand these capacities. The newer technologies also give computational instance to neural networks and other biological metaphors.

Despite significant research in semantic parsing, computational progress is slow. There are considerable discrepancies between language-in-use and reconstructed grammars. More problematic is the often spurious connection between formal grammars, on the one hand, and tacit understanding, knowledge, and meaning, on the other hand. We still have much to learn about the role of language in the human production, storage, retrieval, and utilization of information. All told, it seems reasonable that it will be some time before either the contextualism of linked lists or the universality of semantic parsing will provide for the intersubjectively verifiable analysis of textual materials.

This paper explores an alternate strategy for improving the intersubjective analysis of textual data, rather than relying solely upon the less systematic and more idiosyncratic subjective textual exegesis. This approach assumes that there is a middle ground between a universal grammar of politics and particularistic meaning contexts. It assumes: (a) that all societies have organizing myths, (b) that these myths can be expressed in metaphors and parables, (c) that there are a finite number of such metaphors and parables shared by and communicated among members of a society, and (d) that a significant subset of these metaphors and parables have cross-cultural instantiations.

The proposed strategy begins with two steps already familiar in text stream analysis. First, a simple graph node system is used to differentiate strings of letters that compose "words." The computational procedure dynamically establishes self-propagating left and right children nodes until a "word" is formed by locating a null terminator. Second, the strategy identifies ordinary sets of words through ordinary language wordlinks such as "and" or "or." At the simplest level, therefore, the procedure breaks a text stream into words and then connects some of these words together when natural language connectors are present in the text stream. These two steps are essentially mechanical. Taken together, these two phases might be thought of as the text pre-processing stage.

The next two phases examine the structure of "meaning" in the preprocessed text. These two phases can be repeated several times to provide alternate "interpretations" of a given text stream. First, the preprocessed text stream is processed in light of one or more possible metaphors/parables. In the preprocessing stage, words are linked together through ordinary language connectors. In the processing stage, words and previously linked words are further linked "as if" the text was an instance of a metaphor/parable found in the "meaning library." Linking at this level is of course specific to interpretive framework, and hence different interpretive frameworks will link words and sets of words in different ways. The specific procedure, to be elaborated shortly, uses matrices for each interpretive framework (a) that link text words to primitives in terms of their fuzzy degree of membership and (b) that create "meaning hypersets" of text words-linked-to-primitives that reflect the "meaning" implicit in a given "interpretive framework." The procedure for building these "meaning hypersets" uses a simple engine of fuzzy inference and composition that captures the logic of each metaphor/parable.

In the second phase of the processing stage, the procedure assesses the "degree of fit" between the "interpretive framework" and the given text. This is essentially a check on the "as if" assumption from the first phase of the processing stage. We thus pass through the text "as if" it were an instance of a particular metaphor/parable and then check to see whether this "as if" assumption reasonably reflects the structure of the text. The system is designed to use a library of metaphors/parables. This means that several "as if" passes can be made over any preprocessed text stream.

The third stage is a post-processing stage. This stage occurs only if a metaphor/parable meets user defined standards of goodness-of-fit. In the first phase of the postprocessing stage, the mapping from words to primitives in the gateway matrix used in the processing stage can be updated in light of a successful fit. This provides for a dynamic "learning" in the gateway between incoming text stream and an interpretive framework in the "meaning library". In the second phase of postprocessing, event projections are made, based on what would appear to follow from this particular interpretive framework. These projections, in turn, can serve as the basis for further testing in a particular action domain from which the original text stream arose (e.g., what Saddam Hussein might be expected to do and to say next).

Only the preprocessing and processing stages will be discussed in this paper. Since the system is in its prototype stage, greater illustration will be drawn from the preprocessor stage. We will, however, demonstrate both the preprocessing and processing stage using the text of Saddam Hussein's speech on the withdrawal of his forces from Kuwait. The Hussein speech was chosen for several reasons. First, the translation was provided through the Foreign Broadcast Information Service (FBIS), which represents a large body of textual materials that have become available for scholarly analysis. Second, the translation is "rough" in the sense that the literal level of translation makes it difficult to easily read the metaphors Hussein uses in the speech. Indeed, several members of the press and of officialdom originally misunderstood this text. Third, the speech includes a complicated notion of time that is normally difficult to discern in semantic parsers.

We also will illustrate only one interpretive framework in this analysis, although the larger system from which this illustration is drawn has been designed to simultaneously fit and assess alternate interpretive frameworks. Our purposes here are more limited, namely, to illustrate how an appropriate "interpretive framework" can be used as a text analysis system. We thus leave what constitutes "appropriate" for another occasion. The same can be said for the automated updating of the parsing gateway and for the event projection flowing from an "appropriate" interpretive framework.

A final word is in order regarding the Hussein speech before we turn to the technical details. During the Gulf War, the President of the United States and the press in the United States interpreted Saddam Hussein's reference to "Mother of All Battles" to suggest a final showdown between the forces of good and evil.

This supposed Armageddon metaphor in Hussein's text led to a number of derisive remarks about Hussein and the Iraqi army, including one that suggested instead of the "Mother of All Battles," Iraq was engaged in the "Mother of All Retreats." We were working on the metaphor analysis program at the time this speech became available through the press, and we originally thought the speech would provide an instantiation of an Armageddon metaphor. We quickly learned, however, that the Armageddon metaphor did not fit the Hussein text. Upon closer review of the text, we discovered that the interpretation assigned to Hussein's speech was in fact wrong. It appears that Hussein was not using an Armageddon metaphor but a trials-and-tribulation metaphor. When we checked the latter metaphor against the speech, we found a very close fit. Nearly two weeks after the serendipitous discovery through our prototype metaphor analysis program, a series of articles began to appear in the *New York Times* and other major U.S. media sources that indicated a misinterpretation of the phrase "Mother of All Battles." In particular, the interpretation that seems to have been intended in the course of the speech was that the land war undertaken by the United States was the greatest in a series of trials put before the Iraqi people. Weathering these successive trials and tribulations today would "prove" the Iraqi people in the eyes of God, thus gain God's favor in a future but final confrontation between the forces of good and evil. Contrast that meeting to an interpretation that would describe the land war as the final confrontation between the forces of good and evil.

The Text Stream

The following text is a FBIS translation of Saddam Hussein's address to the Iraqi people on the withdrawal of his forces from Kuwait. This text stream serves as the basis for the discussion in the sections that follow.

Saddam Hussein's Speech on the "Withdrawal" of His Army From Kuwait

In the name of God, the merciful, the compassionate.

O great people; O stalwart men in the forces of holy war and faith, glorious men of the mother of battles; O zealous, faithful and sincere people in our glorious nations, and among all Muslims and all virtuous people in the world; O glorious Iraqi women:

In such circumstances and times, it is difficult to talk about all that which should be talked about, and it is difficult to recall all that which has to be recalled. Despite this, we have to remind of what has to be reminded of, and say part — a principal part — of what should be said.

We start by saying that on this day, our valiant armed forces will complete their withdrawal from Kuwait. And on this day our fight against aggression and the ranks of infidelity, joined in an ugly coalition comprising 30 countries, which officially entered war against us under the leadership of the United States of America — our fight against them would have lasted from the first month of this year, starting with the night of 16-17 [January], until this moment in the current month, February of this year.

It was an epic duel which lasted for two months, which came to clearly confirm a lesson that God has wanted as a prelude of faith, impregnability and capability for the faithful, and a prelude of an [abyss], weakness and humiliation which God Almighty has wanted for the infidels, the criminals, the traitors, the corrupt and the deviators.

To be added to this time is the time of the military and nonmilitary duel, including the military and economic blockade, which was imposed on Iraq and which lasted throughout 1990 until today, and until the time God Almighty wishes it to last.

Before that, the duel lasted, in other forms, for years before this period of time. It was an epic struggle between right and wrong; we have talked about this in detail on previous occasions.

It gave depth to the age of the showdown for the year 1990, and the already elapsed part of the year 1991.

Hence, we do not forget, because we will not forget this great struggling spirit, by which men of great faith stormed the fortifications and the weapons of deception and the Croesus [Kuwaiti rulers] treachery on the honorable day of the call. They did what they did within the context of legitimate deterrence and great principled action.

All that we have gone through or decided within its circumstances, obeying God's will and choosing a position of faith and chivalry, is a record of honor, the significance of which will not be missed by the people and nation and the values of Islam and humanity.

Their days will continue to be glorious and their past and future will continue to relate the story of a faithful, jealous and patient people, who believed in the will of God and in the values and stands accepted by the Almighty for the Arab nation in its leading role and for the Islamic nation in the essentials of its true faith and how they should be.

These values — which had their effect in all those situations, offered the sacrifices they had offered in the struggle, and symbolized the depth of the faithful character in Iraq — will continue to leave their effects on the souls.

They will continue to reap their harvest, not only in terms of direct targets represented in the slogans of their age — whether in the conflict between the oppressed poor and the unjust and opportunist rich, or between faith and blasphemy, or between injustice, deception and treachery on the one hand and fairness, justice, honesty and loyalty on the other — but also the indirect targets as well.

This will shake the opposite ranks and cause them to collapse after everything has become clear. This will also add faith to the faithful now that the minds and eyes have been opened and the hearts are longing for what the principles, values and stances should long for and belong to.

The stage that preceded the great day of the call on 2 August 1990 had its own standards, including dealing with what is familiar and inherited during the bad times, whether on the level of relations between the ruler and the ruled, or between the leader and the people he leads.

The relations between the foreigners among the ranks of infidelity and oppression and among the region's states and the world had their own standards, effects and privileges that were created by the Arab homeland's circumstances, and which were facilitated by propaganda, which no one could expose more than it has now been exposed.

The conflict was exacerbated by the vacuum that was created by the weaknesses of one of the two poles that used to represent the two opposite lines in the world. However, after the second of August 1990, new concepts and standards were created.

This was preceded by a new outlook in all walks of life, in the relations among peoples, relations among states, and the relations between the ruler and the ruled, and by standards of faith and positions; patriotism, pan-Arabism, and humanitarianism; holy war, faith, Islam, fear and non-fear; restlessness and tranquility; manhood and its opposite; struggle, holy war and sacrifice, and readiness to do good things and their opposite.

When new measures spring forth and the familiar, failed, traitorous, subservient and corrupt [people], and tyrants are rejected, then the opportunity for the cultivation of the pure soil will increase in its scope, and the seeds of this plant will take root deep in the good land, primarily, the land of the Arabs, the land of the revelation and the messages, and the land of prophets.

God says: "Like a goodly tree, whose root is firmly fixed, and its branches reach to the heavens. It brings forth its fruit at all times, by the leave of its Lord." [Koranic verses]

Then everything will become possible on the road of goodness and happiness that is not defiled by the feet of the invaders nor by their evil will or the corruption of the corrupt among those who have been corrupted, and who spread corruption in the land of the Arabs.

Moreover, the forces of plotting and treachery will be defeated for good. Good people and those who are distinguished by their faith and by their faithful, honorable stands of holy war will become the real leaders of the gathering of the faithful everywhere on earth, and the gathering of corruption, falsehood, hypocrisy and infidelity will be defeated and meet the vilest fate.

The earth will be inherited, at God's order, by His righteous slaves. "For the earth is God's, to give as a heritage to such of his servants as he pleaseth; and the end is best for the righteous." [Koranic verses]

When this happened, the near objectives will not only be within reach, available and possible, but also the doors will be open without any hindrance which might prevent the achievement of all the greater, remoter and more comprehensive objectives, to the Arabs, Muslims and humanity at large.

Then, also, it will be clear that the harvest does not precede the seeding, and that the threshing floor and the yield are the outcome of a successful seeding and a successful harvest.

The harvest in the mother of battles has succeeded. After we have harvested what we have harvested, the greater harvest and its yield will be in the time to come, and it will be much greater than what we have at present, in spite of what we have at present in terms of the victory, dignity and glory that was based on the sacrifices of a deep faith which is generous without any hesitation or fear.

It is by virtue of this faith that God has bestowed dignity upon the Iraqi mujahedeen, and upon all the depth of this course of holy war at the level of the Arab homeland and at the level of all those men whom God has chosen to be given the honor of allegiance, guidance and honorable position, until He declares that the conflict has stopped, or amends its directions and course and the positions in a manner which would please the faithful and increase their dignity.

O valiant Iraqi men, O glorious Iraqi women. Kuwait is part of your country and was carved from it in the past.

Circumstances today have willed that it remain in the state in which it will remain after the withdrawal of our struggling forces from it. It hurts you that this should happen.

We rejoiced on the day of the call when it was decided that Kuwait should be one of the main gates for deterring the plot and for defending all Iraq from the plotters. We say that we will remember Kuwait on the great day of the call, on the days that followed it, and in documents and events, some of which date back 70 years.

The Iraqis will remember and will not forget that on 8 August, 1990, Kuwait became part of Iraq legally, constitutionally and actually. They remember and will not forget that it remained throughout this period from 8 August 1990 and until last night, when withdrawal began, and today we will complete withdrawal of our forces, God willing.

Today certain circumstances made the Iraqi Army withdraw as a result of the ramifications which we mentioned, including the combined aggression by 30 countries. Their repugnant siege has been led in evil and aggression by the machine and the criminal entity of America and its major allies.

These malicious ranks took the depth and effectiveness of their aggressiveness not only from their aggressive premeditated intentions against Iraq, the Arab nation and Islam, but also from the position of those who were deceived by the claim of international legitimacy. Everyone will remember that the gates of Constantinople were not opened before the Muslims in the first struggling attempt, and that the international community [placed] dear Palestine's freedom and independence in oblivion.

Whatever the suspect parties try, by virtue of the sacrifices and struggle of the Palestinians and Iraqis, Palestine has returned anew to knock at the doors closed on evil.

Palestine returned to knock on those doors to force the tyrants and the traitors to a solution that would place it at the forefront of the issues that have to be resolved; a solution that would bring dignity to its people and provide better chances for better progress.

The issue of poverty and richness, fairness and unfairness, faith and infidelity, treachery and honesty and sincerity, have become titles corresponding to rare events and well-known people and trends that give priority to what is positive over what is negative, to what is sincere over what is treacherous and filthy, and to what is pure and honorable over what is corrupt, base and lowly. The confidence of the nationalists and the faithful mujahedeen and the Muslims has grown bigger than before, and great hope more and more.

Slogans have come out of their stores to strongly occupy the facades of the pan-Arab and human holy war struggle. Therefore, victory is [great] now and in the future, God willing.

Shout for victory, O brothers; shout for your victory and the victory of all honorable people, O Iraqis. You have fought 30 countries, and all the evil and the largest machine of war and destruction in the world that surrounds them. If only one of these countries threatens anyone, this threat will have a swift and direct effect on the dignity, freedom, life, or freedom of this or that country, people and nation.

The soldiers of faith have triumphed over the soldiers of wrong, O stalwart men. Your God is the one who granted your victory. You have triumphed when you rejected, in the name of faith, the will of evil which the evildoers wanted to impose on you to kill the fire of faith in your hearts.

You have chosen the path which you have chosen, including the acceptance of the Soviet initiative, but these evildoers persisted in their path and methods, thinking that they can impose their will on their Iraq, as they imagined and hoped.

This hope of theirs may remain in their heads, even after we withdraw from Kuwait. Therefore, we must be cautious, and preparedness to fight must remain at the highest level.

O you valiant men; you have fought the armies of 30 states and the capabilities of an even greater number of states which supplied them with the means of aggression and support. Faith, belief, hope and determination continue to fill your chests, souls and hearts.

They have even become deeper, stronger, brighter and more deeply rooted. God is great; God is great; may the lowly be defeated.

Victory is sweet with the help of God.

Preprocessing the Text

The first phase of the preprocessing stage begins by representing each letter of the alphabet (and other ascii characters as well) as a node in a graph. Letters following this first letter become list linked to second nodes, further letters become further nodes, until a graph branch reaches a null terminator, meaning that there are no more characters except a white space read as a null terminator on the character string. The characters from start to null terminator are "words." The illustrations that follow start with the second node, namely, two characters together. (For our purposes, the graph below is functionally equivalent to the actual link list system used. The fully elaborated link list system is more difficult to depict in a small illustration.) The extract found in table 9.1 is part of the accounting trace produced by the computer program.

The numbers in brackets following the word nodes and words in table 9.1 reflect the frequency count for that particular set of letters. Thus for example, in the first and second line of table 9.1, the word "about" has three occurrences at the node ABO and there are three words that contain ABO. In this particular case, the word about accounts for the three frequencies at the ABO node and also accounts for the three words containing the sequence ABO.

We shall look at the root "ac" drawn from the sample output table above. At root "ac," as calculated from the Hussein text, there are five derivative words:

TABLE 9.1. Nodes and Words: Letters A through B

```
Root = ab
     about      Nodes[3]     Words[3]
     abyss      Nodes[1]     Words[1]
     Root = abo
           about      Nodes[3]     Words[3]
     Root = aby
           abyss      Nodes[1]     Words[1]
Root = ac
     acceptance     Nodes[1]     Words[1]
     accepted     Nodes[1]     Words[1]
     achievement     Nodes[1]     Words[1]
     action     Nodes[1]     Words[1]
     actually     Nodes[1]     Words[1]
     Root = acc
           acceptance     Nodes[1]     Words[1]
           accepted     Nodes[1]     Words[1]
           Root = acce
                 acceptance     Nodes[1]     Words[1]
                 accepted     Nodes[1]     Words[1]
                 Root = accep
                       acceptance     Nodes[1]     Words[1]
                       accepted     Nodes[1]     Words[1]
                       Root = accept
                             acceptance     Nodes[1]     Words[1]
                             accepted     Nodes[1]     Words[1]
                             Root = accepta
                                   acceptance     Nodes[1]     Words[1]
                             Root = accepte
                                   accepted     Nodes[1]     Words[1]
     Root = ach
           achievement     Nodes[1]     Words[1]
     Root = act
           action     Nodes[1]     Words[1]
           actually     Nodes[1]     Words[1]
           Root = acti
                 action     Nodes[1]     Words[1]
           Root = actu
                 actually     Nodes[1]     Words[1]
Root = ad
     add     Nodes[2]     Words[1]
     added     Nodes[1]     Words[1]
     Root = add
           add     Node Count[2]     Whole Word Count[1]
           added     Nodes[1]     Words[1]
           Root = adde
                 added     Nodes[1]     Words[1]
Root = af
     after     Nodes[5]     Words[5]
```

(Continued)

TABLE 9.1. **Continued**

Root = ag
    against   Nodes[4]   Words[4]
    age   Nodes[2]   Words[2]
    aggression   Nodes[4]   Words[4]
    aggressive   Nodes[2]   Words[1]
    aggressiveness   Nodes[1]   Words[1]
    Root = aga
        against   Nodes[4]   Words[4]
    Root = age
        age   Node Count[2]   Whole Word Count[2]
    Root = agg
        aggression   Nodes[4]   Words[4]
        aggressive   Nodes[2]   Words[1]
        aggressiveness   Nodes[1]   Words[1]
        Root = aggr
            aggression   Nodes[4]   Words[4]
            aggressive   Nodes[2]   Words[1]
            aggressiveness   Nodes[1]   Words[1]
            Root = aggre
                aggression   Nodes[4]   Words[4]
                aggressive   Nodes[2]   Words[1]
                aggressiveness   Nodes[1]   Words[1]
                Root = aggres
                    aggression   Nodes[4]   Words[4]
                    aggressive   Nodes[2]   Words[1]
                    aggressiveness   Nodes[1]   Words[1]
                    Root = aggress
                        aggression   Nodes[4]   Words[4]
                        aggressive   Nodes[2]   Words[1]
                        aggressiveness   Nodes[1]   Words[1]
                        Root = aggressi
                            aggression   Nodes[4]   Words[4]
                            aggressive   Nodes[2]   Words[1]
                            aggressiveness   Nodes[1]   Words[1]
                            Root = aggressio
                                aggression   Nodes[4]   Words[4]
                            Root = aggressiv
                                aggressive   Nodes[2]   Words[1]
                                aggressiveness   Nodes[1]   Words[1]
                                Root = aggressive
                                    aggressive Node Count[2] Whole Word Count[1]
                                    aggressiveness   Nodes[1]   Words[1]
                                  Root = aggressiven
                                      aggressiveness   Nodes[1]   Words[1]
Root = al
    all   Nodes[16]   Words[14]
    allegiance   Nodes[1]   Words[1]
    allies   Nodes[1]   Words[1]
    almighty   Nodes[3]   Words[3]

TABLE 9.1. Continued

```
        already    Nodes[1]    Words[1]
        also    Nodes[5]    Words[5]
    Root = all
            all    Node Count[16]    Whole Word Count[14]
            allegiance    Nodes[1]    Words[1]
            allies    Nodes[1]    Words[1]
            Root = alle
                allegiance    Nodes[1]    Words[1]
            Root = alli
                allies    Nodes[1]    Words[1]
        Root = alm
            almighty    Nodes[3]    Words[3]
        Root = alr
            already    Nodes[1]    Words[1]
        Root = als
            also    Nodes[5]    Words[5]
Root = am
    amends    Nodes[1]    Words[1]
    america    Nodes[2]    Words[2]
    among    Nodes[6]    Words[6]
    Root = ame
        amends    Nodes[1]    Words[1]
        america    Nodes[2]    Words[2]
        Root = amen
            amends    Nodes[1]    Words[1]
        Root = amer
            america    Nodes[2]    Words[2]
    Root = amo
        among    Nodes[6]    Words[6]
Root = an
    and    Nodes[148]    Words[148]
    anew    Nodes[1]    Words[1]
    any    Nodes[3]    Words[2]
    anyone    Nodes[1]    Words[1]
    Root = and
        and    Node Count[148]    Whole Word Count[148]
    Root = ane
        anew    Nodes[1]    Words[1]
    Root = any
        any    Node Count[3]    Whole Word Count[2]
        anyone    Nodes[1]    Words[1]
        Root = anyo
            anyone    Nodes[1]    Words[1]
Root = ar
    arab    Nodes[7]    Words[4]
    arabs    Nodes[3]    Words[3]
    are    Nodes[4]    Words[4]
    armed    Nodes[1]    Words[1]
    armies    Nodes[1]    Words[1]
```

(*Continued*)

TABLE 9.1. Continued

```
    army    Nodes[1]    Words[1]
    Root = ara
        arab    Nodes[7]    Words[4]
        arabs   Nodes[3]    Words[3]
        Root = arab
            arab    Node Count[7]    Whole Word Count[4]
            arabs   Nodes[3]    Words[3]
            Root = arabs
                arabs    Node Count[3]    Whole Word Count[3]
    Root = are
        are    Node Count[4]    Whole Word Count[4]
    Root = arm
        armed    Nodes[1]    Words[1]
        armies   Nodes[1]    Words[1]
        army    Nodes[1]    Words[1]
        Root = arme
            armed    Nodes[1]    Words[1]
        Root = armi
            armies    Nodes[1]    Words[1]
        Root = army
            army    Node Count[1]    Whole Word Count[1]
Root = as
    as    Node Count[6]    Whole Word Count[6]
Root = at
    at    Node Count[11]    Whole Word Count[10]
    attempt    Nodes[1]    Words[1]
    Root = att
        attempt    Nodes[1]    Words[1]
Root = au
    august    Nodes[4]    Words[4]
Root = av
    available    Nodes[1]    Words[1]
Root = ba
    back    Nodes[1]    Words[1]
    bad     Nodes[1]    Words[1]
    base    Nodes[2]    Words[1]
    based   Nodes[1]    Words[1]
    battles    Nodes[2]    Words[2]
    Root = bac
        back    Nodes[1]    Words[1]
    Root = bad
        bad    Node Count[1]    Whole Word Count[1]
    Root = bas
        base    Nodes[2]    Words[1]
        based   Nodes[1]    Words[1]
        Root = base
            base    Node Count[2]    Whole Word Count[1]
            based    Nodes[1]    Words[1]
```

TABLE 9.1. Continued

```
                  Root = based
                          based    Node Count[1]    Whole Word Count[1]
          Root = bat
                  battles    Nodes[2]    Words[2]
Root = be
          be    Node Count[52]    Whole Word Count[21]
          became    Nodes[1]    Words[1]
          because    Nodes[1]    Words[1]
          become    Nodes[5]    Words[5]
          been    Nodes[4]    Words[4]
          before    Nodes[4]    Words[4]
          began    Nodes[1]    Words[1]
          belief    Nodes[1]    Words[1]
          believed    Nodes[1]    Words[1]
          belong    Nodes[1]    Words[1]
          best    Nodes[2]    Words[1]
          bestowed    Nodes[1]    Words[1]
          better    Nodes[2]    Words[2]
          between    Nodes[8]    Words[8]
          Root = bec
                  became    Nodes[1]    Words[1]
                  because    Nodes[1]    Words[1]
                  become    Nodes[5]    Words[5]
                  Root = beca
                          became    Nodes[1]    Words[1]
                          because    Nodes[1]    Words[1]
                          Root = becam
                                  became    Nodes[1]    Words[1]
                          Root = becau
                                  because    Nodes[1]    Words[1]
                  Root = beco
                          become    Nodes[5]    Words[5]
          Root = bee
                  been    Nodes[4]    Words[4]
          Root = bef
                  before    Nodes[4]    Words[4]
          Root = beg
                  began    Nodes[1]    Words[1]
          Root = bel
                  belief    Nodes[1]    Words[1]
                  believed    Nodes[1]    Words[1]
                  belong    Nodes[1]    Words[1]
                  Root = beli
                          belief    Nodes[1]    Words[1]
                          believed    Nodes[1]    Words[1]
                          Root = belie
                                  belief    Nodes[1]    Words[1]
                                  believed    Nodes[1]    Words[1]
```

(Continued)

TABLE 9.1.   Continued

```
                    Root = belief
                        belief     Node Count[1]     Whole Word Count[1]
                    Root = believ
                        believed     Nodes[1]     Words[1]
          Root = belo
              belong     Nodes[1]     Words[1]
    Root = bes
        best     Nodes[2]     Words[1]
        bestowed     Nodes[1]     Words[1]
        Root = best
            best     Node Count[2]     Whole Word Count[1]
            bestowed     Nodes[1]     Words[1]
            Root = besto
                bestowed     Nodes[1]     Words[1]
    Root = bet
        better     Nodes[2]     Words[2]
        between     Nodes[8]     Words[8]
        Root = bett
            better     Nodes[2]     Words[2]
        Root = betw
            between     Nodes[8]     Words[8]
Root = bi
    bigger     Nodes[1]     Words[1]
Root = bl
    blasphemy     Nodes[1]     Words[1]
    blockade     Nodes[1]     Words[1]
    Root = bla
        blasphemy     Nodes[1]     Words[1]
    Root = blo
        blockade     Nodes[1]     Words[1]
Root = br
    branches     Nodes[1]     Words[1]
    brighter     Nodes[1]     Words[1]
    bring     Nodes[2]     Words[1]
    brings     Nodes[1]     Words[1]
    brothers     Nodes[1]     Words[1]
    Root = bra
        branches     Nodes[1]     Words[1]
    Root = bri
        brighter     Nodes[1]     Words[1]
        bring     Nodes[2]     Words[1]
        brings     Nodes[1]     Words[1]
        Root = brig
            brighter     Nodes[1]     Words[1]
        Root = brin
            bring     Nodes[2]     Words[1]
            brings     Nodes[1]     Words[1]
            Root = bring
```

TABLE 9.1. Continued

bring	Node Count[2]	Whole Word Count[1]
brings	Nodes[1]	Words[1]
Root = brings		
brings	Node Count[1]	Whole Word Count[1]
Root = bro		
brothers	Nodes[1]	Words[1]
Root = bu		
but	Nodes[4]	Words[4]
Root = by		
by	Node Count[21]	Whole Word Count[21]

acceptance, accepted, achievement, action, and actually. Three nodes flow from "ac": "acc," "ach," "act." From node "acc" an additional "acce" node follows, then "accep," then "accept," after which the two derivative words are uniquely identified by "accepta" and "accepte." No further branching is needed to reach null terminators for "acceptance" and "accepted." From node "ach" only one unique word flow, namely "achievement." Finally, from node "act" flows two subnodes, "acti" and "actu." At those subnodes "action" and "actually" are uniquely identified. A simple flow chart depicts this node system for "ac" (figure 9.1).

The second phase of text preprocessing involves the creation of word sets using ordinary language connectors. These connectors work much like the connectors in Boolean logic. Consider the use of "and" in an English sentence, linking predecessor and successor words. The Hussein text has 148 occurrences of "and." The resulting word links are illustrated in the following link lists for the "and" node in the word graph.

The lists linked together in table 9.2 are lists of letters linked to other lists of letters with the word and. In the second paragraph of Hussein's speech, for example, the phrase occurs "Oh zealous, faithful and sincere people in our glorious nations." In this instance the word "faithful" is linked with its predecessor word, "zealous" and both, in turn, are linked to the successor words "sincere" "people" through the node word "and," thus "oh zealous, faithful and sincere people" now has two words "faithful" and "sincere" linked with each other as well as their antecedent words in the text stream.

Processing the Text

The mechanical phases in the pre-processing stage have provided words and sets of words for subsequent analysis. The first phase of the processing stage must tackle a more difficult problem, namely, determining what-words-goes-with-

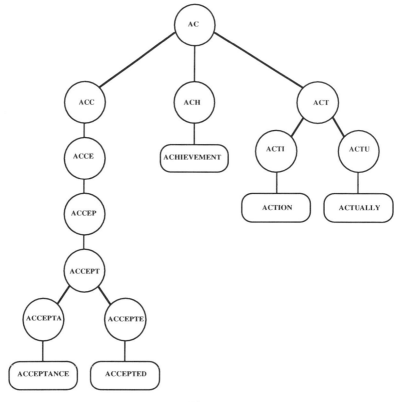

Fig. 9.1

what. We shall not search for universal principles linking words together through semantic parsing; nor shall we rely upon brute mechanical repetition to train machines to recognize "similarity sets" within an otherwise amorphous stream of words. Both of these approaches essentially attempt to solve the "what-goes-with-what" problem in order to facilitate "meaning analysis," or why "this-goes-with-that."

Recall our basic assumptions: (a) that all societies have organizing myths, (b) that these myths can be expressed in metaphors and parables, (c) that there are a finite number of such metaphors and parables shared by and communicated among members of a society, and (d) that a significant subset of these metaphors and parables have cross-cultural instantiations. Instead of solving the "what-goes-with-what" problem in order to facilitate study of "why-this-goes-with-that," we feel justified in reversing the process, namely, using possible answers to "why-this-goes-with-that," as a basis for determining "what-goes-with-what." This approach presumes the existence of alternate interpretive frameworks through which to analyze text streams. Indeed, our larger project is designed to contain libraries of such interpretive frameworks. (A system that could generate alternate interpretive frameworks or hybridize existing interpretive frameworks would render this strategy far more general.) Although less general than a universal semantic parser, if such a universal device is indeed possible, our proposed use of alternate interpretive frameworks is more general than the

TABLE 9.2. Graph Node "And": Boolean Links

and   general   0.5000   Node Count[148]   Whole Word Count [148]

faithful : zealous	for : long	belong : to
sincere : people	increase : their	familiar : is
among : all	was : carved	among : region's
all : virtuous	for : defending	which : were
about : talked	it : followed	concepts : new
it : is	in : documents	standards : were
of : reminded	documents : in	by : standards
on	evil : in	positions : patriotism
on : day	machine : by	tranquility : manhood
ranks : of	its : major	manhood : tranquility
impregnability : faith	depth : took	its : opposite
faithful : for	effectivness : of	readiness : to
weakness : abyss	islam : but	things : good
corrupt : traitors	that : international	familiar : failed
economic : blockade	independence : in	subservient : traitorous
which : lasted	provide : better	corrupt : people
right : between	richness : fairness	scope : its
wrong : we	sincerity : have	land : of
weapons : of	well-known : people	its : branches
great : principled	filthy : and	goodness : of
values : of	filthy : and	corrupted : been
islam : of	to : what	by : their
glorious : be	pure : is	earth : on
in : values	faithful : mujahedeen	end : is
values : in	great : hope	available : reach
for : islamic	more : hope	possible : but
how : they	human : holy	more : comprehensive
unjust : and	in : future	that : threshing
unjust : and	all : evil	floor : threshing
hand : one	evil : all	its : yield
ranks : opposite	largest : machine	come : to
cause : them	path : their	it : will
minds : that	imagined : they	dignity : victory
eyes : have	hope : belief	upon : all
hearts : are	brighter : stronger	at : level
values : principles	more : deeply	directions : its
		positions : in
		faithful : please

knowledge base associated with the idiosyncratic "machine learning" underlying "inheritance" (link-list) learning systems.

We shall use "interpretive frameworks" (i.e., metaphors/parables) as statements of "why-this-goes-with-that." We introduce a sample framework below. Using that framework, in turn, we shall illustrate how such an interpretive framework can be used to guide answers to "what-goes-with-what" in the word stream from the preprocessing stage.

Interpretive Framework: Trials and Tribulations

In the biblical book of Genesis, God is said to have tested Abraham by asking him to sacrifice his son Isaac as a burnt offering. When Abraham had constructed the wooden alter, laid his son Isaac upon it, and drew his knife for the sacrifice, an angel of the Lord called to him to stop the proceedings, for Abraham had demonstrated his fear of God through his willingness to offer his only son Isaac. The angel of the Lord is then said to have called a second time, telling Abraham that, because he had been willing to follow the command of God, the Lord would greatly bless Abraham, greatly multiply his seed, and promise that Abraham's seed would possess the gate of their enemies.

This is an organizing myth of considerable power, in part because it applies regardless of the outcome of human struggles. (Like the myth of pink elephants, it cannot be falsified.) In essence, God's calling creates a test for the believer, and associated with that test is some evil threat. Successful struggle means immediate reward and the defeat of evil. Unsuccessful struggle sows the seed for future struggles which, in turn, will result in reward for the chosen and the defeat of evil. Figure 9.2 shows this in simple schematic form.

Trials and Tribulations: Primitives

We use five primitives for representing the Trials and Tribulations interpretive framework. These are: Actor, Act, Consequence, Time, and Context. In the Biblical mythology of human struggles, there typically are forces for good and forces for evil, with God representing the purest form of the good and Satan representing the purest form of evil. If we represent Actor as a single fuzzy set, membership can be typologized in the following manner:

Actor

$f(Actor) = 1.0$	God
$0.5 < f(Actor) < 1.0$	forces for good
$f(actor) = 0.5$	unclear
$0.0 < f(Actor) < 0.5$	forces of evil
$f(Actor) = 0.0$	Satan

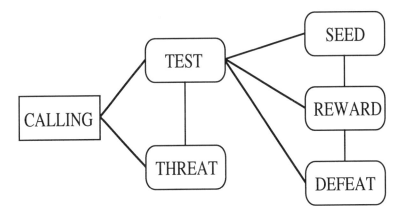

Fig. 9.2

A similar membership structure can be assigned to Acts:

Act

f(Act) = 1.0	Calling
0.5 < f(Act) < 1.0	test
f(Act) = 0.5	unclear
0.0 < f(Act) < 0.5	threat
f(Act) = 0.0	Temptation

Actions lead to consequences, and in this interpretive framework, those consequences are understood ultimately in terms of Godly Rewards and Satanic Defeats. Thus:

Consequences

f(Consequence) = 1.0	Reward by God
0.5 < f(Consequence) < 1.0	victory & harvest
f(Consequence) = 0.5	unclear
0.0 < f(Consequence) < 0.5	tribulations but seeds sown
f(Consequence) = 0.0	Defeat of Satan

Two other primitives add richness and power to the simple trials-and-tribulations mythology. The first is Time, which, for example, might allow tribulations to be seen as today's contributions to tomorrow's victories. Thus:

Time

f(Time) = 1.0	End of Time
0.5 < f(Time) < 1.0	future
f(Time) = 0.5	present
0.0 < f(Time) < 0.5	past
f(Time) = 0.0	Beginning of Time

The final primitive is Context. This provides for greater sophistication, because a seeming tribulation in one context can then be read as a victory in another context. An illustration of this phenomenon would be Hussein's effort to link the Kuwait context to the Palestinian context. Thus:

Context

f(Context) = 1.0	Will of God
0.5 < f(Context) < 1.0	favorable
f(Context) = 0.5	unclear
0.0 < f(Context) < 0.5	struggle
f(Context) = 0.0	Deception of Satan

Trials and Tribulations: Gateway

We have introduced the Trials and Tribulations interpretive framework and its associated primitives as a basis for better understanding the text processing stage where "why-this-goes-with-that" determines "what-words-goes-with-what." Before we introduce the system for mapping between words and meaning, we briefly highlight some relevant features of fuzzy sets. Recall that fuzzy set memberships range from 0.0 to 1.0, with the former being the set complement of the latter. At 0.5, therefore, an element's degree of membership in a set is the same as its degree of membership in the set complement. To illustrate, if set A represents the quality "blue," then ~A is the quality "not blue." If element (a) has a degree of membership in A above 0.5, the element has more of the quality "blue" than "not blue." At fuzzy membership 0.5, however, element (a) has a special ambiguity with respect to the quality "blue."

The gateway linking interpretive frameworks and words drawn from the preprocessed text stream is a matrix of words from the text stream with some fuzzy degree of membership in one or more of the primitives in a given interpretive framework. Thus, for example, the word "abyss" drawn from the Hussein speech has a fuzzy membership in the "trials-and-tribulations" primitive labeled "consequence." In the special case where a "word" has membership in all "trials-and-tribulations" primitives, the "word" is said to have generic or undifferentiated applicability for that interpretive framework. General words (listed as general in the second column of table 9.3) are set to fuzzy memberships of 0.5 in all primitives in the interpretive framework. Other words have varying degrees of fuzzy membership in their corresponding primitive.

The larger system from which this illustration is drawn uses a semi-automated process for establishing the fuzzy membership of words vis-à-vis primitives. The system does require an initial seeding or initial data base. The design utilizes automated updating once the initial seeding is complete. Elaboration of these procedures must be left for later exposition and are, in any event, secondary to the general strategy being illustrated here. Although the semi-automated and automated procedures are much faster, the same work can be accomplished by human coders who have become familiar with a particular interpretive framework. Table 9.3 is an initial matrix seeding for the trials-and-tribulations framework. It shows how "primitives" in an "interpretive framework" are associated with each null-terminated node.

Trials and Tribulations: Linking Rules

We will start the linking process with the "general words" found in the gateway segment (A-B) in table 9.3. What we are about to do is computationally build

TABLE 9.3. Gateway Matrix

Word	Primitive	f( )	NodeCnt	WordCnt
about	general	0.5000	Nodes[3]	Words[3]
abyss	consequence	0.1000	Nodes[1]	Words[1]
acceptance	act	0.7000	Nodes[1]	Words[1]
accepted	act	0.7000	Nodes[1]	Words[1]
achievement	consequence	0.7000	Nodes[1]	Words[1]
action	act	0.5000	Nodes[1]	Words[1]
actually	general	0.5000	Nodes[1]	Words[1]
add	act	0.5000	Nodes[2]	Words[1]
added	act	0.5000	Nodes[1]	Words[1]
after	time	0.7000	Nodes[5]	Words[5]
against	general	0.5000	Nodes[4]	Words[4]
age	time	0.5000	Nodes[2]	Words[2]
aggression	act	0.3000	Nodes[4]	Words[4]
aggressive	act	0.3000	Nodes[2]	Words[1]
aggressiveness	act	0.3000	Nodes[1]	Words[1]
all	general	0.5000	Nodes[16]	Words[14]
allegiance	act	0.7000	Nodes[1]	Words[1]
allies	actor	0.5000	Nodes[1]	Words[1]
almighty	actor	1.0000	Nodes[3]	Words[3]
already	time	0.3000	Nodes[1]	Words[1]
also	general	0.5000	Nodes[5]	Words[5]

(Continued)

TABLE 9.3. Continued

Word	Primitive	f( )	NodeCnt	WordCnt
amends	act	0.5000	Nodes[1]	Words[1]
america	actor	0.1000	Nodes[2]	Words[2]
among	general	0.5000	Nodes[6]	Words[6]
and	general	0.5000	Nodes[148]	Words[148]
anew	time	0.5000	Nodes[1]	Words[1]
any	general	0.5000	Nodes[3]	Words[2]
anyone	actor	0.5000	Nodes[1]	Words[1]
arab	actor	0.5000	Nodes[7]	Words[4]
arabs	actor	0.5000	Nodes[3]	Words[3]
are	general	0.5000	Nodes[4]	Words[4]
armed	act	0.5000	Nodes[1]	Words[1]
armies	actor	0.5000	Nodes[1]	Words[1]
army	actor	0.5000	Nodes[1]	Words[1]
as	general	0.5000	Nodes[6]	Words[6]
at	general	0.5000	Nodes[11]	Words[10]
attempt	act	0.5000	Nodes[1]	Words[1]
august	time	0.5000	Nodes[4]	Words[4]
available	general	0.5000	Nodes[1]	Words[1]
back	time	0.3000	Nodes[1]	Words[1]
bad	general	0.3000	Nodes[1]	Words[1]
base	act	0.3000	Nodes[2]	Words[1]
based	general	0.5000	Nodes[1]	Words[1]
battles	act	0.5000	Nodes[2]	Words[2]
be	general	0.5000	Nodes[52]	Words[21]
became	time	0.3000	Nodes[1]	Words[1]
because	general	0.5000	Nodes[1]	Words[1]
become	time	0.7000	Nodes[5]	Words[5]
been	time	0.3000	Nodes[4]	Words[4]
before	time	0.3000	Nodes[4]	Words[4]
began	time	0.3000	Nodes[1]	Words[1]
belief	act	0.5000	Nodes[1]	Words[1]
believed	act	0.5000	Nodes[1]	Words[1]
belong	general	0.5000	Nodes[1]	Words[1]
best	general	0.7000	Nodes[2]	Words[1]
bestowed	act	0.7000	Nodes[1]	Words[1]
better	general	0.7000	Nodes[2]	Words[2]
between	general	0.5000	Nodes[8]	Words[8]
bigger	general	0.7000	Nodes[1]	Words[1]
blasphemy	act	0.1000	Nodes[1]	Words[1]
blockade	act	0.5000	Nodes[1]	Words[1]
branches	general	0.5000	Nodes[1]	Words[1]
brighter	general	0.7000	Nodes[1]	Words[1]
bring	general	0.5000	Nodes[2]	Words[1]
brings	general	0.5000	Nodes[1]	Words[1]
brothers	actor	0.7000	Nodes[1]	Words[1]
but	general	0.5000	Nodes[4]	Words[4]

packages of words that involve any word designated as general in the gateway matrix. We will build these word packages by linking a general word in the text stream with its predecessor and successor word in the stream. Words already connected by ordinary language conjunctions or other general words are also incorporated into these word packages.

Table 9.4 provides a sample product of the general word linking process. Note that some of these links now point to words that were linked through natural language conjunctions.

In the third paragraph of Hussein's speech, we find the phrase "it is difficult to talk about all that which should be talked about, and it is difficult to recall that which has to be recalled." At the outset of table 9.4, you will note that the word "about" links to two phrases found in this third paragraph of the text. Thus, the component "all" that links the two words "all that" following the use of general word "about" and similarly the use of "about" and "it" are linked together in table

TABLE 9.4. General Word Links

about	general	0.5000	Node Count[3]	WholeWordCount[3]
	all : that			
	and : it			
	in : detail			
actually	general	0.5000	Node Count[1]	Whole Word Count[1]
	and : constitutionally			
against	general	0.5000	Node Count[4]	Whole Word Count[4]
all	general	0.5000	Node Count[16]	Whole Word Count[14]
	among : and			
	and : muslims			
	about : talk			
	that : which			
	that : which			
	that			
	that : we			
	in : effect			
	in : outlook			
	at : fruit			
	of : achievement			
	greater : remoter			
	upon : and			
	depth : of			
	of : level			
	of : victory			
	and : countries			
	evil : and			

(*Continued*)

TABLE 9.4. Continued

also	general	0.5000	Node Count[5]	Whole Word Count[5]
	but : —			
	indirect : targets			
	but : possible			
	doors : will			
	it : will			
	but : islam			
	from : position			

among	general	0.5000	Node Count[6]	Whole Word Count[6]
	and : nations			
	all : muslims			
	ranks : of			
	and : oppression			
	corrupt : of			

are	general	0.5000	Node Count[4]	Whole Word Count[4]
	hearts : and			
	distinguished : by			

as	general	0.5000	Node Count[6]	Whole Word Count[6]
	wanted : has			
	targets : indirect			
	heritage : to			

at	general	0.5000	Node Count[11]	Whole Word Count[10]
	fruit : its			
	all : times			
	have : we			
	have : we			
	level : of			
	and : homeland			
	level : of			
	doors : closed			
	it : place			
	forefront : of			
	highest : level			

available	general	0.5000	Node Count[1]	Whole Word Count[1]
	and : possible			

based	general	0.5000	Node Count[1]	Whole Word Count[1]
	was : that			
	on : sacrifices			

be	general	0.5000	Node Count[52]	Whole Word Count[21]
	should : which			
	to : has			
	to : has			
	should : what			

TABLE 9.4. Continued

to
not : will
to : continue
glorious : and
should : they
only : not
within : reach
clear : that
in : time
much : greater
to : chosen
should : Kuwait
one : of
to : have
must : we

because	general	0.5000	Node Count[1]	Whole Word Count[1]

belong   general   0.5000   Node Count[1]   Whole Word Count[1]
and : for

between   general   0.5000   Node Count[8]   Whole Word Count[8]
right : and
or : rich
or : blasphemy
or : ruled

branches   general   0.5000   Node Count[1]   Whole Word Count[1]
its : and

bring   general   0.5000   Node Count[2]   Whole Word Count[1]
would : that
dignity : to

brings   general   0.5000   Node Count[1]   Whole Word Count[1]
it

by   general   0.5000   Node Count[21]   Whole Word Count[21]
spirit : struggling
which : men
created : were
reated : was
weaknesses : of
and : ruled
standards : of
feet : of
nor : invaders
distinguished : are
and : faith
order : god's
is : it
30 : countries
machine : and

9.4. In this illustration, the word "about" is linked to the word "all" which has already been linked to the word "that." Similarly, the second instance of the word "about" is linked to the word "and" which in turn has already been linked to the word "it."

The next linking step looks for non-general words in the gateway that have fuzzy memberships of 0.5 in specific primitives drawn from an interpretive framework. Instead of linking these words with preceding and succeeding words in the text stream, here we link non-general words with 0.5 membership values with the preceding word in the text stream. Fluff words like "the" are ignored. The preceding word can be a single word or a word package produced in the previous step. Table 9.5 illustrates this further step in building hypersets of words drawn from the text stream. These examples are again drawn from the A-B section of the alphabet.

In the fourth paragraph of Hussein's speech, we find the phrase "our valiant armed forces will complete their withdrawal from Kuwait." From this phrase the word "armed," which can be seen in table 9.5, is linked with the previous word "valiant."

The computation system also keeps tract of sentences from the original text stream. The occurrence of any word and its associated word hypersets can then be located within the original sentence or sentences where the word occurred in the text stream. The example in table 9.6 covers some of the words from the text stream that begin with the alphabet letter "a." Asterisks indicate the sentence place of the word; fluff words have been removed.

TABLE 9.5. Non-General Word Links

action principled	act	0.5000		Nodes[1]		Words[1]		
add will also	act	0.5000		Nodes[2]		Words[1]		
added to be	act	0.5000		Nodes[1]		Words[1]		

age
  it   gave   depth   to
  their
	time	0.5000		Nodes[2]		Words[2]		

allies america and its major	actor	0.5000		Nodes[1]		Words[1]		
amends until he declares that conflict has stopped or	act	0.5000		Nodes[1]		Words[1]		

TABLE 9.5. Continued

anew palestine	time has	0.5000 returned	Nodes[1]	Words[1]
anyone threatens	actor	0.5000	Nodes[1]	Words[1]
arab almighty privileges holy iraq	actor for that war	0.5000 were at	created level	Nodes[7] by of	Words[4]
arabs good corruption comprehensive	actor land in objectives	0.5000 primarily land	land of of	Nodes[3] of to	Words[3]
armed valiant	act	0.5000	Nodes[1]	Words[1]
armies fought	actor	0.5000	Nodes[1]	Words[1]
army iraqi	actor	0.5000	Nodes[1]	Words[1]
attempt struggling	act	0.5000	Nodes[1]	Words[1]
august great after not not	time day second forget forget	0.5000 of call of that on that it	on 8 remained	Nodes[4] 2 throughout	Words[4] period from 8
battles mother mother	act of of	0.5000	Nodes[2]	Words[2]
belief faith	act	0.5000	Nodes[1]	Words[1]
believed patient	act people	0.5000 who	Nodes[1]	Words[1]
blockade to nonmilitary	act be duel	0.5000 added to including	time is military	Nodes[1] time of and	Words[1] military and economic

TABLE 9.6. Sentence Sets

---

about   general   0.5000   Node Count[3]   Whole Word Count [3]
{ great, people, stalwart, men, in, forces, of, holy, war, and, faith, glorious, men, of, mother, of, battles, zealous, faithful, and, sincere, people, in, our, glorious, nations, and, among, all, muslims, and, all, virtuous, people, in, world, glorious, iraqi, women, in, such, circumstances, and, times, it, is, difficult, to, talk, *, all, that, which, should, be, talked, *, and, it, is, difficult, to, recall, all, that, which, has, to, be, recalled, }
{ great, people, stalwart, men, in, forces, of, holy, war, and, faith, glorious, men, of, mother, of, battles, zealous, faithful, and, sincere, people, in, our, glorious, nations, and, among, all, muslims, and, all, virtuous, people, in, world, glorious, iraqi, women, in, such, circumstances, and, times, it, is, difficult, to, talk, *, all, that, which, should, be, talked, *, and, it, is, difficult, to, recall, all, that, which, has, to, be, recalled, }
{ it, was, epic, struggle, between, right, and, wrong, we, have, talked, *, in, detail, on, previous, occasions, }

abyss   consequence 0.1000   Node Count[1]   Whole Word Count [1]
{ it, was, epic, duel, which, lasted, for, two, months, which, came, to, clearly, confirm, lesson, that, god, has, wanted, as, prelude, of, faith, impregnability, and, capability, for, faithful, and, prelude, of, *, weakness, and, humiliation, which, god, almighty, has, wanted, for, infidels, criminals, traitors, corrupt, and, deviators, }

acceptance   act   0.7000   Node Count[1]   Whole Word Count [1]
{ you, have, chosen, path, which, you, have, chosen, including, *, of, soviet, initiative, but, evildoers, persisted, in, their, path, and, methods, thinking, that, they, can, impose, their, will, on, their, iraq, as, they, imagined, and, hoped, }

accepted   act   0.7000   Node Count[1]   Whole Word Count [1]
{ their, days, will, continue, to, be, glorious, and, their, past, and, future, will, continue, to, relate, story, of, faithful, jealous, and, patient, people, who, believed, in, will, of, god, and, in, values, and, stands, *, by, almighty, for, arab, nation, in, its, leading, role, and, for, islamic, nation, in, essentials, of, its, true, faith, and, how, they, should, be, }

achievement consequence 0.7000   Node Count[1]   Whole Word Count [1]
{koranic, verses, when, happened, near, objectives, will, not, only, be, within, reach, available, and, possible, but, also, doors, will, be, open, without, any, hindrance, which, might, prevent, *, of, all, greater, remoter, and, more, comprehensive, objectives, to, arabs, muslims, and, humanity, at, large, }

action   act   0.5000   Node Count[1]   Whole Word Count [1]
{ they, did, what, they, did, within, context, of, legitimate, deterrence, and, great, principled, *, }

actually   general   0.5000   Node Count[1]   Whole Word Count [1]
{ iraqis, will, remember, and, will, not, forget, that, on, 8, august, 1990, kuwait, became, part, of, iraq, legally, constitutionally, and, *, }

add   act   0.5000   Node Count[2]   Whole Word Count [1]
{ will, also, *, faith, to, faithful, now, that, minds, and, eyes, have, been, opened, and, hearts, are, longing, for, what, principles, values, and, stances, should, long, for, and, belong, to, }

added   act   0.5000   Node Count[1]   Whole Word Count [1]
{ to, be, *, to, time, is, time, of, military, and, nonmilitary, duel, including, military, and, economic,

TABLE 9.6. Continued

blockade, which, was, imposed, on, iraq, and, which, lasted, throughout, 1990, until, today, and, until, time, god, almighty, wishes, it, to, last, }

after   time   0.7000 Node Count[5]   Whole Word Count [5]
{ will, shake, opposite, ranks, and, cause, them, to, collapse, *, everything, has, become, clear, }
{ however, *, second, of, august, 1990, new, concepts, and, standards, were, created, }
{ *, we, have, harvested, what, we, have, harvested, greater, harvest, and, its, yield, will, be, in, time, to, come, and, it, will, be, much, greater, than, what, we, have, at, present, in, spite, of, what, we, have, at, present, in, terms, of, victory, dignity, and, glory, that, was, based, on, sacrifices, of, deep, faith, which, is, generous, without, any, hesitation, or, fear, }
{ circumstances, today, have, willed, that, it, remain, in, state, in, which, it, will, remain, *, withdrawal, of, our, struggling, forces, from, it, }
{ hope, of, theirs, may, remain, in, their, heads, even, *, we, withdraw, from, kuwait, }

against   general   0.5000 Node Count[4]   Whole Word Count [4]
{ and, on, day, our, fight, *, aggression, and, ranks, of, infidelity, joined, in, ugly, coalition, comprising, 30, countries, which, officially, entered, war, *, us, under, leadership, of, united, states, of, america, —, our, fight, *, them, would, have, lasted, from, first, month, of, year, starting, with, night, of, 16-17, january, until, moment, in, current, month, february, of, year,}
{ and, on, day, our, fight, *, aggression, and, ranks, of, infidelity, joined, in, ugly, coalition, comprising, 30, countries, which, officially, entered, war, *, us, under, leadership, of, united, states, of, america, —, our, fight, *, them, would, have, lasted, from, first, month, of, year, starting, with, night, of, 16-17, january, until, moment, in, current, month, february, of, year,}
{ and, on, day, our, fight, *, aggression, and, ranks, of, infidelity, joined, in, ugly, coalition, comprising, 30, countries, which, officially, entered, war, *, us, under, leadership, of, united, states, of, america, —, our, fight, *, them, would, have, lasted, from, first, month, of, year, starting, with, night, of, 16-17, january, until, moment, in, current, month, february, of, year,}
{ malicious, ranks, took, depth, and, effectivness, of, their, aggressiveness, not, only, from, their, aggressive, premeditated, intentions, *, iraq, arab, nation, and, islam, but, also, from, position, of, who, were, deceived, by, claim, of, international, legitimacy, }

age   time   0.5000 Node Count[2]   Whole Word Count [2]
{ it, gave, depth, to, *, of, showdown, for, year, 1990, and, already, elapsed, part, of, year, 1991,}
{ they, will, continue, to, reap, their, harvest, not, only, in, terms, of, direct, targets, represented, in, slogans, of, their, *, —, whether, in, conflict, between, oppressed, poor, and, unjust, and, opportunist, rich, or, between, faith, and, blasphemy, or, between, injustice, deception, and, treachery, on, one, hand, and, fairness, justice, honesty, and, loyalty, on, other, -, but, also, indirect, targets, as, well, }

aggression   act   0.3000 Node Count[4]   Whole Word Count [4]
{ and, on, day, our, fight, against, *, and, ranks, of, infidelity, joined, in, ugly, coalition, comprising, 30, countries, which, officially, entered, war, against, us, under, leadership, of, united, states, of, america, —, our, fight, against, them, would, have, lasted, from, first, month, of, year, starting, with, night, of, 16-17, january, until, moment, in, current, month, february, of, year, }
{ today, certain, circumstances, made, iraqi, army, withdraw, as, result, of, ramifications, which, we, mentioned, including, combined, *, by, 30, countries, }
{ their, repugnant, siege, has, been, led, in, evil, and, *, by, machine, and, criminal, entity, of, america, and, its, major, allies, }
{ you, valiant, men, you, have, fought, armies, of, 30, states, and, capabilities, of, even, greater, number, of, states, which, supplied, them, with, means, of, *, and, support, }

(Continued)

TABLE 9.6. Continued

aggressive   act   0.3000   Node Count[2]   Whole Word Count [1]
{ malicious, ranks, took, depth, and, effectivness, of, their, aggressiveness, not, only, from, their, *, premeditated, intentions, against, iraq, arab, nation, and, islam, but, also, from, position, of, who, were, deceived, by, claim, of, international, legitimacy, }

aggressiveness act   0.3000   Node Count[1]   Whole Word Count [1]
{ malicious, ranks, took, depth, and, effectivness, of, their, *, not, only, from, their, aggressive, premeditated, intentions, against, iraq, arab, nation, and, islam, but, also, from, position, of, who, were, deceived, by, claim, of, international, legitimacy, }

all   general   0.5000   Node Count[16]   Whole Word Count [14]
{ great, people, stalwart, men, in, forces, of, holy, war, and, faith, glorious, men, of, mother, of, battles, zealous, faithful, and, sincere, people, in, our, glorious, nations, and, among, *, muslims, and, *, virtuous, people, in, world, glorious, iraqi, women, in, such, circumstances, and, times, it, is, difficult, to, talk, about, *, that, which, should, be, talked, about, and, it, is, difficult, to, recall, *, that, which, has, to, be, recalled, }
{ great, people, stalwart, men, in, forces, of, holy, war, and, faith, glorious, men, of, mother, of, battles, zealous, faithful, and, sincere, people, in, our, glorious, nations, and, among, *, muslims, and, *, virtuous, people, in, world, glorious, iraqi, women, in, such, circumstances, and, times, it, is, difficult, to, talk, about, *, that, which, should, be, talked, about, and, it, is, difficult, to, recall, *, that, which, has, to, be, recalled, }
{ great, people, stalwart, men, in, forces, of, holy, war, and, faith, glorious, men, of, mother, of, battles, zealous, faithful, and, sincere, people, in, our, glorious, nations, and, among, *, muslims, and, *, virtuous, people, in, world, glorious, iraqi, women, in, such, circumstances, and, times, it, is, difficult, to, talk, about, *, that, which, should, be, talked, about, and, it, is, difficult, to, recall, *, that, which, has, to, be, recalled, }
{ great, people, stalwart, men, in, forces, of, holy, war, and, faith, glorious, men, of, mother, of, battles, zealous, faithful, and, sincere, people, in, our, glorious, nations, and, among, *, muslims, and, *, virtuous, people, in, world, glorious, iraqi, women, in, such, circumstances, and, times, it, is, difficult, to, talk, about, *, that, which, should, be, talked, about, and, it, is, difficult, to, recall, *, that, which, has, to, be, recalled, }
{ *, that, we, have, gone, through, or, decided, within, its, circumstances, obeying, god's, will, and, choosing, position, of, faith, and, chivalry, is, record, of, honor, significance, of, which, will, not, be, missed, by, people, and, nation, and, values, of, islam, and, human-ity, }
{ values, —, which, had, their, effect, in, *, situations, offered, sacrifices, they, had, offered, in, struggle, and, symbolized, depth, of, faithful, character, in, iraq, —, will, continue, to, leave, their, effects, on, souls, }
{ was, preceded, by, new, outlook, in, *, walks, of, life, in, relations, among, peoples, relations, among, states, and, relations, between, ruler, and, ruled, and, by, standards, of, faith, and, positions, patriotism, pan-arabism, and, humanitarianism, holy, war, faith, islam, fear, and, non-fear, restlessness, and, tranquility, manhood, and, its, opposite, struggle, holy, war, and, sacrifice, and, readiness, to, do, good, things, and, their, opposite, }
{ it, brings, forth, its, fruit, at, *, times, by, leave, of, its, lord, }
{ koranic, verses, when, happened, near, objectives, will, not, only, be, within, reach, available, and, possible, but, also, doors, will, be, open, without, any, hindrance, which, might, prevent, achievement, of, *, greater, remoter, and, more, comprehensive, objectives, to, arabs, muslims, and, humanity, at, large, }
{ it, is, by, virtue, of, faith, that, god, has, bestowed, dignity, upon, iraqi, mujahedeen, and, upon, *, depth, of, course, of, holy, war, at, level, of, arab, homeland, and, at, level, of, *, men, whom, god,

TABLE 9.6. Continued

has, chosen, to, be, given, honor, of, allegiance, guidance, and, honorable, position, until, he, declares, that, conflict, has, stopped, or, amends, its, directions, and, course, and, positions, in, manner, which, would, please, faithful, and, increase, their, dignity, }

{ it, is, by, virtue, of, faith, that, god, has, bestowed, dignity, upon, iraqi, mujahedeen, and, upon, *, depth, of, course, of, holy, war, at, level, of, arab, homeland, and, at, level, of, *, men, whom, god, has, chosen, to, be, given, honor, of, allegiance, guidance, and, honorable, position, until, he, declares, that, conflict, has, stopped, or, amends, its, directions, and, course, and, positions, in, manner, which, would, please, faithful, and, increase, their, dignity, }

{ we, rejoiced, on, day, of, call, when, it, was, decided, that, kuwait, should, be, one, of, main, gates, for, deterring, plot, and, for, defending, *, iraq, from, plotters, }

{ shout, for, victory, brothers, shout, for, your, victory, and, victory, of, *, honorable, people, iraqis, }

{ you, have, fought, 30, countries, and, *, evil, and, largest, machine, of, war, and, destruction, in, world, that, surrounds, them, }

allegiance   act   0.7000   Node Count[1]   Whole Word Count [1]
{ it, is, by, virtue, of, faith, that, god, has, bestowed, dignity, upon, iraqi, mujahedeen, and, upon, all, depth, of, course, of, holy, war, at, level, of, arab, homeland, and, at, level, of, all, men, whom, god, has, chosen, to, be, given, honor, of, *, guidance, and, honorable, position, until, he, declares, that, conflict, has, stopped, or, amends, its, directions, and, course, and, positions, in, manner, which, would, please, faithful, and, increase, their, dignity, }

allies   actor   0.5000   Node Count[1]   Whole Word Count [1]
{ their, repugnant, siege, has, been, led, in, evil, and, aggression, by, machine, and, criminal, entity, of, america, and, its, major, *, }

almighty   actor   1.0000   Node Count[3]   Whole Word Count [3]
{ it, was, epic, duel, which, lasted, for, two, months, which, came, to, clearly, confirm, lesson, that, god, has, wanted, as, prelude, of, faith, impregnability, and, capability, for, faithful, and, prelude, of, abyss, weakness, and, humiliation, which, god, *, has, wanted, for, infidels, criminals, traitors, corrupt, and, deviators, }

{ to, be, added, to, time, is, time, of, military, and, nonmilitary, duel, including, military, and, economic, blockade, which, was, imposed, on, iraq, and, which, lasted, throughout, 1990, until, today, and, until, time, god, *, wishes, it, to, last, }

{ their, days, will, continue, to, be, glorious, and, their, past, and, future, will, continue, to, relate, story, of, faithful, jealous, and, patient, people, who, believed, in, will, of, god, and, in, values, and, stands, accepted, by, *, for, arab, nation, in, its, leading, role, and, for, islamic, nation, in, essentials, of, its, true, faith, and, how, they, should, be, }

already   time   0.3000   Node Count[1]   Whole Word Count [1]
{ it, gave, depth, to, age, of, showdown, for, year, 1990, and, *, elapsed, part, of, year, 1991, }

also   general   0.5000   Node Count[5]   Whole Word Count [5]
{ they, will, continue, to, reap, their, harvest, not, only, in, terms, of, direct, targets, represented, in, slogans, of, their, age, —, whether, in, conflict, between, oppressed, poor, and, unjust, and, opportunist, rich, or, between, faith, and, blasphemy, or, between, injustice, deception, and, treachery, on, one, hand, and, fairness, justice, honesty, and, loyalty, on, other, —, but, *, indirect, targets, as, well,}

(Continued)

TABLE 9.6. Continued

{ will, *, add, faith, to, faithful, now, that, minds, and, eyes, have, been, opened, and, hearts, are, longing, for, what, principles, values, and, stances, should, long, for, and, belong, to, }

{ koranic, verses, when, happened, near, objectives, will, not, only, be, within, reach, available, and, possible, but, *, doors, will, be, open, without, any, hindrance, which, might, prevent, achievement, of, all, greater, remoter, and, more, comprehensive, objectives, to, arabs, muslims, and, humanity, at, large, }

{ then, *, it, will, be, clear, that, harvest, does, not, precede, seeding, and, that, threshing, floor, and, yield, are, outcome, of, successful, seeding, and, successful, harvest, }

{ malicious, ranks, took, depth, and, effectivness, of, their, aggressiveness, not, only, from, their, aggressive, premeditated, intentions, against, iraq, arab, nation, and, islam, but, *, from, position, of, who, were, deceived, by, claim, of, international, legitimacy, }

amends	act	0.5000	Node Count[1]	Whole Word Count [1]

{ it, is, by, virtue, of, faith, that, god, has, bestowed, dignity, upon, iraqi, mujahedeen, and, upon, all, depth, of, course, of, holy, war, at, level, of, arab, homeland, and, at, level, of, all, men, whom, god, has, chosen, to, be, given, honor, of, allegiance, guidance, and, honorable, position, until, he, declares, that, conflict, has, stopped, or, *, its, directions, and, course, and, positions, in, manner, which, would, please, faithful, and, increase, their, dignity, }

america	actor	0.1000	Node Count[2]	Whole Word Count [2]

{ and, on, day, our, fight, against, aggression, and, ranks, of, infidelity, joined, in, ugly, coalition, comprising, 30, countries, which, officially, entered, war, against, us, under, leadership, of, united, states, of, *, —, our, fight, against, them, would, have, lasted, from, first, month, of, year, starting, with, night, of, 16-17, january, until, moment, in, current, month, february, of, year, }

{ their, repugnant, siege, has, been, led, in, evil, and, aggression, by, machine, and, criminal, entity, of, *, and, its, major, allies, }

Linking Text Hypersets to Primitives

The serial application of three link rules (natural language conjunction, general words in the gateway matrix, and non-general words with 0.5 membership values) now have provided hypersets of text that build upon but extend far beyond the original matrix linking text words to primitives in an interpretive framework. These textual hypersets can now be related back to the primitives in the interpretive framework. Doing so sets the stage for "meaning analysis."

The first step is a straightforward application of fuzzy set operations. We would like to assign fuzzy membership values to the word packages or hypersets, but at this point all we have is fuzzy membership values for individual words within the word packages or hypersets. We must begin with a distinction between types of elements linked in the word packages or hypersets: some hyperset elements have membership values in the same primitive, while other hyperset elements have membership values in different primitives. The first is a simple problem of seeing how instances of the same primitive combine to provide a single membership value for the hyperset as a whole. The second creates multi-dimensional sets that have membership values in two or more primitives. We shall consider each briefly in turn.

When elements of a hyperset have fuzzy membership values in the same primitive, there are a set of simple fuzzy rules for estimating the hyperset value. Consider first the case where the elements are consistent, such as "faithful patient people." We can relate the hyperset "faithful patient people" to the primitive "actor" by dilating the larger membership value by the smaller, that is, taking the membership value of the larger element and raising it to the power of the smaller. Since all fuzzy membership values range between zero and one, this essentially produces a hyperset with even greater membership in the primitive "Actor." Thus:

if:

$$f(Actor_{faithful}) = .7$$
$$f(Actor_{patient}) = .6$$

then:

$$f(Actor_{faithful\&patient}) = .7^{.6}$$

There are of course other rules, such as taking the maximum elements membership to stand for the hyperset. In the larger project from which this illustration is drawn, all eligible rules are used and results are compared to the fitting process examined in the next section. The optimal rule sets are then chosen for interpreting text streams in light of a particular framework, such as Saddam Hussein's speech being interpreted through a Trials and Tribulations framework.

If there are inconsistent elements in a hyperset with common memberships in a single primitive, then the converse of a consistency rule is applied. In the previous example, the consistency rule was dilation. In this counter-illustration, the inconsistency rule will be concentration. Consider the hyperset set "faithful repugnant people." We first determine which is larger, the set membership of the element above 0.5 or the complement of the set element below 0.5. In the illustration below, the set complement of repugnant is 0.6, and hence the larger membership is faithful at 0.7. The winning value becomes the base taken to the power of one plus the other element's set membership. Thus:

if:

$$f(Actor_{faithful}) = .7$$
$$f(Actor_{repugnant}) = .4$$

then:

$$f(Actor_{faithful\&repugnant}) = .7^{1+.4}$$

If the set complement had been the larger value, then, once the above operation were completed, the resulting value would be transformed into its set complement and then assigned as the value of the hyperset. In both operations, the hyperset's membership value in a primitive is moved toward 0.5, weighted by the relative strengths of the opposing words.

A rather different set of rules are invoked when elements in the hyperset have memberships in different primitives. Thus, for example, a hyperset might include "faithful people under attack." In this illustration we have memberships in Actor and Act, with the Actor being evaluated among the forces of good and the Act being evaluated as a tribulation. Such sets may also involve another dimension such as Time. How advanced set composition is performed varies with the interpretive framework. In the present framework, with Time being a third variable, we use the equivalent of a staged composition where "weathering the tribulation" produces the quality of faithful (see the presentation of the interpretive framework above) and this in turn "seeds" the soil for future rewards. Without Time being explicit, the Cartesian product of the two is simultaneously related to both its relevant primitives, namely Actor and Act. The Cartesian product of Actor/Act can be thought of as a particular constellation of Actor/Act in this interpretive framework that is only a trajectory either toward reduced faithfulness or toward reduced tribulation. We currently are expanding the program's library of compositional rules.

Degree of Fit

The last item to be discussed in the processing stage is the degree of fit between a text and possible interpretive frameworks. The focus here is on explicit or implicit if-then logics found within any interpretive framework. The goodness-of-fit process essentially comes down to checking to see whether the expected "thens" follow from observed "ifs" in an if-then static account of why-this-goes-with-that. All of this is still a bit abstract, and so we will elaborate using the interpretive framework described above.

Recall that the Trials and Tribulations framework postulates a Calling from God which puts a good people to a Test that typically also involves some Threat from the Forces of Evil. During the course of that test, either the forces of evil suffer a direct setback or the seeds are sown for a future victory and final reward. During the course of a trial, gains might be made in another context besides the one in which the direct tribulation occurs. Static if-then rules have been constructed to represent these various linkages. Although the rules are written in a fuzzy relational form, they can easily be represented in ordinary language for easier exposition.

The simplest set of if-then rules set up expected relationships between actors and actions/rewards under different time frames. The set of inference rules associated with the Trials-and-Tribulations interpretive frame are summarized in table 9.7.

These are simple rules, but then the interpretive framework is also simple. The goodness-of-fit test is designed to see whether this interpretive framework generates interpretive expectations that are indeed found in the text logic. The better the assessed fit, the more comparative utility will flow from using this interpretive framework as opposed to other frameworks in analyzing the text. We illustrate the process in table 9.8. Entries in that table were drawn from the computational fitting analysis. The table is heavily edited, given its original length and the redundancy among time references, in order to provide a greater overview of the power of the interpretive framework in structuring the text from

TABLE 9.7. Trials-and-Tribulation Inference Rules

If:	The actor is God, sometime in the past or present,
then:	expect a calling to have occurred
If:	The actor is Satan, sometime in the past or present,
then:	expect a temptation to have occurred
If:	The actor is forces of good, sometime in the past or present,
then:	expect a test or trial
If:	The actor is forces of evil, sometime in the past or present,
then:	expect a threat
If:	The actor is God, sometime in the future,
then:	expect a Reward
If:	The actor is Satan, sometime in the future,
then:	expect a Temptation
If:	The actor is forces of good, sometime in the future,
then:	expect victory and harvest
If:	The actor is forces of evil, sometime in the future,
then:	expect reduced threat
If:	The act is a threat or Temptation, sometime in the past, present, of future,
then:	expect victory or harvest in another context

TABLE 9.8. Static Fit

almighty		**actor**	**1.0000**	
epic		time	0.3000	
	revelation		act	0.9000
lasted		time	0.3000	
	revelation		act	0.9000
months		time	0.5000	
	revelation		act	0.9000
prelude		time	0.3000	
	revelation		act	0.9000
prelude		time	0.3000	
	revelation		act	0.9000
time		time	0.5000	
	revelation		act	0.9000
time		time	0.5000	
	revelation		act	0.9000
lasted		time	0.3000	
	revelation		act	0.9000
throughout		time	0.5000	
	revelation		act	0.9000
1990		time	0.3000	
	revelation		act	0.9000
until		time	0.7000	
	freedom		consequence	0.9000
	glory		consequence	0.9000
today		time	0.5000	
	revelation		act	0.9000
until		time	0.7000	
	freedom		consequence	0.9000
	glory		consequence	0.9000
time		time	0.5000	
	revelation		act	0.9000
last		time	0.3000	
	revelation		act	0.9000
days		time	0.5000	
	revelation		act	0.9000
continue		time	0.7000	
	freedom		consequence	0.9000
	glory		consequence	0.9000
past		time	0.3000	
	revelation		act	0.9000
future		time	0.7000	
	freedom		consequence	0.9000
	glory		consequence	0.9000
continue		time	0.7000	
	freedom		consequence	0.9000
	glory		consequence	0.9000
america		**actor**	**0.1000**	
day		time	0.5000	

TABLE 9.8. Continued

aggression	act		0.3000
aggressive	act		0.3000
aggressiveness	act		0.3000
base	act		0.3000
blasphemy	act		0.1000
collapse	act		0.3000
corruption	act		0.3000
deceived	act		0.3000
deception	act		0.3000
defiled	act		0.3000
deviators	act		0.3000
exacerbated	act		0.3000
failed	act		0.3000
falsehood	act		0.3000
fear	act		0.3000
hesitation	act		0.3000
hindrance	act		0.3000
humiliation	act		0.3000
hurts	act		0.3000
hypocrisy	act		0.3000
infidelity	act		0.1000
injustice	act		0.3000
jealous	act		0.3000
malicious	act		0.3000
missed	act		0.3000
negative	act		0.3000
oppression	act		0.3000
plot	act		0.3000
plotting	act		0.3000
premeditated	act		0.3000
prevent	act		0.3000
propaganda	act		0.3000
repugnant	act		0.3000
siege	act		0.3000
spite	act		0.3000
stormed	act		0.3000
threat	act		0.3000
threatens	act		0.3000
traitorous	act		0.1000
treacherous	act		0.1000
treachery	act		0.1000
ugly	act		0.3000
withdraw	act		0.3000
withdrawal	act		0.3000
swift		time	0.5000
blasphemy	act		0.1000
infidelity	act		0.1000
traitorous	act		0.1000
treacherous	act		0.1000

(*Continued*)

TABLE 9.8. Continued

		treachery		act	0.1000
arab			**actor**		**1.0000**
	days		time		0.5000
		revelation		act	0.9000
	continue		time		0.7000
		freedom		consequence	0.9000
		glory		consequence	0.9000
	past		time		0.3000
		revelation		act	0.9000
	future		time		0.7000
		freedom		consequence	0.9000
		glory		consequence	0.9000
	continue		time		0.7000
		freedom		consequence	0.9000
		glory		consequence	0.9000
	now		time		0.5000
		revelation		act	0.9000
	been		time		0.3000
		revelation		act	0.9000
	until		time		0.7000
		freedom		consequence	0.9000
		glory		consequence	0.9000
community			**actor**		**0.7000**
	before		time		0.3000
		acceptance		act	0.7000
		accepted		act	0.7000
		allegiance		act	0.7000
		bestowed		act	0.7000
		chances		act	0.7000
		chivalry		act	0.7000
		compassionate		act	0.7000
		complete		act	0.7000
		comprehensive		act	0.7000
		confidence		act	0.7000
		confirm		act	0.7000
		constitutionally		act	0.7000
		cultivation		act	0.7000
		defending		act	0.7000
		deterrence		act	0.7000
		deterring		act	0.7000
		expose		act	0.7000
		exposed		act	0.7000
		facilitated		act	0.7000
		fairness		act	0.7000
		faith		act	0.7000
		firmly		act	0.7000

TABLE 9.8. Continued

fixed	act	0.7000
fought	act	0.7000
grown	act	0.7000
guidance	act	0.7000
harvested	act	0.7000
honesty	act	0.7000
honor	act	0.7000
honorable	act	0.7000
humanitarianism	act	0.7000
inherited	act	0.7000
initiative	act	0.7000
leading	act	0.7000
leads	act	0.7000
legally	act	0.7000
longing	act	0.7000
loyalty	act	0.7000
non-fear	act	0.7000
obeying	act	0.7000
offered	act	0.7000
patient	act	0.7000
patriotism	act	0.7000
please	act	0.7000
pleaseth	act	0.7000
preparedness	act	0.7000
principled	act	0.7000
privileges	act	0.7000
reach	act	0.7000
rejoiced	act	0.7000
remember	act	0.7000
remind	act	0.7000
reminded	act	0.7000
represent	act	0.7000
represented	act	0.7000
resolved	act	0.7000
revelation	act	0.9000
role	act	0.7000
root	act	0.7000
rooted	act	0.7000
sacrifice	act	0.7000
sacrifices	act	0.7000
sacrifies	act	0.7000
seeding	act	0.7000
seeds	act	0.7000
shake	act	0.7000
shout	act	0.7000
stands	act	0.7000
strongly	act	0.7000
struggle	act	0.7000

(*Continued*)

TABLE 9.8. Continued

struggling	act		0.7000
succeeded	act		0.7000
successful	act		0.7000
valiant	act		0.7000
zealous	act		0.7000
criminal	**actor**		**0.3000**
been		time	0.3000
aggression	act		0.3000
aggressive	act		0.3000
aggressiveness	act		0.3000
base	act		0.3000
blasphemy	act		0.1000
collapse	act		0.3000
corruption	act		0.3000
deceived	act		0.3000
deception	act		0.3000
defiled	act		0.3000
deviators	act		0.3000
exacerbated	act		0.3000
failed	act		0.3000
falsehood	act		0.3000
fear	act		0.3000
hesitation	act		0.3000
hindrance	act		0.3000
humiliation	act		0.3000
hurts	act		0.3000
hypocrisy	act		0.3000
infidelity	act		0.1000
injustice	act		0.3000
jealous	act		0.3000
malicious	act		0.3000
missed	act		0.3000
negative	act		0.3000
oppression	act		0.3000
plot	act		0.3000
plotting	act		0.3000
premeditated	act		0.3000
prevent	act		0.3000
propaganda	act		0.3000
repugnant	act		0.3000
siege	act		0.3000
spite	act		0.3000
stormed	act		0.3000
threat	act		0.3000
threatens	act		0.3000
traitorous	act		0.1000
treacherous	act		0.1000

TABLE 9.8. Continued

	treachery	act		0.1000
	ugly	act		0.3000
	withdraw	act		0.3000
	withdrawal	act		0.3000
lasted		time	0.3000	
	blasphemy	act		0.1000
	infidelity	act		0.1000
	traitorous	act		0.1000
	treacherous	act		0.1000
	treachery	act		0.1000
evildoers	**actor**		**0.1000**	
persisted		time	0.3000	
	aggression	act		0.3000
	aggressive	act		0.3000
	aggressiveness	act		0.3000
	base	act		0.3000
	blasphemy	act		0.1000
	collapse	act		0.3000
	corruption	act		0.3000
	deceived	act		0.3000
	deception	act		0.3000
	defiled	act		0.3000
	deviators	act		0.3000
	exacerbated	act		0.3000
	failed	act		0.3000
	falsehood	act		0.3000
	fear	act		0.3000
	hesitation	act		0.3000
	hindrance	act		0.3000
	humiliation	act		0.3000
	hurts	act		0.3000
	hypocrisy	act		0.3000
	infidelity	act		0.1000
	injustice	act		0.3000
	jealous	act		0.3000
	malicious	act		0.3000
	missed	act		0.3000
	negative	act		0.3000
	oppression	act		0.3000
	plot	act		0.3000
	plotting	act		0.3000
	premeditated	act		0.3000
	prevent	act		0.3000
	propaganda	act		0.3000
	repugnant	act		0.3000
	siege	act		0.3000
	spite	act		0.3000

(Continued)

TABLE 9.8. Continued

	stormed	act		0.3000	
	threat	act		0.3000	
	threatens	act		0.3000	
	traitorous	act		0.1000	
	treacherous	act		0.1000	
	treachery	act		0.1000	
	ugly	act		0.3000	
	withdraw	act		0.3000	
	withdrawal	act		0.3000	
forces		**actor**		**0.5000**	
forces		**actor**		**0.5000**	
forces		**actor**		**0.5000**	
forces		**actor**		**0.5000**	
forces		**actor**		**0.5000**	
	times	time		0.5000	
	start	time		0.5000	
	day	time		0.5000	
	today	time		0.5000	
	after	time		0.7000	
	throughout	time		0.5000	
	period	time		0.5000	
	august	time		0.5000	
	1990	time		0.3000	
	until	time		0.7000	
	last	time		0.3000	
	night	time		0.5000	
	when	time		0.5000	
	began	time		0.3000	
	today	time		0.5000	
foreigners		**actor**		**0.3000**	
	now	time		0.5000	
		aggression	act		0.3000
		aggressive	act		0.3000
		aggressiveness	act		0.3000
		base	act		0.3000
		blasphemy	act		0.1000
		collapse	act		0.3000
		corruption	act		0.3000
		deceived	act		0.3000
		deception	act		0.3000
		defiled	act		0.3000
		deviators	act		0.3000
		exacerbated	act		0.3000
		failed	act		0.3000
		falsehood	act		0.3000
		fear	act		0.3000
		hesitation	act		0.3000

TABLE 9.8. Continued

hindrance	act		0.3000
humiliation	act		0.3000
hurts	act		0.3000
hypocrisy	act		0.3000
infidelity	act		0.1000
injustice	act		0.3000
jealous	act		0.3000
malicious	act		0.3000
missed	act		0.3000
negative	act		0.3000
oppression	act		0.3000
plot	act		0.3000
plotting	act		0.3000
premeditated	act		0.3000
prevent	act		0.3000
propaganda	act		0.3000
repugnant	act		0.3000
siege	act		0.3000
spite	act		0.3000
stormed	act		0.3000
threat	act		0.3000
threatens	act		0.3000
traitorous	act		0.1000
treacherous	act		0.1000
treachery	act		0.1000
ugly	act		0.3000
withdraw	act		0.3000
withdrawal	act		0.3000
infidels	**actor**		**0.1000**
epic	time		0.3000
aggression	act		0.3000
aggressive	act		0.3000
aggressiveness	act		0.3000
base	act		0.3000
blasphemy	act		0.1000
collapse	act		0.3000
corruption	act		0.3000
deceived	act		0.3000
deception	act		0.3000
defiled	act		0.3000
deviators	act		0.3000
exacerbated	act		0.3000
failed	act		0.3000
falsehood	act		0.3000
fear	act		0.3000
hesitation	act		0.3000
hindrance	act		0.3000

(*Continued*)

TABLE 9.8. Continued

humiliation	act	0.3000
hurts	act	0.3000
hypocrisy	act	0.3000
infidelity	act	0.1000
injustice	act	0.3000
jealous	act	0.3000
malicious	act	0.3000
missed	act	0.3000
negative	act	0.3000
oppression	act	0.3000
plot	act	0.3000
plotting	act	0.3000
premeditated	act	0.3000
prevent	act	0.3000
propaganda	act	0.3000
repugnant	act	0.3000
siege	act	0.3000
spite	act	0.3000
stormed	act	0.3000
threat	act	0.3000
threatens	act	0.3000
traitorous	act	0.1000
treacherous	act	0.1000
treachery	act	0.1000
ugly	act	0.3000
withdraw	act	0.3000
withdrawal	act	0.3000

iraq   **actor**   **0.9000**

    time   time   0.5000

acceptance	act	0.7000
accepted	act	0.7000
allegiance	act	0.7000
bestowed	act	0.7000
chances	act	0.7000
chivalry	act	0.7000
compassionate	act	0.7000
complete	act	0.7000
comprehensive	act	0.7000
confidence	act	0.7000
confirm	act	0.7000
constitutionally	act	0.7000
cultivation	act	0.7000
defending	act	0.7000
deterrence	act	0.7000
deterring	act	0.7000
expose	act	0.7000
exposed	act	0.7000
facilitated	act	0.7000

TABLE 9.8. Continued

fairness	act	0.7000
faith	act	0.7000
firmly	act	0.7000
fixed	act	0.7000
fought	act	0.7000
grown	act	0.7000
guidance	act	0.7000
harvested	act	0.7000
honesty	act	0.7000
honor	act	0.7000
honorable	act	0.7000
humanitarianism	act	0.7000
inherited	act	0.7000
initiative	act	0.7000
leading	act	0.7000
leads	act	0.7000
legally	act	0.7000
longing	act	0.7000
loyalty	act	0.7000
non-fear	act	0.7000
obeying	act	0.7000
offered	act	0.7000
patient	act	0.7000
patriotism	act	0.7000
please	act	0.7000
pleaseth	act	0.7000
preparedness	act	0.7000
principled	act	0.7000
privileges	act	0.7000
reach	act	0.7000
rejoiced	act	0.7000
remember	act	0.7000
remind	act	0.7000
reminded	act	0.7000
represent	act	0.7000
represented	act	0.7000
resolved	act	0.7000
revelation	act	0.9000
role	act	0.7000
root	act	0.7000
rooted	act	0.7000
sacrifice	act	0.7000
sacrifices	act	0.7000
sacrifies	act	0.7000
seeding	act	0.7000
seeds	act	0.7000
shake	act	0.7000
shout	act	0.7000

(Continued)

TABLE 9.8. Continued

stands	act		0.7000
strongly	act		0.7000
struggle	act		0.7000
struggling	act		0.7000
succeeded	act		0.7000
successful	act		0.7000
valiant	act		0.7000
zealous	act		0.7000
kuwait	**actor**		**0.3000**
start		time	0.5000
aggression	act		0.3000
aggressive	act		0.3000
aggressiveness	act		0.3000
base	act		0.3000
blasphemy	act		0.1000
collapse	act		0.3000
corruption	act		0.3000
deceived	act		0.3000
deception	act		0.3000
defiled	act		0.3000
deviators	act		0.3000
exacerbated	act		0.3000
failed	act		0.3000
falsehood	act		0.3000
fear	act		0.3000
hesitation	act		0.3000
hindrance	act		0.3000
humiliation	act		0.3000
hurts	act		0.3000
hypocrisy	act		0.3000
infidelity	act		0.1000
injustice	act		0.3000
jealous	act		0.3000
malicious	act		0.3000
missed	act		0.3000
negative	act		0.3000
oppression	act		0.3000
plot	act		0.3000
plotting	act		0.3000
premeditated	act		0.3000
prevent	act		0.3000
propaganda	act		0.3000
repugnant	act		0.3000
siege	act		0.3000
spite	act		0.3000
stormed	act		0.3000
threat	act		0.3000
threatens	act		0.3000
traitorous	act		0.1000

TABLE 9.8. Continued

				treacherous	act	0.1000
				treachery	act	0.1000
				ugly	act	0.3000
				withdraw	act	0.3000
				withdrawal	act	0.3000

leader		**actor**			**0.7000**	
preceded		time			0.3000	
		acceptance	act			0.7000
		accepted	act			0.7000
		allegiance	act			0.7000
		bestowed	act			0.7000
		chances	act			0.7000
		chivalry	act			0.7000
		compassionate	act			0.7000
		complete	act			0.7000
		comprehensive	act			0.7000
		confidence	act			0.7000
		confirm	act			0.7000
		constitutionally	act			0.7000
		cultivation	act			0.7000
		defending	act			0.7000
		deterrence	act			0.7000
		deterring	act			0.7000
		expose	act			0.7000
		exposed	act			0.7000
		facilitated	act			0.7000
		fairness	act			0.7000
		faith	act			0.7000
		firmly	act			0.7000
		fixed	act			0.7000
		fought	act			0.7000
		grown	act			0.7000
		guidance	act			0.7000
		harvested	act			0.7000
		honesty	act			0.7000
		honor	act			0.7000
		honorable	act			0.7000
		humanitarianism	act			0.7000
		inherited	act			0.7000
		initiative	act			0.7000
		leading	act			0.7000
		leads	act			0.7000
		legally	act			0.7000
		longing	act			0.7000
		loyalty	act			0.7000
		non-fear	act			0.7000
		obeying	act			0.7000
		offered	act			0.7000

(*Continued*)

TABLE 9.8. Continued

patient	act	0.7000
patriotism	act	0.7000
please	act	0.7000
pleaseth	act	0.7000
preparedness	act	0.7000
principled	act	0.7000
privileges	act	0.7000
reach	act	0.7000
rejoiced	act	0.7000
remember	act	0.7000
remind	act	0.7000
reminded	act	0.7000
represent	act	0.7000
represented	act	0.7000
resolved	act	0.7000
revelation	act	0.9000
role	act	0.7000
root	act	0.7000
rooted	act	0.7000
sacrifice	act	0.7000
sacrifices	act	0.7000
sacrifies	act	0.7000
seeding	act	0.7000
seeds	act	0.7000
shake	act	0.7000
shout	act	0.7000
stands	act	0.7000
strongly	act	0.7000
struggle	act	0.7000
struggling	act	0.7000
succeeded	act	0.7000
successful	act	0.7000
valiant	act	0.7000
zealous	act	0.7000

leaders   **actor**   **0.7000**

become   time   0.7000

achievement	consequence	0.7000
freedom	consequence	0.9000
glory	consequence	0.9000
happiness	consequence	0.7000
harvest	consequence	0.7000
reap	consequence	0.7000
triumphed	consequence	0.7000
victory	consequence	0.7000

leadership   **actor**   **0.5000**

day   time   0.5000

lasted   time   0.3000

TABLE 9.8. Continued

first	time	0.3000	
month	time	0.5000	
year	time	0.5000	
starting	time	0.5000	
night	time	0.5000	
january	time	0.5000	
until	time	0.7000	
moment	time	0.5000	
current	time	0.5000	
month	time	0.5000	
february	time	0.5000	
year	time	0.5000	
muslims	**actor**	**0.7000**	
times	time	0.5000	
acceptance	act		0.7000
accepted	act		0.7000
allegiance	act		0.7000
bestowed	act		0.7000
chances	act		0.7000
chivalry	act		0.7000
compassionate	act		0.7000
complete	act		0.7000
comprehensive	act		0.7000
confidence	act		0.7000
confirm	act		0.7000
constitutionally	act		0.7000
cultivation	act		0.7000
defending	act		0.7000
deterrence	act		0.7000
deterring	act		0.7000
expose	act		0.7000
exposed	act		0.7000
facilitated	act		0.7000
fairness	act		0.7000
faith	act		0.7000
firmly	act		0.7000
fixed	act		0.7000
fought	act		0.7000
grown	act		0.7000
guidance	act		0.7000
harvested	act		0.7000
honesty	act		0.7000
honor	act		0.7000
honorable	act		0.7000
humanitarianism	act		0.7000
inherited	act		0.7000
initiative	act		0.7000

(*Continued*)

TABLE 9.8. Continued

leading	act	0.7000
leads	act	0.7000
legally	act	0.7000
longing	act	0.7000
loyalty	act	0.7000
non-fear	act	0.7000
obeying	act	0.7000
offered	act	0.7000
patient	act	0.7000
patriotism	act	0.7000
please	act	0.7000
pleaseth	act	0.7000
preparedness	act	0.7000
principled	act	0.7000
privileges	act	0.7000
reach	act	0.7000
rejoiced	act	0.7000
remember	act	0.7000
remind	act	0.7000
reminded	act	0.7000
represent	act	0.7000
represented	act	0.7000
resolved	act	0.7000
revelation	act	0.9000
role	act	0.7000
root	act	0.7000
rooted	act	0.7000
sacrifice	act	0.7000
sacrifices	act	0.7000
sacrifies	act	0.7000
seeding	act	0.7000
seeds	act	0.7000
shake	act	0.7000
shout	act	0.7000
stands	act	0.7000
strongly	act	0.7000
struggle	act	0.7000
struggling	act	0.7000
succeeded	act	0.7000
successful	act	0.7000
valiant	act	0.7000
zealous	act	0.7000

Saddam Hussein's speech. Note how the static structure also serves to identify which Actors and Acts "go together."

To illustrate, consider the first set of connections in table 9.8. In this connection, the actor is the almighty; as indicated for set membership the almighty has a membership value of 1.0 in the set actor. The time word "epic" has membership value of .3 in the set time, meaning that it is in the past. Based on the trials and tribulations inference rules from table 9.7, if the actor is god sometime in the past or the present then we should have expected a calling to have occurred. The word that follows in table 9.8, is "revelation," which has a degree of membership in the act primitive at .9. In short, there is a good fit between the static rule and this particular set of connections between the almighty in epic time and revelation.

Conclusion

This chapter outlines an alternate strategy for the systematic analysis of textual material. The approach begins with libraries of interpretive frameworks and works backward to the structuring of text streams. Although the volume of textual information is great indeed, a relatively small number of interpretive frameworks can cover much of the textual material of general interest to political scientists. An interpretive framework that meets the user's goodness-of-fit standards can, in turn, serve as the basis for generating projections that utilize dynamic components of each interpretive framework.

This illustration has focused on a single speech and a single interpretive framework. The process involves a preprocessing, processing, and postprocessing stage. Only the first two of these stages were discussed in detail. At the preprocessing stage, a stream of text letters were linked into a simple graph node system for distinguishing among letter sequences and words. Ordinary language conjunctions were then used to link nodes in the graph tree. At the processing stage we introduced a gateway matrix. From this matrix general words were used to link preceding and succeeding words in the text stream. This was done having one graph node point to other graph nodes. Non-general words from the same matrix were then used to link a given word with its text stream predecessor. These operations produced word packages or text hypersets which serve as the building blocks for meaning analysis. A series of fuzzy operations are used to prepare the hypersets for inference analysis. Once each hyperset has a fuzzy membership value on one or more primitives, we move to the final processing phase. Here, if-then rules implicit in the interpretive framework are used to set up a "goodness-of-fit" check. A good fit occurs when conjoined primitives in the interpretive framework are mirrored by conjoined hypersets in the text stream.

Although this work is not funded under the Data Development in International Relations (DDIR) project, it bears upon many of the tasks being undertaken there. The operating prototype already has a small but growing library of metaphors and parables. All of the tables provided in this illustration are outputs from the computer program, except the text stream input speech, the library input gateway in table 9.3, and the library input inference rules in table 9.7. The system has been designed so that it can tie directly into either press wires (AP, UPI) or into FBIS tapes. When complete, the system can provide a "meaning analysis" on any generic text stream.

Combined References

Alker, H. R., Jr. 1975. "Polimetrics: Its Descriptive Foundations." In Vol. 7 of *Handbook of Political Science*. Eds. Greenstein, F. and N. Polsby. 139-210. Reading, MA: Addison-Wesley.

___. 1984. "Historical Argumentation and Statistical Inference: Towards More Appropriate Logics for Historical Research." *Historical Methods* 17, 3 (Summer): 164-173 (plus Erratum on p. 270 of the next issue).

___. 1988a. "Bit Flows, Rewrites, Social Talk: Towards More Adequate Information Ontologies." Reprinted in *Between Rationality and Cognition*. Ed. Campanella, M. 237-256. Torino: Albert Meynier.

___. 1988b. "Toward Globalized Event-Data Research on Avoidable War." *DDIR Update* 3, 2 (October): 2-5.

___. 1989. "An Orwellian Lasswell for Today." In *The Orwellian Moment: Hindsight and Foresight in the Post-1984 World*. Eds. Savage, R. L., J. Combs and D. Nimmo. 131-155. Fayetteville: University of Arkansas Press.

Alker, H. R., Jr., J. P. Bennet and D. Mefford. 1982. "Generalized Precedent Logics for Resolving Insecurity Dilemmas." *International Interactions* 7, 2: 165-206.

Alker, H. R., Jr. and C. Christensen. 1972. "From Causal Modelling to Artificial Intelligence: The Evolution of a UN Peace-Making Simulation." In *Experimentation and Simulation in Political Science*. Eds. Laponce, J. and P. Smoker. 177-224. Toronto: University of Toronto Press.

Alker, H. R., Jr., G. Duffy, R. Hurwitz and J. C. Mallery. 1991. "Text Modeling for International Politics: A Tourist's Guide to RELATUS." In *Artificial Intelligence and International Politics*. Ed. Hudson, V. M. 97-126. Boulder: Westview Press.

Alker, H. R., Jr. and W. J. Greenberg. 1971. "The UN Charter: Alternate Pasts and Alternate Futures." In *The United Nations: Problems and Prospects*. Ed. Fedder, E. H. 113-142. St. Louis: University of Missouri, Center for International Studies.

Alker, H. R., Jr. and F. L. Sherman. 1982. "Collective Security-Seeking Practices Since 1945." In *Managing International Crises*. Ed. Frei, D. 113-145. Beverly Hills, CA and London: Sage Publications.

Alvarado, S. J. 1990. *Understanding Editorial Text: A Computer Model of Argument Comprehension*. Boston: Kluwer Academic Publishers.

Andriole, S. J. 1978. "The Levels of Analysis Problems and the Study of Foreign International, and Global Affairs: A Review Critique, and Another Final Solution." *International Interactions* 5, 2-3: 113-133.

___. 1984. "Detente: A Quantitative Analysis." *International Interactions* 11, 3-4: 381-395.

Andriole, S. J. and G. W. Hopple. 1984. "The Rise and Fall of Event Data: From the Basic Research to Applied Use in the U.S. Department of Defense." *International Interactions* 10, 3-4: 293-309.

Azar, E. E. 1970a. "Analysis of International Events." *Peace Research Reviews* 4, 1: 1-113.

___. 1970b. "Methodological Developments in the Quantification of Event Data." Paper prepared for the Cooperation/Conflict Research Group of Event Data Conference. Michigan State University, East Lansing, MI, April 15-16.

___. 1975. "Ten Issues in Events Research." In *Theory and Practice of Events Research: Studies in International Actions and Interactions*. Eds. Azar, E. E. and T. D. Ben-Dak. 1-17. New York: Gordon and Breach.

___. 1980. "The Conflict and Peace Data Bank (COPDAB)." *Journal of Conflict Resolution* 24, 1 (March): 143-152.

___. 1982. *The Codebook of the Conflict and Peace Data Bank (COPDAB)*. College Park, MD: University of Maryland, Center for International Development and Conflict Management.

___. 1990. *The Management of Protracted Social Conflict: Theory and Cases*. Aldershot, UK: Dartmouth.

Azar, E. E. and T. Havener. 1976. "Discontinuities in the Symbolic Environment: A Problem in Scaling." *International Interactions* 2, 4: 231-246.

Azar, E. E. and S. Lerner. 1981. "The Use of Semantic Dimensions in the Scaling of International Events." *International Interactions* 7, 4: 361-378.

Azar, E. E. and T. J. Sloan. 1975. *Dimensions of Interaction: A Sourcebook for the Study of the Behavior of 31 Nations from 1948 through 1973*, Occasional Paper #8. Pittsburgh, PA: International Studies Association.

Bloomfield, L. P. and A. C. Leiss. 1969. *Controlling Small Wars: A Strategy for the 1970's*. New York: Alfred A. Knopf.

Brecher, M. and J. Wilkenfeld. 1982. "Crises in World Politics." *World Politics* 34, 3 (April): 380-417.

Brecher, M., J. Wilkenfeld and S. Moser. 1988. *Crises in the Twentieth Century: Volume I Handbook of International Crises*. New York: Pergammon Press.

Brody, R. A. 1972. "International Events: Problems of Measurement and Analysis." In *International Events Interaction Analysis: Some Research Considerations*. Sage Professional Paper in International Studies, Vol. 1, Series No. 02-001. Beverly Hills, CA and London: Sage Publications.

Bull, H. 1977. *The Anarchical Society*. New York: Columbia University Press.

Burgess, P. M. and R. W. Lawton. 1972. *Indicators of International Behavior: An Assessment of Events Data Research*. Sage Professional Paper in International Studies, Vol. 1, Series No. 02-010. Beverly Hills, CA and London: Sage Publications.

___. 1974. *Indicators of International Behavior: An Assessment of Events Data Research*. Beverly Hills, CA and London: Sage Publications.

Burrowes, R., D. Muzzio and B. Spector. 1974. "Mirror, Mirror on the Wall. . .:A Source Comparison Study of Inter-Nation Event Data." In *Comparing Foreign Policy: Theories, Findings and Methods*. Ed. Rosenau, J. N. 383-406. Beverly Hills, CA and London: Sage Publications.

Butterworth, R. L. 1980. *Managing Interstate Conflict, 1945-1979: Data with Synopses*, Final Report, February.

Butterworth, R. L. and M. E. Scranton. 1976. *Managing Interstate Conflict, 1945-1974: Data with Synopses*. Pittsburgh, PA: University of Pittsburgh, University Center for International Studies.

Calhoun, H. L. 1971. "The Measurement and Scaling of Event Data Using the Semantic Differential." Paper presented at the 25th annual meeting of the Western Political Science Association. University of New Mexico, Albuquerque, NM, April 7-10.

___. 1972. "Exploratory Applications to Scaled Event Data." Paper presented at the 13th annual convention of the International Studies Association. Dallas, TX, March 15-17.

___. 1974. *The Joint Application of Two New Technologies to the Problem of Estimating*, Arlington, VA: CACI. Mimeograph.

___. 1977. *The Measurement and Scaling of Event Data Using the Semantic Differential with Theoretical Applications*. Doctoral Dissertation, University of Southern California, Los Angeles, CA.

___. 1991. Visit with Tomlinson, March 1-3.

Chomsky, N. and G. Miller. 1963. "Finite State Languages." In *Readings in Mathematical Psychology*. Eds. Luce, R. D., Bush, R. R., and E. Galanter. 156-171. Vol II. New York: John Wiley.

Choucri, N. and R. C. North. 1975. *Nations in Conflict: National Growth and International Violence*. San Francisco, CA: W.H. Freeman.

Clarke, D. D. 1983. *Language and Action: A Structural Model of Behavior*. International Series in Experimental Social Psychology, 7. Oxford: Pergamon Press.

Cohen, P. R., J. Morgan and M. E. Pollack. 1990. *Intentions in Communication*. Cambridge, MA: MIT Press.

Corson, W. H. 1970. "Conflict and Cooperation in East-West Crisis: Measurement and Prediction." Paper prepared for Event Data Conference. Michigan State University, East Lansing, MI, April 15-16.

Cox, R. W. and H. K. Jacobson. 1973. "The Stratification of Power." In *The Anatomy of Influence: Decision Making in International Organizations*. By Cox, R. W., H. K. Jacobson, et al. 437-443. New Haven, CT and London: Yale University Press

Daly, J. A. and S. Andriole. 1980. "The Use of Events/Interaction Research by the Intelligence Community." *Policy Sciences* 12, 2 (August): 215-236.

Davies, J. L. and C. K. McDaniel. Forthcoming. "A New Generation of International Event-Data." *International Interactions*.

___. 1991. "The Global Event-Data System." Paper presented at the 32d annual convention of the International Studies Association. Vancouver, BC, March 19-21.

Doran, C. F., R. E. Pendley and G. E. Antunes. 1973. "A Test of Cross-National Event Reliability: Global Versus Regional Data Sources." *International Studies Quarterly* 17, 2: 175-201.

Fan, D. P. 1988. *Predictions of Public Opinion from the Mass Media*. Westport, CT: Greenwood Press.

Farris, L., H. R. Alker, Jr., K. Carley and F. L. Sherman. 1980. "Phase/Actor Disaggregated Butterworth-Scranton Codebook." Cambridge, MA: The Massachusetts Institute of Technology, Center for International Studies. Working paper.

Forsyth, R. and R. Rada. 1986. *Machine Learning: Applications in Expert Systems and Information Retrieval*. New York: Wiley/Halstead.

Gerner, D. J. 1990. "Evolution of a Revolution: The Palestinian Uprising, 1987-1989." Paper presented at the 31st annual convention of the International Studies Association. Washington, DC, April 10-14.

Goldstein, J. S. and J. R. Freeman. 1988. "Reciprocity in U.S.-Soviet-Chinese Relations." Paper presented at the 84th annual meeting of the American Political Science Association. Washington, DC, September 2.

___. 1990. *Three Way Street: Reciprocity in World Politics.* Chicago: University of Chicago Press.

Gurr, T. R. and J. R. Scarritt. August 1989. "Minorities' Rights at Risk: A Global Survey." *Human Rights Quarterly* 11, 3 (August): 375-405.

Haas, E. B. 1968. "Collective Security and the Future International System." Monograph No. 1. Monograph Series in World Affairs, Vol. 5, No. 1. Denver, CO: University of Denver.

___. 1983. "Regime Decay: Conflict Management and International Organizations, 1945-1981." *International Organization* 37, 2 (Spring): 189-256.

Haas, E. B., R. L. Butterworth and J. S. Nye. 1972. *Conflict Management by International Organizations.* Morristown, NJ: General Learning Press.

Habermas, J. 1984. *Theory of Communicative Action.* Vol. 1. Boston: Beacon Press.

___. 1989. *Theory of Communicative Action.* Vol. 2. Boston: Beacon Press.

Hayes, R. E. 1973. "Identifying and Measuring Changes in the Frequency of Event Data." *International Studies Quarterly* 17, 4 (December): 471-493.

Hermann, C. F. 1982. "Foreword." In *Describing Foreign Policy Behavior.* Eds. Callahan, P., L. P. Brady and M. G. Herman. 7-10. Beverly Hills, CA and London: Sage Publications.

___. 1989. "Two Kinds of Event Data." *DDIR Update* 3, 2 (January): 1-2.

Hermann, C. F., M. A. East, M. G. Hermann, B. G. Salmore and S. A. Salmore. 1973. *CREON: A Foreign Events Data Set,* Sage Professional Papers in International Studies, Vol. 1, Series No. 02-024. Beverly Hills, CA and London: Sage Publications.

Hoggard, G. D. 1974. "Differential Source Coverage and the Analysis of International Interactions Data." In *Comparing Foreign Policy: Theories, Findings and Methods.* Ed. Rosenau, J. N. 353-381. Beverly Hills, CA and London: Sage Publications.

Howell, L. D. 1983. "A Comparative Study of the WEIS and COPDAB Data Sets." *International Studies Quarterly* 27, 2: 149-159.

___. 1984. "Comparative Analysis with Events Data: A Reply to McClelland." *International Studies Quarterly* 28, 1 (March): 111-113.

___. 1985. "Arms Transfer Events." *Comparative Foreign Policy Notes* 12, 2 (January): 5-8.

___. 1987. "Changing Priorities: Putting the Data Back into Events Data Analysis." *Foreign Policy Analysis Notes* 14, 3 (Winter): 22-32.

Jenks, C. 1973. "The Problem of "Reality Coverage" in International Events Data." Paper presented at the 14th annual convention of the International Studies Association. New York, March 14-17.

Jensen, L. 1988. *Bargaining for National Security: The Postwar Disarmament Negotiations.* Columbia: University of South Carolina Press.

Johnson, L. E. 1981. "Analysis of Foreign Affairs in a Governmental Environment." *Comparative Foreign Policy Notes* 8, 3 (Winter): 31-39.

Joshi, A. K. 1991. "Natural Language Processing." *Science* 253, (September 13): 1242-1249.

Kegley, C. W., Jr. and E. R. Wittkopf. 1987. *American Foreign Policy: Pattern and Process.* 3d ed. New York: St. Martin's Press.

Kolodner, J. L. and C. K. Riesbeck, Eds. 1986. *Experience, Memory & Reasoning.* Hillsdale, NJ: Erlbaum.

Kratochwil, F. 1989. *Rules, Norms, and Decisions: On the Conditions of Practical and Legal Reasoning in International Relations and Domestic Affairs.* New York: Cambridge University Press.

Krippendorff, K. 1980. *Content Analysis.* Beverly Hills, CA and London: Sage Publications.

Lasswell, H. D. 1936. *Politics: Who gets What, When, How.* New York: McGraw-Hill.

___. 1971. *A Pre-View of Policy Sciences.* New York: Elsevier.

Lasswell, H. D. and D. Blumenstock. 1939. *World Revolutionary Propaganda: A Chicago Study.* New York and London: Alfred A. Knopf.

Lasswell, H. D. and M. A. Kaplan. 1950. *Power and Society.* New Haven: Yale University Press.

Laurance, E. J. 1990. "Events Data and Policy Analysis: Improving the Potential for Applying Academic Research to Foreign and Defense Policy Problems." *Policy Sciences* 23, 2 (May): 111-132.

Lehnert, W., C. Cardie, D. Fisher, E. Riloff and R. Williams. "University of Massachusetts: MUC-4 Test Results and Analysis." in *Proceedings of the Third Message Understanding Conference.* 151-158. San Mateo, CA: Morgan Kaufmann.

Lehnert, W. and B. Sundheim. 1991. "A Performance Evaluation of Text Analysis Technologies." *AI Magazine* 12, 3: 81-94.

Leng, R. J. 1973. "The Future of Events Data Marriages: A Question of Compatability." Paper presented at the 14th annual convention of the International Studies Association. New York, March 14-17.

___. 1978. "Event Data Validity: Comparing Coding Schemes." In *Measuring International Behavior: Public Sources, Events, and Validity.* Ed. Munton, D. Halifax, NS: Dalhousie University.

___. 1986. *Coder's Manual for Describing and Coding International Actions,* 6th ed. Middlebury, VT: Middlebury College. Mimeograph.

___. 1987. "The Future of Event Data: A Backward Glance." Middlebury, VT: Middlebury College. Mimeograph.

Leng, R. J. and J. David Singer. 1988. "Militarized Interstate Crisis: The BCOW Typology and Its Applications." *International Studies Quarterly* 32, 2 (June): 155-173.

Levinson, S. C. 1983. *Pragmatics.* Cambridge Textbooks in Linguistics. Cambridge, Eng.: Cambridge University Press.

Lichbach, M. 1984. "The International News About Governability: A Comparison of the New York Times and Six News Wires." *International Interactions* 10, 3-4: 311-340.

Lovins, J. B. 1968. "Development of a Stemming Algorithm." *Mechanical Translation and Computational Linguistics* 11, 1-2: 11-31.

Mallery, J., R. Hurwitzs and G. Duffy. 1987. "Hermeneutics." In Vol. 1 of *Encyclopedia of Artificial Intelligence.* Ed. Shapiro, S. C., Eckroth, D. and G. A. Vallasi. 362-376. New York: John Wiley.

Mansbach, R. W. and J. A. Vasquez. 1981. "The Effect of Actor and Issue Classifications on the Analysis of Global Conflict-Cooperation." *The Journal of Politics* 43, 3 (August): 861-874.

Maoz, Z. 1989. "Conflict Datasets: Concepts and Measurement." Paper presented at the 30th annual convention of the International Studies Association. London, Eng., March 28-April 1.

McClelland, C. A. 1968. "International Interaction Analysis: Basic Research and Practical Applications." Technical Report #2, World Event/Interaction Survey, in support of ARPA/ONR contract #N00014-67-A-0269-0004. Los Angeles, CA: University of Southern California, School of International Relations. Mimeograph.

___. 1970. "Conceptualization, Not Theory." In *A Design for International Relations Research: Scope, Theory, Methods, and Relevance*. Ed. Norman Palmer. 72-75. Philadelphia: American Academy of Political and Social Science.

___. 1983. "Let the User Beware." *International Studies Quarterly* 27, 2 (June): 169-177.

___. 1991. Interview with Tomlinson, Nipomo, CA, January.

McClelland, C. A., R. G. Tomlinson, R. G. Sherwin, G. A. Hill, H. A. Calhoun, P. H. Fenn and J. D. Martin. 1971. "The Management and Analysis of International Event Data: A Computerized System for Monitoring and Projecting Event Flows." Report in support of ARPA/ONR Contract #N00014-67-A-0269-0004 for Short-Term Conflict Prediction. Los Angeles, CA: University of Southern California, School of International Relations. Mimeograph.

McDaniel, C. K. and J. L. Davies. 1991. "A Speech Act Perspective for Event-Data Research." Paper presented at the International Conference· Vancouver, BC.

McDougal, M. S., H. D. Lasswell and J. C. Miller. 1967. *The Interpretation of Agreements and World Public Order*. New Haven: Yale University Press.

McGowan, P. 1971. "Estimating the Comparability of Different Sets of Political Events Data: A Research Note." Syracuse: Syracuse University, Department of Political Science. Mimeograph.

___. 1974. "Problems in the Construction of Positive Foreign Policy Theory." In *Comparing Foreign Policy: Previous Findings and Methods*. Ed. Rosenau, J. N. 25-44. Beverly Hills, CA and London: Sage Publications.

McGowan, P., H. Starr, G. Hower, R. L. Merritt and D. A. Zinnes. 1988. "International Data as a National Resource." *International Interactions* 14, 2: 101-113.

Mead, G. H. 1962. *Mind, Self and Society*. Ed. Morris, C. Chicago: University of Chicago Press.

Mefford, D. 1991. "Steps Toward Artificial Intelligence: Rule-Based, Case-Based, and Explanation-Based Models of Politics." In *Artificial Intelligence and International Politics*. Ed. Hudson, V. M. 56-96. Boulder: Westview Press.

Merritt, R. L. 1990. "Data in International Research: Confluence of Interest and Possibility." *DDIR Update* 4, 3 (April): 1-11.

___. 1992. "Measuring Events for International Political Analysis." *International Interactions* 18, 2.

Moon, D. 1975. "The Logic of Political Inquiry: A Synthesis of Opposed Perspectives." In Vol. 1 of *Handbook of Political Science*. Eds. Greenstein, F. I. and N. W. Polsby. 131-228. Reading, MA: Addison-Wesley.

Moses, L. E., R. A. Brody, O. R. Holsti, J. B. Kadane and J. S. Milstein. 1967. "Scaling Data on Inter-Nation Action: A Standard Scale is Developed for Comparing International Conflict in a Variety of Situations." *Science* 156, 3778 (26 May): 1054-1059.

Mowlana, H. 1976. "A Paradigm for Source Analysis in Events Data Research: Mass Media and the Problems of Validity." *International Interactions* 2, 1: 33-44.

Munton, D. 1977. "Validity Issues in Measuring International Behavior." Vancouver, BC: University of British Columbia. Mimeograph.

___. 1978. "Measuring International Behavior: Public Sources, Events and Validity." Halifax, NS: Dalhousie University.

Nye, J. S. 1971. *Peace in Parts: Integration and Conflict in Regional Organization.* Boston, MA: Little, Brown and Company.

Osgood, C. E., G. J. Suci and P. H. Tannenbaum. 1957. *The Measurement of Meaning.* Urbana: University of Illinois Press.

Patchen, M. 1990. "Conflict and Cooperation in American-Soviet Relations: What Have We Learned from Quantitative Research?" Paper presented at the 31st annual convention of the International Studies Association. Washington, DC, April 13.

Pazzani, M. J. 1990. *Creating a Memory of Causal Relationships.* Hillsdale, NJ: Erlbaum.

Peterson, S. 1975. "Research on Research: Events Data Studies, (1961-1972)." In *Sage International Yearbook of Foreign Policy Studies.* Ed. McGowan, P. J. 263-309. Beverly Hills, CA and London: Sage Publications.

Pierce, J. R. 1980. *An Introduction to Information Theory.* New York: Dover.

Rajmaira, S. and M. D. Ward. 1990. "Reciprocity and Evolving Norms in the Reagan and Gorbachev Eras." Paper presented at the 86th annual meeting of the American Political Science Association. San Francisco, CA, August 29-September 2.

Riesbeck, C. K. and R. C. Schank. 1989. *Inside Case-Based Reasoning.* Hillsdale, NJ: Erlbaum.

Rummel, R. J. 1964. "Dimensions of Conflict Behavior Within and Between Nations." In *General Systems: Yearbook of the Society for General Systems Research.* Ed. von Bertalanffy, L. and A. Rapoport. Vol. 8. 1-50. Ann Arbor, MI: Society for General Systems Research.

___. 1972. *The Dimensions of Nations.* Beverly Hills, CA and London: Sage Publications.

___. 1976. "The Roots of Faith." In *In Search of Global Patterns.* Ed. Rosenau, J. N. 10-30. New York: Free Press.

Salton, G. 1989. *Automatic Text Processing.* Reading, MA: Addison-Wesley.

Schank, R. C. and R. P. Abelson. 1977. *Scripts, Plans, Goals and Understanding.* Hillsdale, NJ: Erlbaum.

Schank, R. C. and C. K. Riesbeck. 1981. *Inside Computer Understanding: Five Programs Plus Miniatures.* Hillsdale, NJ: Erlbaum.

Schrodt, P. A. and C. Donald. 1990. "Machine Coding of Event Data." Paper presented at the 31st annual convention of the International Studies Association. Washington, DC, April 10-14.

Schrodt, P. A. and D. Leibsohn. 1985. "An Algorithm for the Classification of WEIS Event Code from WEIS Textual Descriptions." Paper presented at the 26th annual convention of the International Studies Association. Washington, DC, March 5-9.

Searle, J. R. 1969. *Speech Acts: An Essay in the Philosophy of Langauge*. New York: Cambridge University Press.

Sherman, F. L. 1987a. "Four Major Traditions of Historical Events Research: A Brief Comparison." Paper presented at the Second DDIR Event Data Conference. Boston, MA, The Massachusetts Institute of Technology, November 13-15.

___. 1987b. "Partway to Peace: The United Nations and the Road to Nowhere." Ph.D. dissertation. State College, PA: The Pennsylvania State University.

___. 1988. "SHERFACS: A New Cross-Paradigm, International Conflict Dataset." Paper presented at the 29th annual convention of the International Studies Association. St. Louis, MO, March 30-April 2.

Sigler, J. H., J. O. Field and M. L. Adelman. 1972. "Applications of Events Data Analysis: Cases, Issues, and Programs in International Interaction." Beverly Hills, CA and London: Sage Publications.

Springer, C. H., R. E. Herlihy and R. I. Beggs. 1965. *Advanced Methods and Models*. Homewood, IL: Richard D. Irwin.

Stone, P. J., D. C. Dunphy, M. S. Smith and D. M. Ogilvie. 1966. *The General Inquirer: A Computer Approach to Content Analysis*. Cambridge: MIT Press.

Taylor, C. L. and D. A. Jodice. 1983. *World Handbook of Political and Social Indicators*, 3d ed. New Haven: Yale University Press.

United States Department of Labor. 1976. *BLS Handbook of Methods*, Bulletin No. 1910. Washington, DC: U.S. Department of Labor, Bureau of Labor Statistics.

van Dijk, T. 1988. *News Analysis: Case Studies of International and National News in the Press*. Hillsdale, NJ: Erlbaum.

van Rijsberger, C. J. 1979. *Information Retrieval*, 2d ed. London: Butterworths.

VanBeers, L. and R. G. Sherwin. 1977. *World Event/Interaction Survey Handbook and Codebook*. Monterey, CA: Department of National Security Affairs, Naval Postgraduate School. Mimeograph.

Vincent, J. E. 1983. "WEIS vs. COPDAB: Correspondence Problems." *International Studies Quarterly* 27, 2 (June): 160-168.

Winograd, T. 1985. "Moving the Semantic Fulcrum." *Linguistics and Philosophy* 8, 1 (February): 91-104.

Wright, Q. 1955. *The Study of International Relations*. New York: Appleton Century Crofts.

Yamani, S. A. 1974. Speech before Sixth Special Session of United Nations General Assembly.

Young, R. A. and W. R. Martin. 1968. "Scaling Events Data." WEIS Project Research Memo. Los Angeles, CA: University of Southern California, School of International Relations. Mimeograph.

Index

Contributors

Hayward R. Alker, Jr., has been a professor of Political Science at MIT since 1968, and is a past president of the International Studies Association. Current research includes collaborative books on *The Dialectics of World Order* and *After Neorealism: Anarchic Institutions of World Politics.*

Gillian Barnes is a Ph.D. candidate in International Relations at The American University, Washington, D.C. Her current interests include political economy in Latin America and the Caribbean, political and ethnic conflict in the Third World, and quantitative approaches to the study of foreign policy.

John L. Davies is research coordinator for the Center for International Development and Conflict Management, director of the Global Event-Data System (GEDS) and Conflict and Peace Data Bank (COPDAB) Projects, and affiliate assistant professor of government and politics, at the University of Maryland at College Park. His interests include the study of social conflict and development, and evaluation of approaches to peace and conflict resolution, with recent and forthcoming publications in the *Journal of Conflict Resolution,* the *Annual Review of Conflict Knowledge and Conflict Resolution,* and *International Interactions.*

Llewellyn D. Howell is professor and chairman of the Department of International Studies at the American Graduate School of International Management (Thunderbird), Glendale, Arizona, specializing in political risk analysis, quantitative research methods, and Southeast Asian studies. His work on event data has been published in *International Interactions* and *International Studies Quarterly.*

Russell J. Leng is the William R. Kenan Professor of Political Science at Middlebury College. He has published numerous articles on interstate crisis behavior, which have been based on Behavioral Correlates of War (BCOW) data. He is in the process of completing a book on interstate crises and war from 1816 to 1980.

Chad K. McDaniel is director of the Academic Software Development Group and Instructional Computing Science Center, and senior fellow at the Center for International Development and Conflict Management, at the University of Maryland at College Park. He has developed several software packages utilizing graphic user interfaces to enhance academic and research productivity, and has an active interest in linguistic and information management issues in the social sciences, with publications in *Science* and *Language and Society,* and forthcoming in *International Interactions.*

Richard L. Merritt, professor of political science and research professor in communications, University of Illinois at Urbana-Champaign, has focused his research on international political communication, quantitative international politics, and German politics. He has been vice-president of the International Political Science Association and International Studies Association.

Robert G. Muncaster is associate professor of mathematics at the University of Illinois at Urbana-Champaign, specializing in applied mathematics. His current research interests are split between theoretical mechanics and international relations. In the latter area he has focused on the development and study of models of international conflict, with recent work published in the *Journal of Conflict Resolution*, *Synthese*, and the *Journal of Theoretical Politics*.

Laura Neack is assistant professor of political science at Miami University, Oxford, Ohio, where she teaches foreign policy analysis. Her research interests include the study of state self-image and structural characteristics, and the impact of both on a state's international conflict and conflict management behavior.

Philip A. Schrodt is professor of political science at the University of Kansas, specializing in international relations and mathematical modelling of political behavior. His current research involves the application of computational modelling and artificial intelligence techniques to the study of international politics, with recent work published in *Political Analysis* and *Social Science Computer Review*.

Steven T. Seitz is associate professor of political science at the University of Illinois at Urbana-Champaign, specializing in public policy analysis. His current research interests involve the application of computational modelling to super power rivalries, the "withdrawal" behaviors of organization employees, the impact of mass marketing campaigns, and forecasting and evaluating alternative public health intervention strategies for the AIDS pandemic both at home and abroad. His work has appeared in inter alia, *Journal of Conflict Resolution*, *Mass Emergencies and Disasters*, and *Journal of Peace Science*.

Frank L. Sherman is assistant professor of political science at The American University, Washington, D.C., Oxford, Ohio, where he teaches international relations and foreign policy. His current research involves updating the SHERFACS dataset and studying the processes of international agenda formation and the nexus of domestic and international conflict.

Rodney G. Tomlinson is professor of international relations at the United States Naval Academy at Annapolis, Maryland, specializing in international conflict structures and processes. His current interests include links between bilateral and multilateral behavior including annual compilation of roll call voting in the United Nations for the U.S. Department of State.

Dina A. Zinnes, Merriam Professor of Political Science at the University of Illinois at Urbana-Champaign, has focused her research on the construction, analysis, and empirical testing of mathematical models of international relations. Her research has appeared in, inter alia, *Journal of Conflict Resolution*, *International Studies Quarterly*, *World Politics*, and *American Political Science Review*. She has also edited a number of volumes devoted to the presentation of mathematical models in international relations and has written a survey of the quantitative research literature in this area, *Contemporary Research in International Relations* (1976).